PETER YAKOVLEVICH CHAADAYEV

Chaadaev, Petr IAkovlevich

PETER YAKOVLEVICH
CHAADAYEV

Philosophical Letters & *Apology of a Madman*

TRANSLATED WITH AN INTRODUCTION BY

Mary-Barbara Zeldin

THE UNIVERSITY OF TENNESSEE PRESS

KNOXVILLE

LIBRARY OF CONGRESS CATALOG CARD NUMBER 79–88186
STANDARD BOOK NUMBER 87049–102–4

FOR JESSE AND XENIA

Preface

THE HISTORY OF THE TEXTS of Peter Yakovlevich Chaadayev's *Philosophical Letters*[1] and *Apology of a Madman* is complicated and unusual. The *Letters* and the *Apology* were written in French, the language with which Chaadayev, like many Russians of his time and background, was most familiar. The *First Letter* was published in Russian translation in the Moscow periodical *Telescope* in 1836. The other letters as well as the *Apology of a Madman* were circulated, in whole or in part, in manuscript copies. In 1862 I. S. Gagarin published *Letters I, VI,* and *VII* (according to the present numbering) and a late version of the *Apology of a Madman* in French in western Europe;[2] he also included in this edition a fourth letter which does not belong to the series of *Philosophical*

[1] The first *Letter* was published in *Telescope* under the title, *Philosophical Letters to Madame * * *: First Letter.* D. I. Shakhovskoy, in his Russian edition of *Letters II, III, IV, V,* and *VIII* (*Literaturnoye nasledstvo*, XXII–XXIV [Moscow, 1935], 10) observes that, in a letter to P. A. Vyazemsky dated March 9 and apparently sent in 1835, Chaadayev said that the title of his book would be *Philosophical Letters addressed to a Lady.* Charles Quénet (*Tchaadaev et les Lettres philosophiques: contribution à l'étude des idées en Russie* [Paris, 1931], p. 230 and n. 2) points out that the practice of writing philosophy in epistolary form and addressing the letters to a woman was not new even in Russia: D. V. Venevitinov had, indeed, recently published *Letters on Philosophy to Countess N. N.* On the other hand, none of the available manuscripts bears more than the simple title, *Philosophical Letters*, with the exception of the manuscript of *Letters VI* and *VII* (Dashkov Collection, F93/Op 3/No. 1355) which was originally entitled "Two Letters on History addressed to a Lady." Further, common usage for the past hundred years has been to call the series of Chaadayev's *Letters*, the *Philosophical Letters* and this usage is followed by both Quénet and Shakhovskoy.

[2] *Oeuvres choisies de Pierre Tchadaïef, publiées pour la première fois par le P. Gagarin de la compagnie de Jésus* (Paris-Leipzig).

Letters. In 1913–1914 M. O. Gershenzon republished Gagarin's text as well as translations of these four letters and of the *Apology of a Madman* in *Sochineniya i pisma P. Ya. Chaadayeva* in Moscow. Finally, in 1935, D. I. Shakhovskoy, a distant relative of Chaadayev's, published Russian translations of the other five letters in the series (*Letters II–V* and *Letter VIII*) in *Literaturnoye nasledstvo*[3] from the French manuscripts found in the Dashkov Collection[4] of the Akademiya Nauk in Leningrad. One hundred and thirty years after the original publication of the Russian translation of the *First Letter*, the complete set of eight letters and an early version of the *Apology of a Madman* first appeared in the French original, edited by Raymond T. McNally.[5]

Meanwhile, the complete *First Letter* has been translated into English and is available in my translation from the Gershenzon French edition in *Russian Philosophy*[6] and, in Marc Raeff's *Russian Intellectual History*, in the translation of Valentine Snow.[7] To my knowledge no other complete translation of the *First Letter* and no complete translation of any of the other letters or of the *Apology* has been published in English.[8]

The present translation returns to the manuscripts. The translations of *Letters III, IV, V,* and *VIII* are made from manuscripts

[3] XXII–XXIV, 18–62.

[4] F93/Op 3/Nos. 1351–54 and 1356.

[5] "Chaadayev's Philosophical Letters Written to a Lady and His Apologia of a Madman," *Forschungen zur osteuropäischen Geschichte* (Osteuropa-Institut an der Freien Universität Berlin, Historische Veröffentlichungen) (Berlin, 1966), XI, 34–117. Unfortunately, this edition contains a number of typographical errors and errors in reading of the manuscripts.

[6] Ed. James M. Edie, James P. Scanlan, and Mary-Barbara Zeldin, with the collaboration of George L. Kline (Chicago, 1965; London, 1967; rev., Chicago, 1969), I, 106–25.

[7] (New York-Chicago, 1966), pp. 160–73.

For detailed study of the manuscripts and of the available editions and translations of the *Letters* see McNally, "Chaadayev's Philosophical Letters," pp. 24–33 and 118–25, and R. J. Kemball, "Russian 19th-Century Thought—Recent Source Material," *Studies in Soviet Thought*, VII (Sept., 1967), 227–33, and "Čaadaev's 'Lettres philosophiques' and 'Apologie d'un fou': More Recent Source Material," *ibid.*, VIII (June-Sept., 1968), 173–80.

[8] While this book was in press and hence too late for me to make use of it, the *Letters* and the *Apology* appeared in the English translation of Raymond T. McNally, *The Major Works of Peter Chaadayev* (Notre Dame, 1969).

in Chaadayev's hand. The translations of *Letters I, II, VI,* and *VII* are made from manuscript copies, the last two bearing corrections in Chaadayev's hand. All manuscripts of the *Letters* are from the Dashkov Collection in the Akademiya Nauk (F93/Op 3/Nos. 1350–1356). The translation of the *Apology of a Madman* is from a manuscript copy with corrections in Chaadayev's hand (F357/Op 2/No. 408). All manuscripts used were made available to me on microfilm by the Akademiya Nauk.

In the case of the *Letters,* in those instances where the reading of the author's handwriting, or his copyist's, was uncertain, reference was made to Shakhovskoy's Russian translation of *Letters II, III, IV, V,* and *VIII*[9] and to McNally's complete published version in the original French.[10] McNally's French text was also used in one major instance: the first pages of *Letter II*[11] are not available in the Dashkov Collection. The only available manuscript is in the Pypin Archives[12] in a copy by M. I. Zhikharev. I was unable to obtain a microfilm of this manuscript. I therefore translated it from McNally's French edition[13] and checked it against the published Russian translation.[14]

In the case of the *Apology of a Madman,* the Akademiya Nauk made two manuscripts available to me on microfilm: F357/Op 2/No. 408 and F309/No. 2688. These are, to my knowledge, the only manuscripts of the *Apology of a Madman* extant. The latter of these is apparently a copy of the former, incorporating the corrections Chaadayev made on it. Although the two manuscripts are thus identical except in a few minor instances, I chose to translate F357/Op 2/No. 408, since Chaadayev's handwritten corrections lent it greater authenticity. In those instances where the reading of the manuscript used was uncertain, reference was made to F309/No. 2688, to McNally's published French edition of

[9] See n. 3, above.
[10] See n. 5, above.
[11] Pp. 52–57, below.
[12] No. 250/542. (Institut Russkoy Literatury, Akademiya Nauk: "Pismo Chaadayeva, ne voshedsheye v 'Oeuvres choisies,' Kopiya Zh.").
[13] McNally, "Chaadayev's Philosophical Letters," pp. 46–49.
[14] *Literaturnoye nasledstvo,* XXII–XXIV, 18–22.

F357/Op 2/No. 408 mentioned above,[15] and to the text of this same manuscript published by Gershenzon as an early version of the *Apology of a Madman* in *Sochineniya i pisma P. Ya. Chaadayeva* (II, 29–40). In addition, the final paragraphs of the version of the *Apology of a Madman* published by Gagarin in 1862[16] and reproduced by Gershenzon in the first volume of *Sochineniya i pisma*[17] have here been translated and appended to the translation of manuscript F357/Op 2/No. 408. They are lacking in the manuscript versions but seemed sufficiently important to warrant inclusion here.

The version of the *Apology of a Madman* selected for translation here is not only clearly earlier than the Gagarin-Gershenzon version, but is written in a much less elegant style than that later version or than the eight *Letters*. Nevertheless, there is a greater presumption of authenticity than in a version of which no manuscript can be found and which Gagarin may well have considerably edited.

In general I have, throughout my translation, followed the style of italicization of the Russian translation: passages heavily underlined in the manuscripts have been italicized, while, for the sake of better English form, light or dubious underlinings have been ignored; Biblical quotations have, as in the Russian translation, been italicized, even if they were not underlined in the manuscript.[18] In translating such quotations I have used the Douay translation, since that is the version traditionally used in Eastern Orthodox publications.

All quotations or paraphrases are given by Chaadayev in French, with the exception of the superscriptions to *Letters I, III,* and *V,* and the superscription to the *Apology of a Madman.* I have followed Chaadayev's form by giving English translations, or English originals, for his quotations, except in the case of the Latin superscriptions to *Letters I* and *III* and to the *Apology of a Madman:*

[15] McNally, "Chaadayev's Philosophical Letters," pp. 109–17.
[16] See n. 2, above.
[17] No. 74, pp. 219–34.
[18] E.g., pp. 61, 63, below.

the superscription to *Letter III* is translated in a footnote, while that to the *First Letter* and the *Apology of a Madman* is obvious; the superscription to *Letter* V is in English in the manuscript. In the frequent cases where Chaadayev's quotations are in fact paraphrases I have so indicated and have translated them as such.

Words in brackets in the text, unless otherwise identified, indicate either my additions or, if they are French, the original words I have translated there. Footnotes are Chaadayev's unless enclosed in brackets: in the latter case they are mine.

In transliterating from Cyrillic I have followed the system proposed by Gregory Razran in *Science*, CXXIX (April 29, 1959), 1111–1113, omitting, however, notations for "hard" and "soft" marks.

I should like to thank the administration of the Akademiya Nauk for making two sets of microfilms of the Dashkov manuscripts and a microfilm of the two manuscripts of the *Apology of a Madman* available to me. I should also like to thank the Fishburn Library of Hollins College for the use of its facilities, and the Ford Foundation Hollins College Humanities Grant as well as the Travel and Research Fund of Hollins College for their financial support in connection with the preparation of this work. I am particularly grateful to Professor Jean Leblon of the Department of Modern Languages of Vanderbilt University who gave me invaluable assistance by his meticulous checking of my translation and his many useful suggestions. My thanks are also due to Mrs. Sue Deaton Ross and Mrs. Betty Stanley Martin for their help in preparing this manuscript, and to the several friends and colleagues whose interest and encouragement led me to complete this work and to make Chaadayev's thought available to English readers.

M.-B. Z.

Hollins College, 1969

Contents

Preface   *page vii*

Introduction   3

Philosophical Letters   29
    Letter One   31
    Letter Two   52
    Letter Three   67
    Letter Four   79
    Letter Five   91
    Letter Six   106
    Letter Seven   134
    Letter Eight   154

Apology of a Madman   161

Bibliography   179

Index   187

Illustrations

P. Ya. Chaadayev, Lithograph done in the 1840's with an inscription by A. I. Herzen: "To Victor Ivanovich Kasotkin from the friend of Chaadayev, A. Herzen; March 18, 1866, Cha/ teau/ de la Bissiere." *Facing page* 32

Cover page of Letter One of *Philosophical Letters*   33

Original manuscript page from Letter Three
of *Philosophical Letters*   48

Original manuscript page from Letter Six
of *Philosophical Letters*   49

PETER YAKOVLEVICH CHAADAYEV

Introduction

ALL THAT PETER YAKOVLEVICH CHAADAYEV published during a lifetime of approximately six decades is contained in the first twenty pages translated in this volume. The whole of his writings, aside from purely personal letters, would constitute but an average-sized book. In addition, Chaadayev was, as his friend Khomyakov pointed out,[1] prominent neither in politics nor in financial circles. He resigned ingloriously from his position as an officer of the Hussars. He was a social and intellectual snob, a neurotic, a hypochondriac, incapable of managing his financial affairs. He took no part in any revolution and preferred, as he admitted himself,[2] to save his skin rather than stand up for his ideals or defend his friends. Unlike Socrates in Athens or even Galileo in Rome, he followed rather the way of Plato's philosopher in the sixth book of the *Republic*, who, like a man in a storm taking refuge by a wall, prefers to save his soul by silence to sacrificing his life by active leadership.[3] Yet he dominated not only the intellectual life of Moscow, but the entire intellectual movement of Russia during the reign of Nicholas I; he was considered a martyr and a champion by the Westernizer Alexander Herzen and "a truly remarkable man" by the Slavophile leader A. S. Khomyakov.[4] Chaadayev was both the call that awakened Russia in the

---

[1] *Polnoye sobraniye sochinenii* (Moscow, 1900), III, 454, cited in A. Gratieux, *A. S. Khomiakov et le mouvement slavophile* (Paris, 1939), II, 181.

[2] Charles Quénet, *Tchaadaev et les Lettres philosophiques: contribution à l'étude du mouvement des idées en Russie* (Paris, 1931), p. 367.

[3] Ed. F. M. Cornford (Oxford, New York, and London, 1958), pp. 203–204.

[4] Cited in Gratieux, *Khomiakov*, II, 181.

3

silence that followed the Decembrist Revolt[5] and the moving force which led to Russia's intellectual development during his lifetime and for at least two generations after his death. This unique position in Russian intellectual history can be referred to two historical facts: the publication of the *First Philosophical Letter* in 1836 and Chaadayev's very presence in Moscow for the next twenty years, during which he became a living symbol of protest, "an embodied veto,"[6] and acted as the inspirer and a critic of all social and religious ideas that arose.

The essence of this inspiration and this criticism was expressed in writing in the eight *Philosophical Letters* translated here. Although these *Letters* do not cover the full development of Chaadayev's thought, they are its first and central expression and present a complete worldview which remains unchanged and from which all his criticism derives. A number of these derivative opinions were modified, particularly those expressed in the *First* and in the *Seventh* and *Eighth Letters*, in the *Apology of a Madman*, and in other subsequent semi-public epistolary statements, but the modifications are changes of emphasis rather than of substance. Even then, the attitude of dissent and of criticism of any form of complacency remains just as it existed some twenty years before the completion of the *First Letter*, when Chaadayev as a boy joined the ranks of those who opposed Alexander I's capitulation to Napoleon at Tilsit.

I

The exact date and place of Chaadayev's birth is unknown. His main biographer, M. I. Zhikharev, suggests both 1792 and 1796 in Nizhni-Novgorod.[7] Chaadayev's father's family was of Lithua-

---

[5] Alexander Herzen, *Sochineniya v devyatitomakh*, V: *Byloye i dumy*, Parts 4–5 (Moscow, 1956), 138; the same view is expressed by Khomyakov: see Gratieux, *Khomiakov*, II, 181.

[6] Alexander Herzen, *My Past and Thoughts: The Memoirs of Alexander Herzen*, trans. Constance Garnett (2nd ed.; 4 vols.; New York and London, 1968), II, 519.

[7] I am indebted to Quénet's classic study, *Tchaadaev et les Lettres philosophiques*, for most of the biographical information below. On Chaadayev's birthdate, see

nian descent, raised to the Russian nobility in 1639.[8] His mother, born Princess Natalia Mikhailovna Shcherbatova, was of the old Russian nobility. Orphaned at a very young age, Peter and his elder brother Mikhail were brought up in the comfortable household of their mother's unmarried sister, Anna Mikhailovna Shcherbatova, in Moscow. From his earliest years Peter was remarkable for his intelligence, culture, and independence. He was also extremely vain of his person and intellect. He entered Moscow University in 1808, where his classmates included the future playwright and dissenter A. S. Griboyedov and the future Decembrists N. I. Turgenev and I. D. Yakushkin.

Upon completing his studies in 1811 or, more probably, in 1812, he followed family tradition and joined the Semenovsky Guards. With them he fought at Borodino; he received the Iron Cross for his role in the battle of Kulm and was part of Alexander I's honor guard when the Tsar entered Paris in 1814. A brilliant military career already well in the making, Chaadayev continued to rise both in military rank and social prestige. By 1819 he was a full captain, the most cultured and sought-after person in Russian high society, with friends in the royal family and with strong Western and liberal sympathies. These sympathies, partly acquired, like most of those of the youth of his day, during his military sojourn in western Europe, were not such, however, as to lead him to join any of the secret societies of political malcontents formed by his colleagues—nor did the young liberals, with the exception of N. I. Turgenev, consider him one of their group. Chaadayev seems already to have recognized himself and to have

---

pp. lxv–lxviii. Other dates given are 1793 and 1794. These two dates are favored by recent Soviet authorities; the *Malaya sovietskaya entsiklopediya* (1931) has "approximately 1796" whereas the 1957 edition of the *Bolshaya sovietskaya entsiklopediya* gives the date as 1794. The other possible birthplace is Moscow (Quénet, p. lxviii).

[8] Quénet observes that the family got its name from an ancestor called "Chaadai" (*ibid.*, lviii); George Vernadsky remarks that Chaadayev "must have been of Mongol ancestry, for Chaaday is a contraction of the Mongol name Jagatay (Chagatay). Presumably Peter Chaadaev was a descendant of Chingis-Khan's son Jagatay" ("The Mongol Impact on Russia," *Readings in Russian Civilization* [Chicago and London, 1964], I, 198).

been recognized by his friends as an intellectual rather than an activist.

During these post-war years, Chaadayev frequented the home of the historian N. M. Karamzin, and it was there, in 1816, that he met Pushkin—a meeting which was to lead to a lifelong friendship. Chaadayev, as Pushkin's senior by some five years, very soon thought of himself as the young poet's intellectual mentor, while Pushkin early saw in Chaadayev the elements which, in a different sense, were to shape the philosopher's life:

> By the lofty will of heaven
> Born in the fettered service of the Tsars,
> In Rome he would have been a Brutus, in
>   Athens Pericles,
> But here he is an officer of the Hussars.[9]

While Pushkin attributed to Chaadayev the source of all his political ideas,[10] it was the poet, according to Quénet,[11] who many years later led Chaadayev to study Peter the Great and thus indirectly influenced the change of emphasis in Chaadayev's opinion of Russia which is evident in his writing after 1831 and particularly in the *Apology of a Madman*.

Perhaps in good part because of his diffidence, detachment, and sense of personal privacy, the major events and turning points in

---

[9] *Sobraniye sochinenii* (Moscow, 1959), I, 124. Chaadayev is the subject of a number of Pushkin's poems. One side of his character is supposed to be the origin of many qualities of Eugene Onegin. Pushkin also associates himself directly with another, more active aspect:

> Come, to our country let us tend
> The noble promptings of the spirit.
> Comrade, believe: joy's star will leap
> Upon our sight, a radiant token;
> Russia will rouse from her long sleep;
> And where autocracy lies, broken,
> Our names shall yet be graven deep.

Trans. by Babette Deutsch, *The Poems, Prose and Plays of Pushkin*, ed. Avram Yarmolinsky (New York, 1926), pp. 51–52. Quénet (*Tchaadayev et les Lettres philosophiques*, p. 33) here sees Pushkin encouraging Chaadayev rather than vice versa.

[10] Quénet, *Tchaadaev et les Lettres philosophiques*, p. 33.

[11] *Ibid.*, pp. 280–81.

6

Chaadayev's life tend to be open to controversy: his birthdate is uncertain; his role in the publication of the *First Letter* is ambiguous; even the cause of his death is undetermined. The details of his resignation of his commission and return to private life are equally subject to speculation. This much alone is fact: in a letter dated March 25, 1820 (O.S.), he wrote to his brother mentioning his hope to retire in the near future.[12] On the night of October 16/17 (O.S.) of the same year, while Alexander I was at the Congress of Troppau, soldiers of the first battalion of the Semenovsky regiment mutinied on a matter of a commanding officer who was considered unduly severe. This battalion was the élite of the guard, part of Alexander's "own" regiment, many of whom the Tsar knew personally. The times were troubled; the mutiny occurred in the capital of the country. It was inevitable that the Tsar should be particularly upset by the incident. A messenger was dispatched to him with the news on October 18 (O.S.); then, the following day, Chaadayev, who had long since (in 1813) been transferred and was now with the Hussar life guards, was chosen to bring Alexander a full report. Chaadayev resigned his commission three months later.

There was and is nothing in fact to connect the two events, but rumors spread quickly: society then and historians since have speculated and theorized. It has been suggested that Chaadayev was slow in reaching Troppau, insisting on traveling in leisurely comfort, and that the Tsar received the report after Metternich had heard and told him the news. Infuriated, Alexander therefore asked for Chaadayev's resignation.[13] Another suggestion is that Chaadayev resigned because he felt, and feared others felt, that he had acted in bad faith toward his former Semenovsky comrades when he reported the mutiny, and that he was at least partly responsible for Alexander's decision to dissolve the regiment.[14] A third suggestion is that Chaadayev resigned because he had, in

---

[12] M. O. Gershenzon, ed., *Sochineniya i pisma P. Ya. Chaadayeva* (Moscow, 1913–1914), I, No. 2, pp. 1–2.
[13] Quénet, *Tchaadaev et les Lettres philosophiques*, pp. 59–64.
[14] *Ibid.*, pp. 64–65.

his opinion, completed his service to the government—a common enough custom of the Russian aristocracy.[15] One uncommon detail, however, is that such resignations were usually accepted with a final promotion: Chaadayev did not receive one. In any event, his resignation became effective on April 29 (O.S.) of 1821, and Chaadayev left St. Petersburg for Moscow six weeks later. There he lived with his aunt for the following two and a half years.

The dispersal of the regiment achieved the reverse of its purpose—if that was to cut off possible rebellion and was not merely an act of recrimination. Malcontents were now scattered throughout the army. Secret societies multiplied. Chaadayev, for once taking an active role, joined the revived Union of Public Welfare. Since the southern, Moscow, branch was, however, never actually constituted, Chaadayev could truthfully say at the time of his arrest at the frontier after the Decembrist Revolt that he had never belonged to a secret society.

For Chaadayev was fortunately abroad when that revolt occurred. He had left Moscow for western Europe in 1823, partly because he longed to revisit the West in a time of peace and partly, it seems, for his health, which began to deteriorate both nervously and physically after the Troppau incident. Apparently, the travel did nothing to improve the latter and seriously affected his finances. He borrowed again and again from his brother and found himself compelled to sell land and serfs, in spite of his abolitionist views. Meanwhile, he grew more and more expatriate, criticizing every aspect of Russian life and seeking any excuse not to return home. Intellectually, aside from dislike of his homeland, the main accomplishment of his stay abroad was that of meeting Schelling in Karlsbad. The German philosopher's influence on Chaadayev continued for the remainder of the Russian's life.

It was thus only in the summer of 1826, six months after the Decembrist Revolt, that Chaadayev finally crossed the frontier back to Russia. Many of his acquaintances had been Decembrists and of them several had been condemned to death, including his

---

[15] *Ibid.*, pp. 65–66.

good friend N. I. Turgenev. It was not surprising, therefore, that Chaadayev was arrested. Fortunately, he could clear himself relatively quickly and so return home by September of that year.

But the home to which he returned was drastically changed: Chaadayev's relations with his brother had cooled, most of his friends were exiled, the oppressive atmosphere of the reign of Nicholas I was already making itself felt. His health unimproved, lonely, in financial difficulties, Chaadayev grew more and more withdrawn. Leaving his aunt's country home, he returned to live in Moscow in 1829, a recluse suffering fits of depression which drove him close to suicide. In 1831, his doctor, despairing of any improvement in Chaadayev's health under such circumstances, virtually dragged him back into society, to the English Club. It was during these years at his aunt's home and in seclusion in Moscow that Chaadayev composed his *Philosophical Letters*, the last of which was completed in 1831.[16]

The English Club immediately had the desired effect. Chaadayev enjoyed his visit, found that people still knew and liked him. He became a regular member and life began for him again—not the early life of the brilliant officer of the Hussars, but the life of the cultured social critic which Chaadayev had become.

But once again Moscow had changed. During the period of seclusion which followed that of foreign travel a new, post-Napoleonic generation who had witnessed unharmed its elder brothers' Decembrist Revolt turned its attention from those brothers' political concerns to quieter, intellectual ones. This was the young generation of Stankevich, Khomyakov, Kireyevsky, Belinsky, and Herzen: they had discovered Schelling and were soon to discover Hegel; some, like Herzen, had also studied St. Simon. Chaadayev's age and experience would normally have excluded him from their midst—nor did he ever, in fact, become associated with any particular one of the groups formed around these men. Nevertheless, he was accepted by them all: for himself, because of his very diffidence, culture, and intelligence and

[16] He continued, however, to revise them.

his foreign experience, and for his position as "the man who knows Schelling personally."[17] More tolerant of Russia because of his disappointment with the West as a result of the French Revolution of 1830, which he considered a sign of decadence,[18] he could sympathize with some of the ideas of those who were later to become the Slavophile leaders; still critical of Russia's present, he was welcome to those who were to be known as the Westernizers. His approval was sought by both and to both he gave his counsel and his criticism. And among them, as well as among the older intellectuals of his own generation, he circulated his writings, in particular manuscript copies of his *Philosophical Letters*. Thus the *Letters* were read and known long before the publication of the first one in *Telescope*.

During the years from 1831 to 1836, Chaadayev continued to write occasional articles, notably a letter to Pushkin on the 1830 revolution in France[19] and the "Memorandum to Benkendorf" in defense of Kireyevsky's article on "The Nineteenth Century."[20] Chaadayev also claimed the main ideas as well as a chapter in P. Y. Yastrebtsov's book *On the System of the Sciences which must be Known by those Children of Today who are to Constitute the Most Cultured Class of our Society*.[21] He also devoted much time to reading: Schelling, the French philosophers, but particularly

[17] Quénet, *Tchaadaev et les Lettres philosophiques*, p. 197.

[18] Letter to Pushkin of Sept. 18, 1831 (O.S.) (Gershenzon, *Sochineniya i pisma*, I, No. 42, pp. 163–66).

[19] *Ibid.*

[20] Gershenzon, *Sochineniya i pisma*, I, No. 42, pp. 335–41. Although the authorship of the "Memorandum" is not certain, it contains ideas so obviously identical with those expressed in the *Philosophical Letters*, and even phrases word-for-word the same, that it would be difficult not to follow Gagarin's lead in attributing it to Chaadayev. It should be noted, however, that many other ideas expressed in it have changed in the direction of those of the *Apology*. Views similar to the latter are found in Chaadayev's letters to A. I. Turgenev of 1835 (*ibid.*, Nos. 53 and 55, pp. 179–82 and 183–90).

For the influence of Chaadayev on Kireyevsky, see Alexander Koyré, "Russia's Place in the World: Peter Chaadayev and the Slavophils," *The Slavonic Review*, V (March 15, 1927), and Koyré's *La philosophie et le problème national en Russie au début du XIXe siècle* (Paris, 1929), Ch. VI, "L'Européen" (pp. 174–93).

[21] Moscow, 1833. Yastrebtsov acknowledges his debt to "P. Ya. Ch." on p. 201. See Quénet, *Tchaadaev et les Lettres philosophiques*, p. 219.

science, concentrating on the value of science as a support for religion. He also probably began to read Karamzin's *History of the Russian State*.[22] At the same time he tried vainly to publish at least parts of the *Philosophical Letters*.

Four months after the first Moscow performance of Gogol's *Inspector General* had scandalized and fascinated Moscow by its critique of Russian society, Chaadayev's bitter, relentless denunciation of Russia was published in *Telescope*. Its reception was very different: the scandalized public had crowded in to see Gogol's play and Nicholas had showered praise on the "comic" poet; the public was equally scandalized by the *First Philosophical Letter*, but there was no praise, only tragedy. Number 15 of *Telescope* appeared in late September. By mid-October all Moscow, according to Zhikharev,[23] was talking about the "incomprehensible" article: the more violent called it anti-nationalistic, stupid, not worthy of notice; others were more restrained; none supported it, not even Chaadayev's lifelong friend, A. I. Turgenev. Nor was St. Petersburg any quieter about a matter that was "not worthy of notice." Alone of Chaadayev's friends, Pushkin—who had expressed criticisms when he read some of the *Letters* in manuscript in 1831[24]—decided not to rise to protect himself with an adverse comment.[25]

The public was insulted, yet it had not been insulted when the *Letters* had been circulated in manuscript; Chaadayev's explanation was that it is easier to appraise opinions when they

[22] See Quénet, *Tchaadaev et les Lettres philosophiques*, pp. 211–15 and 276–78. Ideas of Karamzin are evident in the "Memorandum to Benkendorf," the letter of July 15, 1833 (O.S.), to Nicholas I (Gershenzon, *Sochineniya i pisma*, I, No. 47, pp. 175–76), the 1835 letters to Turgenev and, finally, in the *Apology* (see pp. 15–16 and 26–28, below).

[23] Quénet, *Tchaadaev et les Lettres philosophiques*, p. 230.

[24] Letter to Chaadayev of July 6, 1831 (O.S.): Pushkin's letter refers primarily to *Letters* VI and VII; see also Pushkin's letter of Aug. 3 (O.S.) of the same year, to P. A. Vyazemsky (*The Letters of Alexander Pushkin*, trans. J. Thomas Shaw [Indiana, 1963], II, 500–501 and 520–21).

[25] Pushkin drafted two variants of a letter to Chaadayev on the occasion of the publication in *Telescope*. He decided not to send either version: "A falcon," he noted, "does not peck out another falcon's eye" (Letter of Oct. 19, 1836 [O.S.], *ibid.*, III, 779–81 and notes, pp. 796–98).

appear in print.[26] To this may be added at least two factors: in manuscript the *Letter* was considered private and the reader could exclude himself from the target of its devastating criticism; moreover, agreement with the unprinted *Letter*'s opinions constituted no danger, whereas to express public approval of such views or merely to defend the right to state them would, under the police state of Nicholas I, be tantamount to courting disaster.

The *Letter*, unsigned, was immediately attributed to Chaadayev. It was also quickly brought to the attention of the Tsar. A commission of inquiry was set up. N. I. Nadezhdin, the editor, and A. V. Boldyrev, the censor who had authorized publication, were brought to St. Petersburg for interrogation, while Chaadayev was declared insane and put under medical care with the express advice of Benkendorf, the head of the Third Section, that he not be allowed to expose himself to the cold, raw air of the late autumn season. Chaadayev's house was searched and all his papers were seized. Meanwhile, the ecclesiastical hierarchy joined in the clamor, accusing Chaadayev of conversion to Roman Catholicism.[27] Chaadayev, Nadezhdin, and Boldyrev attempted to clear themselves by mutual accusations. Both Chaadayev and Nadezhdin argued that the *Letter* did not properly express their views on Russia and was intended only as an attack on false patriotic pride. Nadezhdin also said that Chaadayev had told him the *Letter* had official approval. Boldyrev stated that he had not studied the *Letter* with care because he was too busy with his duties as rector of Moscow University and that Nadezhdin had read only acceptable passages to him while the censor was playing a game of cards. Chaadayev, obviously anxious to please the authorities, seriously upset by the charge of insanity which the nervous illness he had suffered since his resignation from the Hussars encouraged him to fear justified, accused Nadezhdin of publishing the *Letter* without permission, adding that he had given permission for its

---

[26] Letter to M. Ya. Chaadayev of 1837 (Gershenzon, *Sochineniya i pisma*, I, No. 68, pp. 203–204); see Quénet, *Tchaadaev et les Lettres philosophiques*, p. 233.

[27] Quénet, *Tchaadaev et les Lettres philosophiques*, pp. 247–49.

publication only when the manuscript was already in proof and passed by the censor.

The upshot of the affair was that Chaadayev was kept under house arrest and daily medical supervision for over a year, although allowed to go for a walk once a day and to receive friends; he was forbidden to publish anything again. Boldyrev was forced to resign his position as censor and lost both his professional rank and his pension, while Nadezhdin, the chief sinner in the eyes of the commission, was deported to Ust-Sysolsk[28] five hundred miles from the provincial capital. Fortunately for Chaadayev, the ever-mercurial public turned sympathetic toward him when the severity of the punishment became known. The rude and uneducated official physician was replaced by a medical friend of Chaadayev's and many of Chaadayev's friends and admirers grew diligent in visiting him, thus restoring somewhat the mental balance which the shock of the affair had threatened permanently to destroy. But the tragedy could not but leave scars: many former acquaintances did not renew their ties; Chaadayev's papers were not all returned; within a few months the sudden death of Pushkin added yet another sorrow to a burden already dangerously heavy for a sensitive, neurotic personality.

Meanwhile, the affair provided Benkendorf and Uvarov, the minister of education, with an excuse to demand and receive an increase in censorship. As for the *Letter* and the incidents surrounding it, no comment on them, favorable or disfavorable, was allowed in print: only complete silence.

Yet Chaadayev was to have champions of whom he was, at the time, quite unaware. The Marquis of Custine, in the record of his travels in Russia, was to make Chaadayev's case a symbol of the oppression he found there and to make it known to the world.[29]

---

[28] Now Syktyvkar, in the Koma A.S.S.R.

[29] *Journey for Our Time* (*The Journals of the Marquis of Custine*), ed. and trans. Phyllis Penn Koehler (New York, 1951), pp. 335–38. It should be noted, however, that Custine is, in this passage, concerned primarily with Chaadayev's criticism of the Russian church in favor of Rome; see also pp. 292–94, and Quénet, *Tchaadev et les Lettres philosophiques*, pp. 294–98.

Herzen, in exile in Vyatka, reading the *First Letter* in his copy of *Telescope*, was, while Chaadayev's troubles were only beginning, to find it a milestone marking the end of ten years of enforced silence.

It was a shot that rang out into the dark night. Whether it was something foundering that proclaimed its own destruction, whether it was a signal, a cry for help, tidings of dawn or of the fact that there would be no dawn, in any event, it forced all to awake.

What, one may ask, is the significance of two or three pages published in a monthly[30] review? Yet such is the strength of what is spoken, such is the power of a word in a silent land unaccustomed to free speech, that Chaadayev's *Letter* shook all thinking Russia to its foundations. And well it might. After *Woe from Wit* there was not a single literary composition that could have made so strong an impression. Between these two works lay ten years of silence, the Fourteenth of December,[31] the gallows, penal servitude, Nicholas. These two works mark the two limits of this void in Russia's Petrine period. The wilderness left by the strong men who were sent to Siberia had not been reclaimed. The intellect languished; it labored, but it produced nothing. To speak was a peril and there was, indeed, nothing to say. Then, suddenly, quietly, a mournful figure arose and requested a hearing in order calmly to voice his *lasciate ogni speranza*.[32]

Four years after Chaadayev's death Khomyakov said: "at a time when, it seems, thought was driven into heavy and unwanted slumber . . . [Chaadayev] kept others awake and, in the thickening darkness, kept the lamp from going out."[33]

Although Chaadayev never published again, he did not stop writing. Even while the inquiry into *Letter I* was being conducted, the idea of the *Apology of a Madman* was taking shape. It is mentioned in his letter to S. G. Stroganov as early as November 8,

---

[30] The *Telescope* was actually supposed to appear every two weeks.
[31] The date (O.S.) of the Decembrist uprising.
[32] *Sochineniya v devyatitomakh*, V: *Byloye i dumy*, Parts 4–5 (Moscow, 1956), 138 (my translation).
[33] *Polnoye sobraniye sochinenii*, cited in Gratieux, *Khomiakov*, II, 181.

1836 (O.S.).[34] The *Apology* was originally intended, of course, as an explanation of the views expressed in the *First Letter*, softening these views both in order to get back into the good graces of the government and, to a lesser extent, of the irate public, and in order to indicate where the author's present views were modified from those he had held when that *Letter* was first written in 1829. Early in 1837, with the same end in view and explaining his position in the whole affair, Chaadayev wrote a letter to his brother, intended for circulation.[35] Such "open" letters continued to occupy him, although, especially in the early years after the *Telescope* affair, Chaadayev also spent much of his time reading. Without his papers and notes, and thus "deprived of the possibility of continuing my work," he wrote to A. I. Turgenev shortly after the search of his house, "I am bored for the first time in my life. This is the time to read, to study."[36]

According to Quénet, Chaadayev's most influential reading at this time was Karamzin's *History of the Russian State*, which he seems to have taken up again in 1837.[37] The evidence of Karamzin's influence in the years immediately following the completion of the *Letters*, particularly in the 1831 "Memorandum to Benkendorf," the letter to Nicholas I, the chapter in Yastrebtsov, and the 1835 letters to A. I. Turgenev,[38] is now considerably stronger. In a letter to A. I. Turgenev in 1837,[39] Chaadayev writes as though he were, Quénet thinks,[40] only now really getting to know Karamzin's ideas. The major "revisions" of the views of the *Letters* expressed in the *Apology*, revisions which Chaadayev was to continue to uphold for the rest of his life, can all be traced to Karamzin: Chaadayev's softened attitude toward Russian Christianity which he now praised for its character of prayer and humility,

---

[34] Gershenzon, *Sochineniya i pisma*, I, No. 61, pp. 194–96. See paragraph below and pp. 26–28, for old and modified ideas in the *Apology*.
[35] *Ibid.*, No. 68, pp. 203–204.
[36] *Ibid.*, No. 60, p. 194.
[37] Quénet, *Tchaadaev et les Lettres philosophiques*, p. 278, and pp. 10–11, above.
[38] See pp. 10–11, above.
[39] Gershenzon, *Sochineniya i pisma*, I, No. 72, pp. 213–17.
[40] Quénet, *Tchaadaev et les Lettres philosophiques*, pp. 276, 277.

his discovery of the advantage of Russia's isolation which has left it "pure," his views of Russia's mission as the instrument of a new revelation to the world, and especially his interpretation of the historical role of the prince, already suggested in the 1831 "Memorandum to Benkendorf," are all ideas which characterize the work of Karamzin. To be sure, other sources may have reinforced them: Kireyevsky, for instance, also held the notion of Russia's mission to the world; the central idea of the *Apology*, that of the role of the prince as embodied in Peter the Great, was without doubt encouraged by Chaadayev's anger against the pre-Slavophile Slavists who had bitterly opposed the views of *Letter I*, as well as by Chaadayev's concentrated study of Peter which started when Pushkin was officially commissioned to write a history of Peter[41] and to which Chaadayev devoted much time during his period of boredom after the confiscation of his papers.[42]

Thus, the few months between the publication of the *First Letter* and the writing of the *Apology* were a time during which study and reading led Chaadayev to give a formulation to his ideas which was to provide fuel to both the young Slavophiles and the young Westernizers. The latter had not yet turned to Peter for support; the former had not previously been challenged to clarify their ideas in the face of nonpolemical, reasoned Westernism.[43]

In his remaining years Chaadayev continued, with varying degrees of emphasis, to hold this position. With both groups he shared a love of Russia and concern with its role in history. Against the Slavophiles, he looked to Peter as the start of Russia's history and to the West as the stimulus for the development of a nation which was by nature static. Against the Westernizers he held up his religious outlook and his Christian interpretation of history. As the major inspiration for both sides and in his capacity both as a moderator between the two camps and an advocate of what he

---

[41] See his letter to Pushkin of Sept. 18, 1831 (O.S.) (Gershenzon, *Sochineniya i pisma*, I, No. 42, p. 166).

[42] Letter to A. I. Turgenev of 1836 (*ibid.*, No. 66, pp. 200–201).

[43] Quénet, *Tchaadaev et les Lettres philosophiques*, p. 283.

considered valuable in either, he was far more Western than the Westernizers who, especially in later years, espoused their views so whole-heartedly that they were blind to any faults on their side and to any virtues on the other's. A notable exception to such doctrinaire partisanship is Herzen, whose great admiration for Chaadayev and friendship with him[44] may well be due to a recognition in his friend of some of his own intellectual characteristics.

These qualities of disengagement, of intellectual liberalism yet of criticism which is rarely dispassionate, are evident in Chaadayev's later semi-public letters. When, in 1845, Khomyakov published his article on "The Opinions of Foreigners on Russia," in reply to the Marquis of Custine,[45] Chaadayev liked its association of Slavophilism with religion sufficiently to translate it into French and to forward it for publication abroad, but he nevertheless wrote a letter to the French publisher, A. de Circourt, which, though asking for the publication of Khomyakov's work, refuted the latter's assertion of the superiority of Russian Christianity to that of the West.[46] In 1847, he defended Gogol's *Selected Passages from Correspondence with Friends* against the attacks of both official Slavists and Westernizers and against the coldness of liberal Slavophiles. He accused the Slavists of leading Gogol astray, the Slavophiles of using him for their own ends, and the Westernizers, through the independent poet and critic N. P. Pavlov who had sided with them, of Jesuit characteristics while they had themselves criticized the religious, the Roman Catholic, and especially the "Jesuit" tone of Gogol's book.[47] When revolution broke out in western Europe, Chaadayev, always opposed to violence, wrote to Khomyakov expressing his disappointment with "what is called Europe" and exalting Russia, but insisting that nevertheless Russia must not isolate herself from the West nor fall into na-

---

[44] See *ibid.*, pp. 308–13.
[45] See p. 13, above.
[46] Letter of 1846 (Gershenzon, *Sochineniya i pisma*, I, No. 105, pp. 268–75).
[47] Letter to Prince P. A. Vyazemsky of April 29, 1847 (O.S.) (*ibid.*, No. 109, pp. 279–85).

tionalistic pride.[48] In 1854, in his observations on Khomyakov's pamphlet on *Western Communions*, Chaadayev was angry; he bitterly accused Orthodoxy of sterility. The spread of Protestantism, he argued, was not stopped at the Russian border by a more powerful faith, as Khomyakov contended; rather, "itself an idea, Protestantism stopped . . . quite naturally at the point where the realm of ideas ended and the realm of brute fact and ceremony began."[49]

His last public statement was written at the end of 1854, after the allied invasion of the Crimea. Chaadayev seized the opportunity to give an extreme expression of Westernism: siding with the liberal patriotism of Peter, Catherine, and Alexander, which respected and was grateful to the West, he attacked the patriotic pride of both the government and the people for whom civilization, prosperity, and progress were of no value, for whom it sufficed merely to be Russian. As a result the government, dragged along by the Slavophiles, had fallen into a fatal blunder. The patriotism of Peter had brought the Russians to Paris; that of 1854 brought the vanguard of Europe to the Crimea.[50]

Chaadayev could not, however, be counted a Westernizer, nor, on the other hand, could he ever join the ranks of the Slavophiles. Whereas the former sought a solution to Russia's problems in a social and political revolution, Chaadayev found a religious solution. Whereas the latter found this religious solution in Russian Orthodoxy and pre-Petrine Russia, Chaadayev found it in the unity expressed by the Catholicism of Rome and the impact of Peter the Great. He disavowed the revolutionary qualities Herzen attributed to him and went so far as both to write to Herzen to thank him for the tribute and to write to A. F. Orlov disassociating himself from the emigré leader,[51] while his Westernizing ideas

---

[48] Letter of Sept. 26, 1849 (O.S.) (*ibid.*, No. 117, pp. 289–90).

[49] "Observations on Two Passages from A. S. Khomyakov's Pamphlet in reply to Laurentie," 1854 (*ibid.*, No. 137, pp. 304–306).

[50] "Extract from a Letter to an Undetermined Correspondent," 1854 (*ibid.*, No. 139, pp. 308–10).

[51] Letter to Herzen of July 26, 1851 (O.S.) (*ibid.*, No. 128, pp. 299–300), and undated letter to Orlov (*ibid.*, No. 127, pp. 298–99).

and, particularly, the very Westernism of his character, shocked the loyal patriotism of the Slavophiles.

Neither group was of Chaadayev's class or generation. Chaadayev was, as Quénet points out,[52] a product of the reign of Alexander I, a liberal aristocrat whose teachers had been Borodino and Paris and the universities of Germany. He was neither a wealthy landowner nor a landowner's natural son. But he was and knew he was a man who had, in the words of the Marquis of Custine, "set Russia on fire,"[53] and who then had become "a living protest,"[54] in what A. I. Turgenev called "his intellectual solitude of Moscow."[55]

The years after 1836 brought increasing material hardships. In 1840 Chaadayev was already in serious financial difficulty; soon he was forced to borrow money not only from his relatives but from his servants. In 1845 his health grew considerably worse and from then on there is hardly a single personal letter in his correspondence that does not mention some symptom of illness. As always, his sickness involved his mental state: in 1845 he mentioned thoughts of suicide.[56] The death in 1852 of the aunt who had brought him up affected him deeply. In 1855 he made out his will. By early 1856 he was speaking seriously of the sudden death he had wanted and anticipated since 1835.[57] On Wednesday of Holy Week of that year he fell suddenly and inexplicably seriously ill. His youthful appearance vanished. According to Zhikharev, Chaadayev seemed to age ten years in twenty-four hours and, on the day of his death, looked two decades older than his sixty years. On the Saturday, April 14 (O.S.), he received Holy Communion. A few hours before the first stroke of the Easter bell resounded from the Kremlin, Chaadayev was dead.

[52] *Tchaadaev et les Lettres philosophiques*, p. 374.
[53] *Journey for Our Time*, p. 337.
[54] Herzen, *My Past and Thoughts*, II, 519.
[55] Quénet, *Tchaadaev et les Lettres philosophiques*, p. 374.
[56] Letter to Princess I. D. Shakhovskoy (Gershenzon, *Sochineniya i pisma*, I, No. 95, p. 262). See also Quénet, *Tchaadaev et les Lettres philosophiques*, pp. 387–88 and 390–91.
[57] Letter to A. I. Turgenev (Gershenzon, *Sochineniya i pisma*, I, No. 55, pp. 189–90).

II

The eight letters which constitute the complete series of the *Philosophical Letters*[58] can be briefly described as follows:

Letter I is a general introduction to the whole series.[59] It introduces not only the ideas Chaadayev will elaborate in the remainder of the series, but immediately, in the very superscription, suggests the basic religious concern and attitude of the *Letters* and, by the second paragraph, sounds the critical tone which, though in a form less violent than in this *First Letter*, characterizes the complete work. Starting with the note of submission to the divine will and of allegiance to Providence, "Thy kingdom come," Chaadayev immediately proceeds to attack the secular status quo, "that baneful state of things which, among us, invades all hearts and souls":[60] semi-awareness is, no matter how painful, one step ahead of complete somnolence.

The doctrine which Chaadayev now begins to present is based, he tells us, on the "principle of unity, and of the direct transmission of truth through an uninterrupted succession of its ministers"[61] since the day when God first impressed fundamental primordial ideas on the mind of the first man. This doctrine im-

[58] Chaadayev's letter to Pushkin of June 17, 1831 (O.S.) (Gershenzon, *Sochineniya i pisma*, I, No. 40, pp. 161–62), indicates that the series is complete: "I have, my friend, completed all I had to do, I have said all I had to say." Heinrich Falk (*Das Weltbild Peter J. Tschaadejews nach seinen acht "Philosophischen Briefen"* [Munich, 1954], pp. 36–37) argues further that the *Apology*'s description of Chaadayev's work as incomplete (p. 173, below) refers to the fact that only the *First Letter* was published and that the author's whole thought was thus not presented in print. Chaadayev may also, in my opinion, have meant that he would like to revise the series further in terms of the modification of his views since 1831.

[59] This is how Chaadayev describes it in the *Apology*. When Pushkin, on July 6, 1831 (O.S.) (*The Letters of Alexander Pushkin*, trans. Shaw, II, 500–501), wrote to Chaadayev his criticism of the manuscript the philosopher had sent him, he complained of the need for an introduction. From the content of Pushkin's letter it seems most likely that what Chaadayev had sent him was the manuscript copy of *Letters VI* and *VII* only. If this is the case, Chaadayev's contention that he had given Nadezhdin the *First Letter* only for reference and not for publication (Quénet, *Tchaadaev et les Lettres philosophiques*, pp. 228–29, 252) may well be true. Unfortunately, Chaadayev's own statements conflict.

[60] P. 31, below.

[61] P. 32, below.

plies the fusion of all moral forces into a single thought, felt in a single feeling, and realized in a total historical social system or church. Each aspect of this doctrine reinforces the others: religious practice awakens religious feeling and strengthens religious faith.

Such a doctrine, Chaadayev continues, encourages and requires a quiet, somewhat detached, and serious life which can observe in peace the pain and emptiness of contemporary reality. But the need for such a life of the mind, although recognized elsewhere, is a novel idea in Russia.

Chaadayev then launches into the bitter critique of Russia and Russian life which both first fully awakened Russian national self-consciousness and aroused the anger with which the publication of the *Letter* was received. Instead of advancing with the rest of the family of nations toward the universal social system Chaadayev's doctrine calls for, Russia, he argues, remained independent of this family and so, belonging to neither East nor West, has had no living share in their education and ideas. As a result of its isolation it has separated itself not only from world history but from history as such: order, steadfastness in even daily living are lacking to it; having never got beyond the confines of childhood, it has never made an idea its own by living with it in stormy adolescence; thus, it now has no maturity, only physical growth; having no moral formation, it thus has no personality: it merely picks up and sheds Western ideas as easily as one puts on and sheds one's clothes. Nor has it any representative leaders to think for it as other nations have had. At best Russia exists to be a lesson to others.

Russia's error lay in its acceptance of isolation by following Byzantium when Byzantium broke off from the Christianity of the West. Then Russia was conquered. Then it turned to slavery. Thus, in order to be one among the family of nations, it must admit its fault and somehow acquire the education it has missed. It must turn toward Western civilization and assimilate Western progress toward the social realization of divine Truth. True civili-

zation and progress belong to the West because the West participated in the historical development of Christian ideas and made
them its history and these ideas are the elements of the establishment of the Kingdom of God on earth.

Chaadayev concludes the letter by paraphrasing what he tells
us is part of an earlier article: the assertion of the pervasive effect
of Christianity, whether that religion is accepted or rejected,
whether the effect is on an individual or on a national scale,
whether a person is of high intelligence or meek or contemplative
or imaginative or pure in heart.

The *Second Letter* develops two of the thoughts of the *First*, the
kind of religious life desirable for serious intellectual meditation—
not a life of rugged isolation from society, but one of comfortable
and quiet sobriety within society—and the role of revelation and
Providence in all moral thought and action, both on the individual
and on the national level.

Letter III returns from religion to philosophy and seeks to support the conclusions stated by revelation by an analysis of empirical facts, thus showing how faith can "enlist the arguments of
reason."[62] Reason, Chaadayev points out, in its cognitive, its
logical, and its moral activities, is successful only when it is submissive—to given data or to an intellectual or moral law. Such submission returns the isolated ego, limited by time and space, to the
immediate awareness of the order of creation and of its role in it,
and thus to its proper existence.

Letter IV analyzes the fundamental principles of science and
scientific method and relates them to the principles of moral
philosophy. Scientific method, limited to finite objects and ruled
by the principle of causality, cannot be used in morals where
the object is infinite and free will obtains, but the basic laws of
the physical world, gravitation and propulsion, are parallel to the
basic laws of the mental world, free will and determination by
Providence. Since these are all laws of motion, they can be reduced to a common denominator, that of an initial external

[62] P. 67, below.

action to which gravitation and free will relate as accessory causes. Such a view cancels neither the existence of the self nor free will, any more than propulsion cancels gravitation: in the first instance, the human self acts and is a human self when and only when it knows, regardless of how the knowledge came to it; in the second instance, it acts freely, both in that it does not wholly know its determination and insofar as it nevertheless does act according to law, i.e., according to that determination. God gave us freedom, but He has also always controlled its direction. Without this control we could, in our free acts, destroy creation, just as a sudden voluntary motion of a molecule would destroy the physical world.

Letter V, basing itself on the notion of a single initial impulse which was derived in *Letter IV*, develops Chaadayev's general metaphysics of a nonsensible total unity of creation which, however, is not pantheistic in the usual sense. The principle of the created world, both physical and mental, is motion, transmitted by contact. Thus, just as contact binds present events to prior events and unites them into one nature, so the contact of ideas binds minds and unites them into the oneness of mankind through the ages, into a cosmic mind which consists of the totality of traditional ideas in human memory. These ideas, gathered in part by every individual like the air he breathes,[63] are ideas of a Supreme Being, of justice, of good and evil. These are ideas impressed on the first man "on the day of his creation by the same hand which thrust this planet into its elliptical orbit"[64] and transmitted from generation to generation. While in physical nature the fundamental motion is seen as a quantitative force, in mental nature it is a tradition. In neither realm is anything ever completely isolated. Thus, the unity of reality is the force of Providence through history.

Letters VI and *VII* verify this view of Providential unity by application to history, for history, Chaadayev argues, is the field of application of moral philosophy, just as nature is that field for

[63] P. 97, below.
[64] P. 104, below.

natural philosophy or science. History should therefore be viewed philosophically; it should be organized in terms of ideas, not facts. If this is done, it becomes clear that historical persons and nations both play Providential roles; they are called into action by their varying historical missions. Rather, therefore, than thinking in terms of national rivalry or in terms of striving for a homogeneous universal society, men should regard nations as each having personal contributions to make toward the achievement of the common goal of unity. Such a view of the role of nations was evident in the federation of Christian peoples, which lasted until the return of pagan disunity brought about by the Reformation and which will someday be restored. It is clear, from this viewpoint, that the beginning of the Christian era is the central fact of history: it provides the great overarching idea which gives meaning to all that came before it as preparation to fit man to desire and know truth, and to all that has come after it as progress toward the realization of that truth, i.e., the unity of all peoples. This unity is to be made visible in the future; it is symbolized now in the institution of the papacy. History, Chaadayev continues in *Letter VII*, has a single field of study and can therefore find a fundamental rule of explanation—in the notion of the unity of all persons, families, and nations. This great and basic idea of unity was first given concrete expression in the history of the Jewish people and in Moses their leader, who endowed them with the concept of a single God.

Letter VIII is intended as a general conclusion. Thought, Chaadayev says there, must today speak the language of reason rather than of feeling, but in so doing it must recognize that all its power and all its science come from Christian revelation, from the abiding principle and passion for truth found in the teachings of Christ. Fortunately, man today recognizes the importance of the past without which there can be no future; but truth, being historically grounded, also develops with time: the Scriptures are thus not the only revelation and do not speak equally intelligibly to all men at all times and in all places. The word which speaks to all men is rather the idea impressed on human memory by God and kept alive by men imbued with it in history. This is the reason for the dogma of the Eucharistic sacrament: it is the actual and final expression of the unity of matter and spirit, of the continuity of the future with the present and the past, of the material presence of the man-God in time, of the goal of "all the labor of the intellectual generations . . . the great apocalyptic synthesis."[65]

The categories on which Chaadayev bases his philosophy are now clear: the unity of reality through the principle of the transmission of primitive ideas, divinely introduced when man was first created and expressed concretely in history in individual men and nations. These men and nations play, by the combined force of free will and Providence, their role in the progress of Christian society toward the achievement of the Kingdom of God on earth, that is, the achievement of the completely harmonious system of every man and of his cognitive, aesthetic, and moral faculties. Reality is one through history, which itself is a history of ideas working through men and of which the principle is identical with that of the physical world, namely motion originating from a divine impulse. History is meaningful and therefore truly history only insofar as it embodies the fundamental divine idea, hence, insofar as it is Christian: neither history nor Christianity can be understood without the other. Christianity is thus the reality and the truth and the unity of the world. The historical focus of unity is Christ, its institutional expression is the church centered in the papacy, and its embodiment, which provides the union of the mental and material realms, is the sacrament of the Eucharist.

Egoism, a result of the perversion of the free will man received from God, shatters the unity and leads to isolation, both in the individual and in nations, and to error both logical and moral. This, as grounded in the schism of Orthodoxy and Roman Catholicism, is the cause of Russia's present nature, its backwardness, its insignificance, its immorality. All reality is united by shared

65 P. 160, below.

traditional ideas: Russia has refused its share and thus, Chaadayev implies, is not part of reality at all.

It is noteworthy that neither the government nor the public ever seriously objected to Chaadayev's philosophical views, but only to his specific criticism of Russia in terms of these views. On the other hand, although neither these views nor the derivation of their implications for Russia is, as such, explicit in the *First Letter*, the general direction of Chaadayev's thought and the details of his bitter criticism were sufficient to make his damnation of Russia clear to any careful reader, and far less than that was enough to arouse the anger of a precariously complacent general public.

But Chaadayev, since 1831, had rescinded his total anathema of Russia and, by 1837, accused it only of not yet readily accepting the Grace proffered to it. Thus, the *Apology of a Madman*, while maintaining the position that Russia is at fault for what it has left undone, opens with an assertion of enlightened patriotism—not the blind patriotism of the fanatical Slavists who love their country right or wrong, but that of one who loves, Chaadayev says, what deserves to be loved and cherished in Russian civilization.

Russia, Chaadayev argues in the *Apology*, has leaned toward the West since Ivan III, but it was Peter the Great who finally provided it with an idea by turning it away from its old ways to face the West, and thus offering it a share in human history in exchange for the denial of an empty past. This was possible only because that past was empty and Russia therefore had no ties to hold it back; both this lack of past and the genius of Peter who understood its meaning are Providential and form part of Russia's particular destiny in history.

For, Chaadayev continues, turning back to the philosophy of history of the *Letters*, "the history of a people is not merely a succession of facts . . . but also a sequence of connected ideas. Facts must be expressed by ideas;"[66] the history of a nation "will begin only on the day when this nation becomes conscious of the idea which was entrusted to it, which it was called upon to realize, and

---

[66] See below, p. 168.

when it sets about to follow it with that enduring though hidden instinct which leads nations to their destinies."[67] This the fanatical Slavists ignore as they search out curios for museums and libraries.

The world, Chaadayev points out, is divided into two parts, each distinguished by its particular idea; the East has a centripetal, meditative, synthetic idea which first enlightened the world but which became exhausted by its submissiveness and inwardness, while the West has a centrifugal, analytic idea which bases itself on law and activity and which, by its energy and vision of a boundless future, completes what the East began. This is the idea which Peter understood and offered to Russia.

Thus, the Slavists in particular and the Russians in general err in their lack of a philosophy of history. A proper understanding of history would make it clear that Russia, by being a latecomer in the development of history, can, from its objective, dispassionate position, arbitrate and resolve all social problems and thus lead the West. This, such a philosophy would show, is its destined role.

Chaadayev concludes the first and only completed part of the *Apology*[68] with an admission of his exaggeration of Russia's position in *Letter I*. Singling out particularly at this point the positive role of the Orthodox Church, he now says that it is this church, in its humble yet often heroic activity, which has provided any content there may be to Russian history prior to Peter the Great. He adds, however, that, although the future of a nation which produced Peter the Great cannot be so dark as he had previously painted it, it is evident from the success of Gogol's cynical comedy and the anger aroused by Chaadayev's austere and profound analysis that the Russian public still has a long way to go before it achieves mature patriotism and serious thought, and that whatever power Russia has is due only to its geographical situation on the one hand and to its princes on the other.

[67] See below, p. 169.

[68] The *Apology*, in the revised Gagarin-Gershenzon version, consists of two parts, the first covering fifteen pages in the present translation, the second only six lines.

The modifications of Chaadayev's thought evident in the *Apology* can thus be reduced to two, both of which in fact are to be found in general terms in the *Letters* themselves: the notions that history is the expression in fact of an idea and that this idea is carried to realization by historical figures provided by Providence. The *Apology*, however, finds such an idea and such a historical figure in Russia: the humility and heroic acts of the Russian Church provide Russia with both the possibility of survival and the possibility of enlightenment from the West, while Peter the Great, in his understanding of this idea and therefore of the destined role of Russia, introduced this enlightenment into this country. Chaadayev's philosophical position has thus not altered; it is only his interpretation of details within this position that has been modified.

Chaadayev's views for the remainder of his life changed only in terms of shifts of emphasis in these details: the strength or obscurity of the Russian idea, the success of Peter's vision, or the obstacles to its realization. Throughout his life, however, Chaadayev continued to unite the religious approach to history, which is identified with the Slavophiles, with the search for Western enlightenment, which the Westernizers, following his lead, symbolized in the figure of Peter the Great.

Philosophical Letters

Adveniat regnum tuum

Madam:

What I like, what I respect most in you, is your candor, your frankness. You can imagine how your letter must have surprised me. It is these attractive qualities in you which charmed me when I met you and which led me to speak to you about religion. Everything about you was such as to enjoin me to be silent. Imagine, then, once more my astonishment when I received your letter! This is all I have to say, Madam, about the opinion which you assume I have of your character. Let us say no more about it and go at once to the serious part of your letter.

First, whence comes this intellectual disturbance which so troubles you, which wearies you, you say, to the point of affecting your health? Here is the sad result of our conversations. Instead of the calm and peace which a new feeling awakened in your heart should have given you, it has caused anguish, qualms, almost remorse. Yet should this surprise me? It is the natural result of that baneful state of things which, among us, invades all hearts and souls. You merely yielded to the action of those forces which here shift everything about, from the highest ranks of society to the slave who exists only for the pleasure of his master.

Besides, how could you have resisted it? The qualities which distinguish you from the crowd surely render you the more open to the noxious influences of the air you breathe. In the midst of all that surrounds you, how could the few things which I was allowed to tell you determine your views? Could I purify the atmosphere in which we live? I should have foreseen the consequences; in fact, I did foresee them. Hence that frequent reticence, hardly likely to carry conviction to your soul and which must naturally have misled you. However, had I not been sure that, whatever pain religious feeling can cause in a heart in which it is but half-awakened, this is nevertheless better than complete somnolence, I would now have no alternative but to repent of my zeal. But those clouds which today darken your sky will one day, I hope, be dispersed into a salutary dew which will bring fertility to the seed cast into your heart; the effect which a few worthless words have had on you is to me a guarantee of the greater effect which the work of your own intelligence will surely produce in the future. Give yourself fearlessly, Madam, to the emotions which religious ideas arouse in you: only pure feelings can spring from this pure source!

As for external matters, it is sufficient for you today to know that the doctrine founded on the supreme principle of unity, and of the direct transmission of truth through an uninterrupted succession of its ministers, cannot but be that which best corresponds to the true spirit of religion, for it is wholly contained in the idea of the fusion of all the moral forces in the world into a single thought, a single feeling, and in the progressive establishment of a social system or church which will make truth reign among men. Any other doctrine, by the mere fact of its separation from the original doctrine, rejects the effect of the sublime invocation of the Savior: *Holy Father, I pray that they may be one, as we also are,*[1] and does not want that God should rule on earth. But it does not follow from this that you are bound to make this truth manifest to the world; this is certainly not your vocation. The very principle from which this truth derives makes it your duty, rather, considering your position in the world, to see it only as the internal light of your faith, no more. I consider myself fortunate in that I contributed in turning your thoughts to religion; but I would consider myself unfortunate indeed, Madam, if at the same time I

[1] [See John 17:11. —*Trans.*]

P. Ya. Chaadayev, Lithograph done in the 1840's with an inscription
by A. I. Herzen: "To Victor Ivanovich Kasotkin from the friend of
Chaadayev, A. Herzen; March 18, 1866, Cha[teau] de la Bissiere."
Institut of Russian Literature, Leningrad.

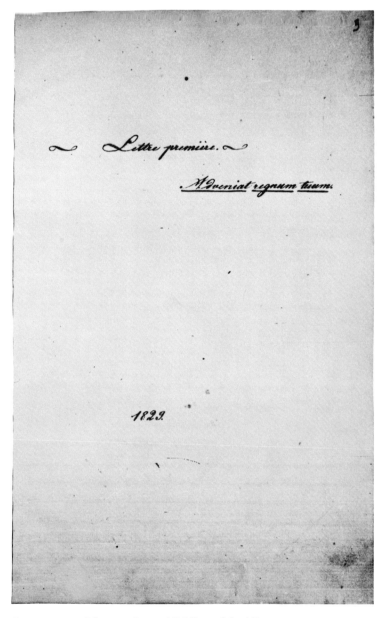

Cover page of Letter One of *Philosophical Letters*

had caused such troubles in your conscience as would, in the end, but quench your faith.

I believe I told you, one day, that the best way to keep religious feeling alive is to observe all the practices prescribed by the Church. This exercise in humility contains more than is usually recognized; the greatest minds have deliberately and thoughtfully practiced it; it is a true worship of God. Nothing so strengthens the spirit in its beliefs as the strict performance of all obligations attached to them. Moreover, most of the Christian rituals, inspired by the Supreme Reason, possess real efficacy for anyone who can be permeated by the truths they express. There is but one exception to this rule, otherwise perfectly general, and that is when one finds in oneself beliefs of a superior order, which elevate the soul to the very source whence flows all our certitude, and which yet do not contradict popular beliefs, but rather reinforce them; then and only then is it permissible to neglect external observance in order the better to devote oneself to more important labors. But let man beware of taking the illusions of his vanity, the deceptions of his reason for extraordinary revelations which exempt him from the general law! In your case, Madam, how can you do better than clothe yourself in that gown of humility which so well becomes your sex? It is, believe me, what can best calm your troubled soul and pour sweetness into your life.

Is there, I ask you, even according to worldly opinion, any condition more natural for a woman whose cultured intellect can find charm in study and in the serious emotions which accompany meditation, than that of a somewhat serious life devoted in great part to the thought and practice of religion? In your reading, you tell me, nothing so touches your imagination as the descriptions of those quiet and serene lives whose view, like that of some beautiful landscape at dusk, gives rest to the soul and removes us, for a moment, from a painful or insipid reality. Well, these pictures are not fantasies: it is up to you to bring one of these charming fictions into being; you lack nothing to accomplish it. You see that I am not enjoining a very austere morality: I am seeking that which can give peace to your soul in your own inclinations and in the most pleasant dreams of your imagination.

A certain portion of man's life pertains not to his physical, but to his mental existence. You must not neglect it. There is a mode of behavior imposed on the soul just as there is on the body: man must learn to submit to it. This is an old truth, I know; but it seems to me that in our country it still has the value of novelty. One of the worst features of our unique civilization is that we have not yet discovered truths that have elsewhere become truisms, even among nations that in many respects are far less advanced than we are. It is the result of our never having walked side by side with other nations; we belong to none of the great families of mankind; we are neither of the West nor of the East, and we possess the traditions of neither. Somehow divorced from time, we have not been touched by the universal education of mankind. That wonderful interconnection of human ideas in the succession of the centuries, that history of the human mind which brought man to the state in which he is today in the rest of the world, has had no influence upon us. That which elsewhere has long constituted the foundation of society and life is still for us but theory and speculation. For example, I must say this to you, Madam: you who are so happily constituted to gather up all that there is in the world of good and true, you who are so fashioned as to overlook nothing which will bring the sweetest and purest joys to the soul, where are you, I ask you, with all these advantages? You are still seeking with what to fill not your life, but your day. The very things which elsewhere provide the necessary framework of life, within which daily events are naturally ordered, this condition, as indispensable to a healthy moral existence as good air is to a healthy physical existence, is completely lacking for you. You understand that I am speaking here not of moral principles or philosophical maxims, but simply of a well-ordered life, of those habits, of those routines of the mind which put the soul at ease, which give it a regulated motion.

Look about you. Don't you think that we are very restless? We

34

all resemble travelers. Nobody has a definite sphere of existence; we have no proper habits; there are no rules, there is no home life, there is nothing to which we could be attached, nothing that would awaken our sympathy or affection—nothing durable, nothing lasting; everything flows, everything passes, leaving no traces either outside or within you. In our own houses we seem to be camping, in our families we look like strangers, in our cities we look like nomads, even more than the nomads who tend their herds on our steppes, for they are more attached to their wastelands than we to our cities. And do not think that this is not important. Poor souls that we are, let us not add to our other afflictions that of not understanding ourselves, let us not aspire to the existence of pure intelligences; let us learn to live sensibly within our given reality. But, first, let us talk a while longer about our country; this will not lead us away from the subject. Without such a preamble, you could not understand what I have to say.

Every nation has its period of stormy agitation, of passionate unease, of hasty activities. In such a period men become wanderers over the world, both in body and spirit. This is a time of great passions, strong emotions, great national undertakings. At such times nations toss about violently, without any apparent object, but not without benefit for future generations. All societies have gone through such phases. Such periods provide them with their most vivid memories, their legends, their poetry, their greatest and most productive ideas; such periods represent the necessary basis of every society. Otherwise, societies would have nothing valuable or cherished in memory; they would value only the dust of the earth they inhabit. This fascinating phase of the history of nations represents their adolescence, the age when their faculties develop most vigorously, and whose remembrance brings both joy and wisdom to their maturity. But we Russians, we are devoid of all this. At first brutal barbarism, then crude superstition, then cruel and humiliating foreign domination, the spirit of which was later inherited by our national rulers—such is the sad history of our youth. We had none of that period of exuberant activity, of the fervent turmoil of the moral forces of nations. Our period of social life which corresponds to this age was filled with a dull and gloomy existence, lacking in force and energy, with nothing to brighten it but crime, nothing to mitigate it but servitude. There are no charming remembrances, no graceful images in the people's memory; our national tradition is devoid of any powerful teaching. Cast a look upon the many centuries in our past, upon the expanse of soil we inhabit, and you will find no endearing reminiscence, no venerable memorial, to speak to you powerfully of the past, and to reproduce it for you in a vivid and colorful manner. We live only in the narrowest of presents, without past and without future, in the midst of a flat calm. And if we happen to bestir ourselves from time to time, it is not in the hope, nor in the desire, of some common good, but in the childish frivolousness of the infant, who raises himself and stretches his hands toward the rattle which his nurse presents to him.

So long as life has not become more regulated, more easy, more gentle than in the midst of the uncertainties of its earliest age, the true development of mankind in society has not yet begun for a nation. So long as societies waver about without convictions and without rules even for daily life, so long as that life has no form, how can the seeds of good ripen in them? This is still the state of chaotic fermentation of the things of the moral world, similar to the revolutions of the earth which preceded the present state of our planet. We are still at that stage.

Our first years, spent in immobile brutishness, have left no traces on our minds; we have nothing that is ours on which to base our thinking; isolated by a strange fate from the universal development of humanity, we have also absorbed none of mankind's ideas of traditional transmission. Yet it is on those ideas that the life of nations is founded; it is from those ideas that their future develops and that their moral growth derives. If we want to have an outlook similar to that of other civilized nations, we have somehow to repeat the whole education of mankind. In this we can be assisted by the history of [other] nations, and we have before us the products of the ages. No doubt this task is difficult, and possibly it is not given to one man to exhaust this vast subject; but, first of all, we must know what we are talking about, what is this education of mankind and what is the place which we occupy in the general order of things.

Nations live but by the mighty impressions which past centuries have left in their minds and by contact with other nations. In this way every man is conscious of his ties with the whole of mankind. "What is the life of man," Cicero asked, "if the memory of past events does not come to bind the present to the past?"[2] But we Russians, like illegitimate children, come to this world without patrimony, without any links with people who lived on the earth before us; we have in our hearts none of these lessons which have preceded our own existence. Each one of us must himself once again seek to tie the broken thread in the family. What is habit, instinct, among other peoples we must get into our heads by hammerstrokes. Our memories go no further back than yesterday; we are, as it were, strangers to ourselves. We walk through time so singly that as we advance the past escapes us forever. This is a natural result of a culture based wholly on borrowing and imitation. There is among us no inward development, no natural progress; new ideas throw out the old ones because they do not arise from the latter, but come among us from Heaven knows where. Since we accept only ready-made ideas, the indelible traces which a progressive movement of ideas engraves on the mind and which gives ideas their forcefulness makes no furrow on our intellect. We grow, but we do not mature; we advance, but obliquely, that is, in a direction which does not lead to the goal. We are like children who have never been made to think for themselves: once they have come of age they have nothing of their own; all their knowledge is on the surface of their being, their whole soul is on the outside. This is exactly our situation.

Nations are moral beings in the same way as individuals are. As years make the education of persons, so centuries make theirs. In

[2] [*Orator*, 120. Chaadayev's rendering is a paraphrase. —*Trans.*]

a way, one can say that as a people we are an exception to the rule. We belong to that number of nations which do not seem to make up an integral part of the human race, but which exist only to teach the world some great lesson. The lesson which we are destined to give will, naturally, not be lost; but who knows when we shall find ourselves once again in the midst of humanity, and what afflictions we shall experience before we accomplish our destiny?

The peoples of Europe have a common aspect, a family resemblance. In spite of the general division of these peoples into Latin and Teutonic branches, into southern and northern, there is a common link which unites them into a fasces, clear to anyone who has studied their general history. You know that even recently all Europe was called Christendom, and that this word had its place in public law. In addition to this general character, each of these peoples has a particular character, which, however, consists of no more than history and tradition. It is what makes up the hereditary intellectual patrimony of these peoples. Every individual has a right to it; each assimilates during his lifetime, without fatigue or labor, these notions scattered in his society, and profits by them. You can draw the parallel yourself and see how many elementary ideas we can thus pick up through simple give-and-take, to make use of them as best we can to direct our lives. And observe that this is not a matter of study or reading, of anything literary or scientific, but simply of the contact of minds, of those ideas which invade a child in the cradle, which surround him in the midst of his play, which his mother breathes on him in her caresses; finally, these are ideas which, in the guise of divers feelings, enter into the marrow of his bones with the very air he breathes, and which have already formed his moral being before he is delivered out into the world and society. Do you wish to know what ideas these are? They are the ideas of duty, of justice, of right, of order. They were brought forth by the very events which set up societies; they are integral elements in the social life of these nations. Such is the atmosphere of the West; this is more than history, more than psychology; it is the physiology of a European. What have we to substitute for this in our country?

I do not know whether one can draw any universal conclusion from what I have just said and thus reach an absolute principle, but one can certainly see how the strange situation of a people which cannot connect its thought with any succession of ideas that have been progressively developed in its society and have slowly devolved one from the other, which has taken no part in the general progress of the human spirit save by blind, superficial, and often very awkward imitation of other nations, must powerfully influence the mind of every individual within it.

You will find that, as a result, a certain poise, a certain method in our thoughts, a certain logic is lacking to us all. The Western syllogism is unknown to us. There is more than frivolity in our best minds. But the best ideas are no more than sterile visions and remain paralyzed in our brains owing to lack of connection and succession. It is a trait of human nature that a man gets lost when he can find no means to bind himself to what has come before him and what will follow upon him. Then all consistency, all certainty escapes him. Lacking the guiding sense of continuous duration he finds himself lost in the world. There are lost souls in every country; but in ours it is a general characteristic. I do not mean the lightness with which one used to reproach the French—actually but an easy manner of conceiving things which did not exclude either depth or breadth of mind and which gave infinite grace and charm to their social intercourse—I mean the flightiness of a life totally lacking in experience and foresight, a flightiness which results simply from the ephemeral existence of an individual detached from the species. Such a life holds dear neither the honor nor the progress of any community of ideas or interests, not even a traditional family outlook or that mass of prescriptions and perspectives which compose, in a state of things founded on memory of the past and awareness of the future, both public and private life. There is absolutely nothing general in our heads; everything in them is individual, and everything is transitory and incomplete.

39

Even in our very expressions I find something strangely vague, cold, uncertain, something which resembles to an extent the aspect of people at the lowest rung of the social ladder. When I was abroad, particularly in the South where faces are so animated and expressive, I often compared the faces of my compatriots with those of the natives, and I was struck by this expressionlessness in our faces.

Foreigners have praised in us a sort of careless rashness which one finds particularly in the lower classes of our nation, but, since they could observe only certain isolated effects of our national character, they could not judge the whole. They did not see that the same principle which makes us sometimes so daring makes us also ever incapable of depth and perseverance. They did not see that what renders us so indifferent to the hazards of life renders us indifferent also to all good, all evil, all truth, all deceit, and that it is precisely this which deprives us of all those powerful motives which lead men to perfect themselves. They did not see that it is precisely this lazy boldness which is responsible for the fact that in our country not even the upper classes, painful though it be to say this, are exempt from the vices which elsewhere exist only among the very lowest. They did not see, finally, that, although we have some of the virtues of a young people not much advanced in civilization, we have none of the virtues of a mature, highly cultured people.

I do not mean, certainly, that we have only vices, while European peoples have only virtues; God forbid! But I do say that in order to judge peoples fairly we must study the general spirit that constitutes their life, for that spirit alone, and not any other specific trait of character, can lead them on the road toward greater moral perfection and indefinite progress.

The masses are subject to certain forces which themselves exist in the top social group. They do not think for themselves; there are among them a certain number of thinkers who think for them, who give the impulse and put in motion the collective intelligence of a nation. While the small number thinks, the rest feels and the general motion occurs. This is true of all races on earth, except for some brutish ones in whom there remains of human nature but the physical form. The primitive peoples of Europe, the Celts, the Scandinavians, the Germans [*Germains*], had their druids, their scalds, their bards: these were, in their way, powerful thinkers. Look at those peoples of North America which the materialistic civilization of the United States is so busily destroying: there are among them men of remarkable profundity. Well, I ask you, where are our wise men, where are our thinkers? Who has ever thought for us? Who thinks for us now?

And yet, situated between the two great divisions of the world, between East and West, with one elbow leaning on China and the other on Germany, we should have combined in us the two great principles of intelligent nature, imagination and reason, and have united in our civilization the past of the entire world. But this is not the part which Providence has assigned to us. Far from it, she seems wholly to have neglected our destiny. Suspending, where we were concerned, her beneficial action on the human mind, she left us completely to ourselves, she wished to have nothing to do with us, she wished to teach us nothing. Historical experience does not exist for us. To behold us it would seem that the general law of mankind had been revoked in our case. Isolated in the world, we have given nothing to the world, we have taken nothing from the world; we have not added a single idea to the mass of human ideas; we have contributed nothing to the progress of the human spirit. And we have disfigured everything we touched of that progress. From the very first moment of our social existence, nothing has emanated from us for the common good of men; not one useful thought has sprouted in the sterile soil of our country; not a single great truth has sprung from our midst; we did not bother to invent anything, while from the inventions of others we borrowed only the deceptive appearances and the useless luxuries.

Strange. Even in the world of science, which touches on all fields, our history makes no connection, explains nothing, proves nothing. If the barbarian hordes which threw the world into confusion had not crossed the land we inhabit before swooping down on the West, we would hardly have provided a chapter to world history. For people to notice us we have had to stretch from the Bering Straits to the Oder. Once, a great man[3] wanted to educate us, and in order to make us eager for enlightenment, he threw us the mantle of civilization: we picked up the mantle but did not touch civilization. Another time, another great Prince,[4] associating us to his glorious mission, led us victorious from one end of Europe to the other: returning home from this triumphal march across the most civilized countries in the world, we brought back nothing but evil ideas and baneful errors which resulted in an immense calamity that set us back by half a century. We have something in our blood which drives off all true progress. In a word, we have lived and we live but to be a great lesson to such distant posterity as will be aware of it; today, whatever anyone says, we mark a void in the intellectual sphere. I cannot tire of marveling at this void and this strange solitude of our social existence. It is due, certainly, in part to some singular destiny, but doubtless in part, too, to man, as is true in all moral events. Let us question history still further: it is history which explains a people.

What were we doing at the time when, from the midst of the struggle between the energetic barbarism of the northern peoples and the high idea of religion, the edifice of modern civilization was being built up? Driven by a baneful fate, we turned to Byzantium, wretched and despised by those nations, for a moral code that was to become the basis of our education. Only a moment earlier an ambitious mind[5] had removed this household from the universal brotherhood: what we got was thus the idea as it had been disfigured by human passion. At the time, in Europe everything was animated by the vivifying principle of unity. All emanated from it and all converged upon it. The whole intellec-

---

3 [Peter the Great. —*Trans.*]
4 [Alexander I. —*Trans.*]
5 Photius.

tual movement of those times tended to build up the unity of human thought, and all incentive had its source in this powerful need to arrive at a universal idea which is the genius of modern times. Strangers to this marvelous principle, we became the prey of conquerors, and when, freed from foreign yoke, we could, had we not been separated from the common family, have profited from the ideas which had blossomed during this time among our Western brothers, we fell instead into an even harsher servitude, sanctified as it was by the fact of our deliverance.

Many glowing rays were already then illuminating Europe, flashing out from the apparent darkness with which it was covered. The greater part of the knowledge in which man prides himself today was already anticipated by individual minds; society already had assumed a definite character; and, by turning back to pagan Antiquity, the Christian world had found the forms of beauty which it lacked up to then. But we locked ourselves up in our religious separatism, and nothing reached us of what was happening in Europe. We had no dealings with the great project of the world. The outstanding qualities with which religion had endowed modern peoples and which, in the opinion of a healthy mind, raises them as much above the Ancients as they in turn were above the Hottentots and the Lapps; these new forces with which it had enriched human mind; these customs which submission to a disarmed authority rendered as gentle as they had at first been brutal, none of this had taken place among us. While the Christian world marched on majestically along the road marked out for it by its divine Creator, carrying along generations, we, although called Christians, stuck to our place. The entire world was being rebuilt, while we built nothing: as before, we hibernated in our hovels built of logs and straw. In a word, the new destiny of mankind was not being fulfilled in our country. We were Christians, but the fruits of Christianity were not ripening for us.

I ask you, is it not absurd to suppose, as is generally done in our country, that we can appropriate in one stroke this progress of the peoples of Europe, made so slowly through the direct and evident action of a unique moral force, and to suppose that we can do this without even trying to find out how it developed?

Nothing is understood of Christianity if it is not seen that Christianity has a purely historical side which is so essentially part of dogma that it contains in a way all the philosophy of Christianity, for it demonstrates what that religion has done for man and what it will do for him in the future. Thus, the Christian religion is seen not only as a moral system conceived in the perishable formulae of the human intellect, but also as a divine, eternal power acting universally in the mental world and whose visible action should be a perpetual teaching to us. This is the true meaning of the dogma expressed symbolically in the belief in a Universal Church.

In the Christian world everything should necessarily concur to the establishment of a perfect order of things on earth, and everything does so concur to it; otherwise, the Word of the Savior would be given the lie by fact. He would not be in His Church until the end of time. The new order, the reign of God which redemption was to effect, would not differ from the old order, the reign of evil, which it was to destroy. There would still only be that imaginary perfectibility which philosophy dreams of and which is refuted by every page of history: a vain agitation of the mind which satisfies only the needs of our material being and which has ever raised a man to a height only to dash him into a still deeper abyss.

But, you will say, are we then not Christians and can one be civilized only in the European manner? Of course we are Christians; and so are the Abyssinians. Of course one can be civilized in a manner other than the European; the Japanese are, and more so, from what one of our compatriots says, than we are in Russia. And do you believe that it is the Christianity of the Abyssinians and the civilization of the Japanese that will bring about that order of things of which I just spoke and which is the final destiny of the human race? Do you believe that it is these absurd aberrations of divine and human truths which will bring Heaven to earth?

44

There are two very distinct things in Christianity. One is its action on the individual; the other is its action on universal mental nature. These are naturally fused in the Supreme Reason and necessarily lead to the same end. But the duration within which the eternal designs of the Divine Wisdom are realized cannot be grasped by our limited vision. We must distinguish divine action as it is manifested in a given time in the life of man from that action which occurs only in the infinite. On the day of the final achievement of the work of redemption all hearts and minds will constitute but one feeling and one thought, and all the walls which separate peoples and communions will fall to the ground. But today each must be cognizant of how he is placed in the scheme of the general vocation of Christians, that is, of what means he can find in him and around him to cooperate in the progress toward the goal set for the whole of human society.

There is thus necessarily a certain sphere of ideas in which participate the minds who belong to the society where this end is destined to be achieved, that is, where revealed thought is to ripen and reach its complete fullness. This sphere of ideas, this moral sphere produces in this society a certain mode of life and a point of view which, without being precisely the same for each, nevertheless, with regard to us as with regard to all non-European peoples, make for a single way of being, the result of that immense intellectual labor of eighteen centuries in which all the passions, all the interests, all the sufferings, all the imaginings, all the efforts of reason have participated.

All the nations of Europe held hands as they traversed the centuries; if now they ever try to go their separate ways, they eventually come back to the same path. In order to understand the close relationship of these peoples, it is not necessary to study history; you have only to read Tasso, and you will see them all prostrated at the foot [of the walls] of Jerusalem. Remember that for fifteen centuries they had but one language with which to worship God; they had but one moral authority; they had but one faith. Consider that for fifteen centuries, every year, on the same day, at the same hour, in the same words, all together they raised their voices to the Supreme Being to celebrate His glory in the greatest of his blessings. Marvelous concert, a thousand times more sublime than all the harmonies of the physical world. Now, since this sphere where men of Europe live and which is the only one within which the human species can reach its final destiny is the result of the influence which religion has exercised among them, then it is clear that, if until now the weakness of our beliefs or the insufficiency of our dogma has kept us outside this universal movement within which the social idea of Christianity was developed and formulated and has thrown us back into the category of peoples who are to profit but indirectly and very late from the full effect of Christianity, we must seek to revive our beliefs by all possible means and to give ourselves a truly Christian impulse, for it is Christianity which has accomplished everything in Europe. This is what I meant to say when I told you that we in Russia must go through the education of mankind from the very beginning.

The whole history of modern society occurs on the level of ideals. There is, thus, a true education to be had there. Originally set up on the basis of ideals, history has gone forward only by means of thought. Ideals have always been the cause of interests; never have interests provoked ideals. All political revolutions were, at the outset, but moral revolutions. People searched for Truth and found freedom and well-being. The phenomenon of modern society and its civilization are to be explained in these terms. Otherwise, they cannot be understood at all.

Religious persecutions, martyrdom, the spreading of Christianity, heresies, councils: these are the events which filled the first centuries. All the movement of this period, including the barbarian invasions, is connected with these [first] efforts of the modern spirit in its infancy. The following period was occupied by the organization of the hierarchy, the centralization of spiritual power, and by the uninterrupted spreading of religious teaching among the northern nations. Next follows the exaltation of religious sentiment to the highest degree and the stabilizing of religious authority. The philosophical and literary development of the mind and the improvement of morals under the dominion of religion complete this history—which could be called sacred with as much right as the history of the ancient chosen people. Finally, once again it was a new religious turn, a new swing of the human mind stimulated by religion, that determined the present order of society. Thus the great interest, one may say the only one, among modern peoples was ever that of an ideal. All material, positive, personal interests were absorbed in it.

I realize that, instead of admiring this prodigious impulse of human nature toward its possible perfection, people have called it fanaticism and superstition. But, whatever one may say, judge for yourself what a deep impression a social development wholly produced by a single sentiment, in good and in evil, must have left on the character of these peoples! Let a superficial philosophy make all the noise it cares about the wars of religion, the stakes kindled by intolerance; we, for our part, can but envy the lot of those peoples who, by the clash of opinions, in the bloody conflicts taking place for the sake of Truth, created for themselves a world of ideas which we cannot even imagine, much less transport ourselves to body and soul, as we claim to do.

Certainly, in the countries of western Europe not everything is permeated with reason, virtue, and religion—far from it. But there everything in a mysterious way obeys that power which reigned sovereign during many centuries; there everything is the effect of that long succession of events and ideas that caused the present state of society. Here is an example that proves this assertion. The English, whose character is so distinct and whose institutions are in full measure permeated by the modern spirit, strictly speaking have no history but a religious one. Their last revolution, to which they owe their freedom and well-being, as well as the whole succession of events which brought about this revolution, beginning with Henry VIII, is but a religious development. During that whole period purely political interest was but a secondary motive and, at times, disappeared altogether or was sacrificed to the idea. And while I am writing these lines,[6] it is still the interest of religion which moves that privileged land. But, in general, what people in Europe would not find in its national conscience, if it made the effort to seek for it, that particular element which, in the form of a holy idea, was the constant vivifying principle, the soul of its social being, for the whole duration of its existence?

The effect of Christianity is by no means limited to its direct and immediate influence upon the minds of men. The great task which it is destined to fulfill can be achieved only through a multitude of moral, intellectual, and social combinations, in which the complete freedom of the human spirit must necessarily have the greatest latitude. Thus, one can say that all that has happened since the first day of our era, or rather since the moment when the Savior of the world said to his disciples: "Go ye . . . preach the Gospel to every creature,"[7] including all attacks directed against Christianity, enters perfectly into this general idea of its influence. It is sufficient to see the empire of Christ exercising its influence in every heart, whether in awareness or in ignorance, with consent or by compulsion, to admit the realization of His prophecies. Thus, in spite of all incompleteness, vice, and guilt in European society as it is today, it is nonetheless true that the reign of God is realized in it to some extent, for it contains the principle of indefinite progress and it possesses the seeds and elements of all that is needed for this reign to be one day definitively established on earth.

Before concluding these reflections on the influence of religion on society, I shall transcribe here what I said about it in the past in a document with which you are not acquainted.

"It is certain," I said, "that so long as one does not perceive the effect of Christianity wherever human thought in any way comes into contact with it, be it but to attack it, one does not have a clear idea of it. Wherever the name of Christ is pronounced, that name alone captivates men, whatever they may try to do about it.

[6] 1829.
[7] [Mark 16:15 —Trans.]

Original manuscript page from Letter Three of *Philosophical Letters*

Original manuscript page from Letter Six
of *Philosophical Letters*

Nothing more clearly indicates the divine origin of this religion than this aspect of absolute universality which allows it to penetrate people's souls in all possible ways, to possess souls without their being aware of it, to dominate them, to subjugate them, even when they most resist it. It does this by bringing into the mind truths which previously were not there, by arousing in the heart emotions which the heart had never felt, by breathing into us feelings which place us, without our being aware of it, in the general order of things. In this way the function of every individual thing is determined by it and it makes everything concur to a single end. When Christianity is considered from this point of view every prophecy of Christ becomes a palpable truth. One then sees distinctly the interplay of all those levers which His almighty hand sets in motion to lead man to his destiny without threatening his freedom, without paralyzing any of his natural powers, but, on the contrary, adding to their intensity and exalting to infinity all of man's real capacity. One sees that in this new economy no moral element remains idle, that the most energetic faculties of thought as well as the ardent expansion of feeling, the heroism of a strong soul as well as the surrender of a submissive spirit, all find in it a place and function. Accessible to every rational being, the revealed idea, associating itself to our every heartbeat no matter of what nature that heartbeat may be, captivates everyone, grows, and even becomes stronger through the very obstacles it meets. In a man of genius it reaches to heights inaccessible for the rest of men; for a timid soul it walks on the ground and goes step by step; for a contemplative mind it is absolute and profound; for a soul subject to imagination it is ethereal and rich in images; in a gentle and loving heart it is transformed into charity and love: it leads every mind that surrenders to it powerfully forward, filling it with ardor, force, and lucidity. Notice what a diversity of characters, what a multiplicity of forces it sets into motion; what a number of different capacities are made one; how many variously constituted hearts beat for but one idea! But the influence of Christianity on society as a whole is still more remarkable. Picture to yourself the entire evolution of the new society, and you will see how Christianity transforms every human interest into its own, everywhere replacing material necessity with a moral one and stimulating in the domain of thought those great disputes unknown to the history of any other age or to any society, those fearful collisions of ideas, when the whole life of peoples became but one great idea and one boundless feeling; you will see how it absorbs everything: private and public life, family and fatherland, science and poetry, reason and imagination, memory and hope, joys and sorrows. Happy are those who, in this great movement impressed on the world by God Himself, are in their hearts aware of the effects they bring about. But not all are active instruments, not all act consciously; multitudes necessarily move blindly, like inanimate atoms, inert masses, without knowing the forces which set them in motion, without perceiving the goal toward which they are pushed."

It is time to return to you, Madam. I admit that I find it difficult to tear myself away from these general observations. It is from the picture which presents itself to me from this height that I derive all my consolation; I take refuge in the sweet belief in the future bliss of mankind when, depressed by the unhappy reality which surrounds me, I feel the need to breathe purer air, to look at a clearer sky. I do not think, however, that I have wasted your time. I had to acquaint you with the point of view from which one should regard the Christian world and with what we, on our side, are doing in this world. What I have said about our country must seem full of bitterness to you, yet I have spoken but the truth, and not even the whole truth. Moreover, Christian consciousness tolerates no blindness, least of all that of national prejudice, since it most of all divides men.

This is a very long letter, Madam. I think that we both need to stop for breath. I thought, when I began, that I could tell you what I had to tell you in a few words: on second thought I find that there is enough for a whole book. Would that suit you, Madam? Let me know. But, in any case, you will not be able to avoid a second letter, for we have but approached the subject. In the meantime I would be very grateful if you would consider the prolixity of the first one as a compensation for the time I kept you waiting. I started to reply the very day I received your letter: unpleasant and dull tasks then took up all my time and I had to get rid of them before I could begin to speak to you of such serious matters; then I had to recopy my scribbling which was completely illegible. This next time you will not wait so long: I am starting in again tomorrow.

Necropolis, 1829, 1 December

If I made myself clear the other day, Madam, you must have understood that I am far from thinking that we lack only enlightenment. There is no profusion of that among us either, I grant you, but we must resign ourselves to dispense for the time being with those vast intellectual riches which the centuries have accumulated elsewhere in the hands of men: we have other business. Besides, even supposing that by study and reflection we could acquire the knowledge we still lack, how would we give ourselves those mighty traditions, that vast experience, that deep awareness of the past, those powerful habits of mind, products of an immense employment of all human faculties, which constitute the moral nature and the true superiority of European nations? At this time the problem is thus not one of enlarging the realm of our ideas, but of rectifying those we have, of giving them a new direction. As for you, Madam, your most urgent need is a situation where the new thoughts which chance has introduced into your mind, the new needs which these thoughts have given your heart, the feelings which they have awakened in your soul, may find real application. A world that is your own must be created for you, since the one you inhabit has become foreign to you.

First, the state of our soul, however elevated we may consider it, depends inevitably on the things that surround us. Concern yourself, therefore, with properly understanding what your position in the world and in your family permits you to do in order to

---

[1] [See Preface, p. ix and p. ix, n. 11–14. —*Trans.*]

harmonize your feelings with those of your way of life, your ideas with your domestic concerns, your beliefs with those of the people you see. A multitude of troubles arises from nothing more than the dissonance between what goes on in our private minds and the demands of society. You say that your income does not permit you to enjoy a pleasant life in the capital. Well, you own a charming country place; what prevents you from installing your household gods there for the remainder of your days? Happy necessity which depends only on you to be rendered as profitable to you as all the most interesting teachings of philosophy. Make that refuge as attractive as possible. Busy yourself embellishing it, decorating it; give it studied refinement, charm: why not? This is not a matter of cultured sensuality; it is not to obtain vulgar pleasures that you would be going to all this trouble: it is to withdraw all the more into your inner life. Do not scorn, I beg you, these material details. We live in a country so lacking in expressions of ideals that if we do not surround ourselves in our personal lives with a little poetry and good taste we run the risk of losing all discrimination, all idea of art. The neglect of the comforts and amenities of life is one of the most striking characteristics of our curious civilization. We hardly think of taking shelter from the inclemencies of the weather—and that in a climate which leads one seriously to doubt that it was ever intended for the habitation of rational beings. If we were dull enough in the past to settle in these brutal climes, let us try at least today to settle ourselves in them in such a way as somewhat to forget their ruggedness.

I remember that you used very much to enjoy reading Plato. Note then how the most idealistic, the most ethereal of the sages of Antiquity took care to surround the characters of his philosophical dramas with the comforts of life. Now you see them walking leisurely along the delightful shores of the Ilissus or the cypress-lined avenues of Gnossos; now they seek the fresh shade of an old plane tree or the sweet rest of some blossoming turf; now, when the heat of day has fallen, they go breathe the scented air and soft breezes of an Attic evening; or, finally, you see them lying

53

careless around the banquet table, crowned with flowers and glass in hand: it is thus only after they are well situated on earth that he carries them to his superlunar regions where he so loves to soar. I could also show you in the writings of the sternest of our Church Fathers, in St. John Chrysostom, in St. Gregory Nazianzen, even in St. Basil, delightful descriptions of the retreats where these great men found peace and the lofty inspirations which made them the luminaries of faith. These holy men did not think that giving care to things which, say what you like, take up a great part of life detracted from their worthiness. There is a veritable cynicism in this indifference, of which some of us make a virtue, to the comforts of life. One of the things which most retards our progress is, I believe, the lack of any idea of art in our private lives.

Next, I would like you, in this refuge which you would have done your best to embellish, to live a perfectly even and methodical life. We all lack a feeling for order and method: let us rectify this defect. There is no point in repeating what has been said in favor of a well-regulated life; what is certain is that only by this constant subjection to an invariable rule can we accustom ourselves to submit without effort to the supreme law of our nature. But in order to follow any rule to the letter nothing must go awry. Frequently one is thrown out of a deliberate routine at the first hours of the morning: then the whole day is out of tune. Thus, nothing is more essential than the first impressions we receive, the first ideas which come to us as we begin to live again after the semblance of death which separates our days. It is these impressions, these ideas which usually determine the state of our soul for the whole day. A day which ends with an irretrievable error begins with a personal vexation. Accustom yourself, therefore, to make the first hours of the day as serious, as solemn as possible; make your soul at once climb to the greatest height it is capable of reaching; try to spend these hours in complete solitude, to shed all that can touch you, that can distract you too sharply: thus prepared you will be able to brave without fear the troublesome influences which will later besiege you and which otherwise would make your whole life a perpetual and endless battle. Besides, once that moment is past, there is no other during which you can be alone, can stop to collect yourself; life seizes you with all its preoccupations of pleasures and annoyances; you merely revolve in the eternal cycle of human pettiness. Let us not allow the only hour of the day when we can be quite by ourselves to pass without benefiting from it.

I feel quite strongly, I admit, about this necessity daily to meditate and put my soul in order; I am convinced that there is no other way to be secure from the encroachments of the things around us: but, as you no doubt realize, that is not enough. You need an idea which spreads over all your life, which is always present to you, which serves you as a torch at all hours of the day. We come into the world with a vague instinct of moral goodness, but we can conceive it fully only in the more complete idea which develops out of that instinct during the course of our lives. It is to this inner activity that everything must be referred; it is in terms of this that all your life must be ordered. But all this must be done in the silence of your heart, for the world has no sympathy for profundity. It averts its eyes from great convictions; the presence of a solemn idea tires it. You, however, need a true feeling and a serious idea which do not hesitate between the various opinions of men, but lead you steadfastly to your goal. Do not envy society's frantic pleasures; you will find in your retreat comforts which it cannot know. I have no doubt that, once accustomed to the calm atmosphere of such a life, you will, from the midst of your refuge, quietly watch the world as it grows restless and rushes on its way before you. You will enjoy with delight the silence of your soul. Meanwhile, you must acquire the inclinations, habits, and attachments which are proper to your new mode of life. You must divest yourself of all the vain curiosity which wastes and mutilates life; you must above all destroy that deep-rooted inclination of the heart which makes novelty attractive, daily gossip interesting, which produces ceaseless longing and expectation of the morrow. Without that you will find neither peace nor well-being, only disgust and boredom. Do you want the waves of the world to break near your peaceful home? Banish from your soul all those restless emotions aroused by the doings of society, all those nervous feelings provoked by the news of the day; close your door to all rumors, all echoes of the world; forbid even your home, if you have the courage to do so, to all that frivolous literature which is, at bottom, but those same sounds put in writing. Nothing to my mind is so incompatible with a well-ordered intellectual regimen than eagerness for the latest journalistic scribblings [*lectures nouvelles*]. One sees only people who have become incapable of serious meditation, of deep feeling, because they nourish themselves on nothing but these ephemeral writings in which everything is touched upon while nothing is thoroughly studied, in which everything is promised while nothing is given, in which everything is shown in a dubious or false light which leaves in the soul only emptiness[2] and uncertainty. If you want to find the mode of life you will have adopted attractive, novelty must never in any matter have a claim for you.

It is certain that the more you acquire tastes and needs relating to this mode of life, the more at ease you will be in it; the more you harmonize the external with the internal, the visible with the invisible, the more pleasant you will make the course you have to traverse. But I must also not conceal from you the obstacles you will have to meet. In our country that road has more of them than one can say. It is not a beaten path, where the wheel of life rolls along a well-traced track; it is a way along which you must push through brambles and thorns, and at times through forests. In the old civilizations of Europe, where all modes of life have long since been worked out, if someone there decides to change his life, he has but to select the new framework within which he wants to settle, his place is prepared for him in advance; the roles are cast; so long as you take the role that belongs to you, men and things

---

[2] [McNally ("Chaadayev's Philosophical Letters," p. 48, l. 33 and p. 48n.) suggests "*vide*" for an illegible word. The Russian translation (*Literaturnoye nasledstvo*, XXII–XXIV, 22) has "*pustota*" and no indication that the word was unclear. —*Trans*.]

group around you by themselves: it is up to you to make fitting use of it. But in our country the situation is quite different. What expense, what hardship before you can find ease in your new sphere of life! What time lost, what strength expended to orient yourself, to accustom men to look at you in your new aspect, to silence the fool, to wear out the surprise! Does anyone here know the power of thought? Has anyone here seen how a great conviction finds its way into one's mind through some event foreign to the usual course of things, through some unexpected light, through some superior teaching,[3] how it seizes the soul, completely overturns your being, and raises it above itself and everything that surrounds it? What wakeful conscience has ever here hastened a heartbeat? What man here has ever devoted himself to the worship of Truth? How can anyone who earnestly lives up to his beliefs not find obstacles and hindrances in the midst of this mob that nothing has ever affected? You must create your own surroundings, Madam, even the air that you breathe, even the soil which you trample. This is literally true: are not the slaves who serve you your atmosphere? Are not the furrows that other slaves have dug by the sweat of their brows the earth that supports you? How many things, how much misery is embraced in the single word "slave"! This is the magic circle in which we flounder helplessly; this is the odious fact which destroys us all; this is what in our country renders our most noble efforts, our most generous impulses vain; this is what paralyzes all our wills, soils all our virtues. Weighed down by this fatal guilt, what soul is so fine that it will not wither under the unbearable burden? What man is so strong that, always at odds with himself, always thinking one way and acting another, he does not in the end find himself repulsive? I have returned unawares to my original thesis; let me say one more word before I return to your concerns.

What is the cause of this horrible wound that is consuming us? How comes it that the most striking feature of Christian society

[3] [The manuscript of the Dashkov Collection (F93/Op 3/No. 1351) begins here. —*Trans.*]

is precisely the one of which the Russian nation, in the very bosom of Christianity, has divested itself? Why does religion have this perverse effect upon us? I do not know, but it seems to me that this circumstance alone could lead one to doubt that Orthodoxy with which we adorn ourselves. As you know, no ancient philosopher thought of imagining a slaveless society, nor even of finding fault with slavery. Aristotle, who can be regarded as the representative of all the wisdom there was in the world before the coming of Christ, stated as a fact that some men were born to be free, others to be in chains. You also know that there is no skeptic so obstinate that he will not agree that the abolition of servitude in Europe is due to Christianity. Further, it is known that the first emancipations were religious acts performed before the altar, and that in the majority of the emancipation charters one finds the expression, *pro redemptione animae*, for the salvation of my soul. Finally, it is known that the clergy everywhere set the example, freeing their own serfs, and that, in those parts of the world subject to their spiritual authority, the abolition of slavery was first instigated by the Roman pontiffs. Why [then] did Christianity not have the same results among us? Why, on the contrary, did the Russian people descend to slavery only after they became Christian, namely in the reigns of Godunov and Shuisky? Let the Orthodox Church explain this phenomenon. Let it say why it did not raise its maternal voice against this detestable usurpation of one part of the people by the other. And note, I pray you, how obscure we Russians are in spite of our power and all our greatness. Only today the Bosphorus and the Euphrates have simultaneously heard our cannon thunder. Yet history, which at this very hour is demonstrating that the abolition of slavery is the work of Christianity, does not suspect that a Christian people of forty million is in chains. Nations are in reality a part of the human race only because of their intellectual powers, and the attention which they arouse is determined by the moral influence they have in the world, and not by the noise they make.

Let us return to our subject.

Letter Two

After what I have told you of the kind of life I should like to see you adopt, you may possibly imagine that I am asking you to engage yourself in a wholly monastic life. But I am speaking only of a sober and thoughtful life which has nothing in common with the dreary rigor of ascetic morality; I am speaking merely of a way of life which differs from that of the masses only by [being guided by] a positive idea, a sincere feeling, to which all other major ideas, all other feelings are referred. Such a life can perfectly well be combined with legitimate pleasures; indeed, it even requires them, and human society is its necessary condition. Solitude has its dangers; at times one finds strange seductions in it. Concentrated within itself, the spirit feeds on vain, self-created images; like St. Anthony, a man then peoples his desert with phantoms, children of his fancy, who in turn pursue him. On the other hand, if a man cultivates religious thought without passion, without violence, he will preserve, even in the midst of all the bustle of society, that inner disposition before which all the enchantments, all the distractions of life are powerless. Thus, what must be found is a certain mental attitude, tender and pliant, an attitude which can without effort combine the idea of the true and the good with all operations of reason and with all emotions of the heart. Above all, one should try to imbue himself with the truths of revelation. The great prerogative of these truths is that they are accessible to all intelligent creatures; they adapt themselves to all types of minds. They can be reached by all possible roads, by the submissive and blind faith professed unthinkingly by the multitude, by profound knowledge, by the native piety of the heart, by the reasoned inspiration of the mind, by the exalted poetry of the soul; but the simplest road is to return to those moments, so frequent in a man's life, when we have most strongly felt the impact of religious feelings upon our souls, when it seems to us that we were deprived of all our own power and that a superior force drove us in spite of ourselves toward the good, raising us from earth and carrying us toward Heaven. Then, in the awareness of our impotence, our spirit will open itself with extraordinary will to thoughts of

Heaven and the highest truths will naturally flow into our hearts.

It is impossible, if we return again and again to the principle of all our moral activity, to the motives of our thoughts and actions, not to see that a great part of all we do is determined by something which in no way belongs to us. What is best and noblest in us, what is most useful to us, is precisely what we do not ourselves produce. All the good that we do is but the effect of our capacity to submit ourselves to the action of an unknown power. The only true principle of our [own] activity is the idea of our own interest within the limits of a given time which we call life; this principle is nothing but the instinct of self-preservation, which we share with all other animate beings, but which we modify in terms of our particular nature. Try as we will, no matter what disinterestedness we place in our feelings and in our actions, this interest, more or less understood, more or less remote, always directs us. However eager our desire to act for the general good, this abstract good that we conceive is none other than the good we want for ourselves. We can never wholly efface ourselves; we always include ourselves in what we desire for others. Indeed, the Supreme Reason, condescending to our natural weakness in the human expression of its law, ordered nothing else when it ordered that we do unto others as we would that they did unto us—a far cry, in this as in everything else, from the morality of the philosophers which claims that it can conceive the absolute, that is, the universal good, as if we could on our own grasp the notion of universal utility, while [in fact] we do not even know what is useful to ourselves! What is the absolute good? It is the immutable law in virtue of which everything tends to its own end: that is all we know about it. But, if the idea of this good had to be our guide in life, would we not have to know something more about it? Up to a certain point we act in accordance with general law, no doubt, since otherwise we would have the principle of our existence within ourselves, which is absurd. But we act this way without knowing why. Driven by an invisible power, we can seize its action, study it in its effects, at times identify ourselves with it, but we cannot possibly deduce from all this the positive law of our moral nature. A vague feeling, a disembodied idea which has no authority—it can never be more than that. All human philosophy is contained in the terrible mockery of the God of the Old Testament: *Behold Adam is become as one of us, knowing good and evil.*[4]

I believe that you now begin to see why a revelation is necessary. The following, in my opinion, demonstrates this necessity. Man learns to conceive physical laws by observing the phenomena of nature succeeding one another before his eyes in accordance with a uniform and invariable law. By bringing together the observations of preceding generations, he attains a systematic knowledge which is confirmed by his own experience and which the great instrument of calculus clothes in the immutable form of mathematical certainty. Although this order of knowledge is far from embracing the whole system of nature and of rising to the universal principle of things, it nevertheless comprehends perfectly [all] positive knowledge, because this knowledge refers to beings whose extension and duration can be either perceived by the senses or predicted by sure analogies. In a word, this is the realm of experience, and as much as experience can give certainty to the ideas it introduces into the mind, just so much can the physical world be known to us. As you know, this certainty goes so far as to let us predict certain phenomena removed from us by vast intervals, and so far as to give us the power to act on inert matter with incredible force.

These are the means man has for certain knowledge. If our reason has, in addition to this, a power of spontaneity or a principle of internal activity not dependent on perception of the material world, still it can exercise its own power only on materials furnished to it [by the material order of things[5]]; but in the moral

---

[4] [See Genesis 3:22. —*Trans.*]

[5] [A note in the published Russian translation here reads: "Several words in the preserved manuscript have evidently been omitted in this place. The words placed in brackets (translated in brackets above) have been inserted in accordance with the sense of the passage and by analogy with corresponding passages in *Letters IV and V*" (*Literaturnoye nasledstvo*, XXII–XXIV, 63, n. 13). —*Trans.*]

order [to what[6]] would man apply this tool? What would he have to observe to discover the law of the moral order? Intelligent nature, surely. But is intelligent nature made like material nature? Is it not free? Does it not follow the law it imposes on itself?[7] By studying intelligent nature in its external and internal effects, what shall we learn? That it is free, that's all. And if by chance we arrive at last, in this line of study, at some absolute certainty, would not the feeling of our freedom at the next instant throw us necessarily back once more into the same order of ideas whence we had but a moment since thought to have escaped? Would we not find ourselves a moment later in the same place? This circle is unavoidable. But that is not all. Suppose we really rose to some truths so fully demonstrated that reason had to admit them absolutely; suppose we did in fact find some general rules to which an intelligent being would have necessarily to submit? Those rules and those truths would refer only to a part of the total life of man, [namely] to his terrestrial life. They would therefore have nothing in common with the other part, which is wholly unknown to us and of which no analogy can discover the mystery for us. How then could they be the true laws of intelligent being, since they would refer only to a part of his existence, a moment in his life? If the laws we thus collect from experience are but the laws of one period of the time covered by [our] moral nature, how can they be the laws of this nature? Would this not be the same thing as saying that there is a special medical science for every age of life, that, for example, it is useless to know the ills of maturity in order to treat children's diseases, that to prescribe properly for youth there is no need of knowing what is proper to man in general, that the state of our health is not determined by the state of health of each moment of our lives, that, finally, we can engage in all sorts of errors and excesses in some periods of our existence without thereby affecting

---

[6] See n. 5, above.   [7] [The French reads: *"la loi qu'il s'impose à elle même,"* thus possibly meaning *". . . à elle même de suivre"*: the law which it is obligated to follow. However, both the Russian editor (*Literaturnoye nasledstvo*, XXII–XXIV, 26) and McNally ("Chaadayev's Philosophical Letters," p. 52, ll. 14–15) read the author's intention as I have. —*Trans.*]

the rest of our days? What strange notion would you have, I ask you, of a man who claimed that there was one set of morals for youth, another for maturity, another for old age, and that education is in no way concerned with the child or the young man? Well, this is exactly what your philosophers' morality is saying. It teaches us what we have to do today; it does not care a fig about how this will affect us tomorrow. [Yet] what is future life but the tomorrow of our present life?

We may conclude from all this that, since the total life of an intelligent being comprehends two worlds of which only one is known to us, and since every instant of this life is indissolubly bound to the whole succession of moments of which life is composed, it is evidently impossible for us to raise ourselves by our own powers to the knowledge of a law which must necessarily refer to both these worlds. Hence, this law must be taught to us by a reason for which there is but one world and but one order of things.

Do not, however, imagine that the morality of the philosophers has no value in our eyes. We know full well that it contains great and noble truths which have long guided men and which at this hour still speak powerfully to men's hearts and souls. But we also know that these truths were not imagined by human reason, but were rather infused into it at different periods of the general life of man. This is one of these primordial truths taught by natural reason and which revealed reason merely consecrates by its supreme authority. Honor to the sages of the earth, but glory to God alone! Man has never walked but by the radiance of divine light; this radiance has always illumined his way, but he could not see the source from which the bright ray fell upon his path. It *"enlighteneth every man that cometh into this world,"* as the Evangelist tells us; *"it was always in the world, but the world knew it not."*[8]

The habits which Christianity introduced into the human mind lead us to see the revealed idea only in the two great revelations of

8 [See John 1:9–10. —*Trans.*]

the Old and New Testaments and to forget the primordial revelation. [Yet] without a clear notion of this first communion of God with the spirit of man there is no way of understanding Christianity. Thus, finding no solution to the great problem of moral being, the Christian naturally turns to the doctrines of the philosophers. But the philosophers can explain man only by man; they thus separate him from God and fill him with the idea of his own self-sufficiency. It is generally thought that Christianity does not explain all we need to know, that there are moral truths which only philosophy can teach us: this is a grave error. No human science can replace divine science. For the Christian the whole movement of the human spirit is but the reflection of the continuous action of God in the world; the study of the results of this movement merely furnishes him new proofs to support his beliefs; he sees in the different philosophical systems, in all the efforts of man, no more than a more or less successful development of the intellectual powers of the world, varying with different situations and different societies; but the mystery of the destiny of man he discovers not in the uneasy and uncertain agitation of human reason, but in the symbols [*symboles*] and profound types bequeathed to humanity by the doctrines whose source is lost in the bosom of God. If he digs among the theories in which terrestrial thought has again and again been formulated, this is to seek there the traces, more or less faint, of the first teaching granted to man by the Creator Himself on the day when He fashioned man by His own hand. If he meditates on the history of the human spirit, this is to find the supernatural lights which have not ceased unconsciously to illumine human reason through all the mists, all the darkness with which it so loves to envelop itself. He recognizes everywhere those powerful and ineradicable ideas fallen onto the earth from Heaven, without which humanity would long ago have been engulfed by its freedom. Finally, he knows that it is again thanks to these same ideas that the human spirit can grasp the more perfect truths which God deigned to impart to him at a more recent time.

Far, therefore, from trying to appropriate all the imaginings that have budded in the human brain, he tries only better to conceive the ways of God in the general life of man. He cherishes [only[9]] celestial tradition; what men have done to disfigure it is of but secondary interest to him. In this way he necessarily comes to understand that there is a sure rule by the aid of which one can discover, in the midst of the ocean of human opinions, the ship of salvation which invariably follows the star placed in the firmament as its guide: an ever-shining star that no cloud has ever veiled, visible to all eyes, in all climates, and which remains day and night above our heads. And once it is demonstrated to him that the whole economy of the moral universe is the result of an admirable combination of the primordial ideas cast by God Himself into our souls and of the action of our reason upon these ideas, it also becomes evident to him that the preservation of these elements, their transmission from age to age, from generation to generation, must have been regulated by some special laws, and that there are certainly some visible signs by which one can recognize, amid all the holy places scattered over the earth, the Holy Ark which contains the immutable pledge of Truth.

Madam, before the world was ripe to receive the new lights which were, one day, to spread over it, while the education of mankind was being completed by the development of all its proper powers, a vague but profound feeling permitted some elected men from time to time to foresee the bright track of the star of Truth pursuing its orbit. Pythagoras, Socrates, Zoroaster, Plato especially, had received some ineffable radiance and their countenances shone with an extraordinary reflection. Their gaze, turned toward the point where the new sun was to rise, had in some way glimpsed its dawning. But they were unable to rise to the knowledge of the true characteristics of absolute Truth, because, ever since man had denatured himself, it had nowhere appeared in all its splendor, and one could not recognize it through the

---

[9] [McNally ("Chaadayev's Philosophical Letters," p. 54, l. 19) inserts *"que"* here and the Russian translation (*Literaturnoye nasledstvo*, XXII–XXIV, 28) adds *"tolko."* Such an insertion is clearly required to preserve the sense. —*Trans.*]

shades with which it was covered. But if, in the new economy, man still fails to recognize these characteristics, this is but the effect of a voluntary blindness; if he turns from the right path, this is but by a sinful self-abandonment to the dark principle which was left in his heart for the sole purpose of rendering his adherence to Truth more effective.

You can see, no doubt, Madam, where all this argument is leading. The consequences which derive from it come to mind of themselves. It is these consequences which will soon concern us. You will grasp them without difficulty, I am sure. Besides, we shall no longer have to be interrupted by digressions, such as those which we have met this time, and we shall be able to talk with more coherence and method. Good day, Madam.

Absorbta est mors ad victoriam[1]

Religious meditation has led us to philosophical reasoning and philosophical reasoning has led us back to the religious idea. Let us now return to the philosophical point of view; we have not yet exhausted it. The religious question, when one tries to consider it in the light of pure reason, merely completes the philosophical question. Besides, however strong one's faith may be, it is good if the soul knows how to make use of the powers it finds within itself. There are souls for whom it is absolutely necessary that faith should, in case of need, be able to enlist the arguments of reason. I believe that such is just the case with you. You are too familiar with the philosophy of the schools, your religion is too recent, your habits are too far removed from that inward life where simple piety is nourished and contented by itself, for you to be guided by feeling alone. Your heart cannot do without reasoning. Granted that feeling conceals many illuminations, that the heart has great powers, things proper to feeling are present to us only so long as they affect us, and emotion cannot endure unceasingly. On the other hand, what we acquire through reasoning is with us at all times. Whatever the state of our soul, an idea that has been carefully deliberated never leaves us, whereas one that has [merely] been felt is always escaping, changing at every instant in accordance with the liveliness of our heartbeat. Moreover, we cannot

---

[1] ["Death is swallowed up in victory": I Corinthians 15:54. —*Trans.*]

choose whatever kind of heart we wish; we must keep the kind we find within us, whereas we always make our own reasoning.

You say that you are naturally disposed to a religious life. I have often thought about this and I cannot agree. You are taking as a natural bent [what is but] a vague feeling provoked by circumstance, a dreamlike fancy of your imagination. When one discovers a vocation in life this uneasy ardor is not the way to it. Rather, one then accepts one's destiny with complete security, with undisturbed conviction. Of course, one can, one must, begin anew. The assurance that this is possible, the feeling that this is our duty are articles of faith for every Christian, the most important of his beliefs. Christianity wholly depends on the principle of the possible and necessary rebirth of our being, and all our efforts should tend toward this. But until we can feel our former nature dissolve and the new, Christ-made man begin to appear within us, we must neglect no means of hastening the moment of this happy revolution, which can, besides, happen to us only insofar as we shall have made every effort to produce it.

As you know, we are not concerned here with exploring the whole field of philosophy; our task is more humble than that. We must rather find what does not lie within this field than what does. I hope that this task will not be beyond our powers. For a religious mind this is the only way of conceiving and using human science; but in addition we must first know what this science is and, as far as possible, leave nothing in it unexplored by our beliefs.

It was Montaigne who said: *"Obedience is the proper duty of a reasonable soul who recognizes a superior and beneficent heavenly Being."*[2] Yet you know that Montaigne is not considered a credulous person. Let us, then, take this skeptic's thought for our text today. It is wise at times to select one's aides from the camp of the enemy, thereby diminishing his forces to that extent.

---

[2] [*Essays*, II, Ch. 12 (ed. Jean Plattard, Société Les Belles Lettres [Paris, 1947], II, Bk. I, p. 226). Chaadayev's quotation is not quite accurate: Montaigne wrote: *"l'obeyr est le principal office d'une ame raisonnable, reconnoissant un celeste superieur et bienfacteur"* (Obedience is the principal duty of a reasonable soul who recognizes a superior and beneficent heavenly Being). —*Trans.*]

In the first place, there is no reason which is not obedient reason: that is quite true. But that is not all. Does man do anything his life long but seek to submit to something? First, he finds in himself a power which he recognizes as different from that which determines motion external to him: he feels himself alive. At the same time he recognizes that his power is limited: he feels his own nothingness. Next he perceives that the power external to him dominates him and that he must submit to it. This is his whole life. From the moment that he begins to reason, these two notions —one of an internal and imperfect power, the other of an external and perfect power—come on their own to fill his mind. And although these two notions do not come as clearly and precisely as do those suggested to us by our senses or those transmitted by means of communication with beings similar to us, yet all our ideas of good, of duty, of virtue, of law, as well as their opposites, come to us only from the need we feel to subordinate ourselves to that which arises, not from our ephemeral nature, not from the restless stirrings of our inconstant will, not from the urgings of our anxious desires: all our activity is but the effect of a force which drives us to place ourselves in the general order of things, in the order of dependence. Whether we consent to this force or whether we resist it is immaterial; we are always under its sway. We have, therefore, no recourse but to try to understand as best we can its action on us and, once we have discovered something about it, to give ourselves up to it with faith and trust, for this force which acts upon us unawares is the never-failing force which leads the universe to its destiny. And what is the great question of life? This: what must we do to discover the action of the sovereign power on our being?

This is how I conceive the principle of the mental world and in this way, as you see, it corresponds perfectly to the principle of the physical world. But one of these principles appears to us as an irresistible force to which everything inevitably submits, whereas the other seems to us to be no more than a power which is combined with our own power and is, to some extent, capable of being modified by our own power. This is the logical aspect imposed on the world by our artificial reason. But this artificial reason, which we have voluntarily substituted for that portion of universal reason which was imparted to us in the beginning, this bad reason which so often upsets observable objects and presents them to us completely differently from the way they are in fact, this reason still does not conceal from us the absolute order of things to such a point that we cannot see in this order the fact that passivity precedes freedom and that the law which we make for ourselves is derived from the general law of the world. Thus, it in no way prevents us, when we accept freedom as a given fact, from recognizing that passivity is the true reality of the moral order, just as it is of the physical order. All powers of the mind, all its means of cognition can, in fact, come to the mind only from its docility. The mind is powerful only because it is submissive. All human reason needs to know is to what it must submit. No sooner does a man except himself from this supreme rule of intellectual and moral activity than he falls instantly into vice, either of reasoning or of will. The whole mission of a good philosophy is, thus, first to demonstrate this rule, and then to show us whence shines the light which must guide us in our lives.

Why is it, for example, that in none of its activities does the mind rise so high as in mathematical computation? What is mathematical computation? An intellectual manipulation, a mechanical working of reason in which reasoning will counts for nothing. Why the prodigious power of analysis in mathematics? Because it is an employment of reason wholly subordinate to a given rule. Why the great efficacy of observation in physics? Because it does violence to the natural bent of the human spirit, because it subjects it to a pace diametrically opposed to its habitual pace, because it places it face-to-face with nature, in the humble posture which is proper to it.[3] How did natural philosophy reach its great certainty? By reducing reason to a wholly passive,

---

[3] Why did the Ancients not know how to observe? Because they were not Christians.

wholly negative activity. And what does logic do—that fine logic which has given this [natural] philosophy such enormous power? It puts reason in chains, curbs it to the universal yoke of obedience, and renders it as blind and submissive as nature itself, the object of its study. *The only road,* says Bacon, *open to man to reign over nature is the same as that which leads to the Kingdom of Heaven: it can be entered only in the humble person of a little child.*[4]

And logical analysis, what is that if not a violence which the mind does to itself? If you let your reason do as it will, it will operate only synthetically. We can proceed analytically only by acting on ourselves with tremendous effort; we always fall back into the natural procedure, into synthesis. Indeed, the human mind began with synthesis; synthesis is what characterizes the science of the Ancients. But however natural and legitimate synthesis may be—and quite often it is more legitimate than analysis—it is certain that it is only to the method of submission, to analysis that the most effective powers of thought belong. On the other hand, if one looks carefully one finds that our greatest discoveries in the natural sciences are never anything but pure, wholly spontaneous intuitions, that is, that they arise only from a synthetic principle. But note this about intuition: although it essentially belongs to human reason and is one of its most active tools, we cannot understand it as we do our other faculties. That is because we do not possess it purely and simply like the others, because there is something in it of a higher intelligence, because its destiny is but to reflect that other intelligence in ours. And that is exactly why we owe to it our most beautiful insights.

Thus, it is clear that human reason is not led to its most positive knowledge by a really internal power, but that its motion must always be impressed on it from without. The true principle of our intellectual power is, therefore, at bottom only a kind of *logical abnegation* identical with moral abnegation and derived from the same law.

---

[4] *Novum Organum.* ["Aphorisms," I, 68; Chaadayev's rendering is a paraphrase. —*Trans.*]

Further, nature offers itself up to us not merely as experience and knowledge, but also as a rule of reasoning. Every natural phenomenon is a syllogism which has its major and minor premises and its conclusion. Thus, nature itself imposes on the human mind the method the mind must follow in order to know it; thus, in that connection, our reason merely submits to a law which is offered to it in the very motion of things. Accordingly, when the Ancients, the Stoics, for example, who had such magnificent presentiments, spoke of imitating nature, of obeying it, of conforming to it, they did so because they lived closer to the origin of things than we and had not yet shattered the world as we have; they were merely proclaiming this primitive principle of intellectual nature, namely, that no power, no rule, comes to us from ourselves.

As for the principle that makes us act and which is simply desire for our good, where would the human race be if the idea of that good were but an invention of our reason? Every century, every nation would have a private idea of it. How would mankind as a whole advance along its indefinite progress if the human heart did not possess a universal notion of a good common to all times and to all places, and consequently not a creation of man? What is the source of the morality of our actions? Is it not that commanding feeling which orders us to submit to law, to respect truth? But law is law only because it does not come from us; truth is truth only because we have not dreamt it up. If it happens that we take as the rule of our conduct what we ought not to take as such, that is because we are not strong enough to free our judgment from the influence of our inclinations; our inclinations then dictate the law we follow, but only because we expect to find in this latter law the general law of the world. Granted, there are people who seem to conform quite naturally to all the precepts of morality; such are a number of the outstanding persons we admire in history. This happens because, in these privileged souls, the feeling of duty was not developed by thought but by those hidden means which lead men unawares, by those great lessons which life teaches without our searching for them, teachings more powerful than our personal thought and which constitute the general thought of man: now an example which strongly affects the mind, now a fortunate coincidence which takes hold of a man and raises him above himself, now the favorable arrangement of a life which makes of him what he would not have been without it—living lessons of history dispensed only to certain individuals according to a law unknown to us. If a vulgar psychology makes little of all these mysterious stimuli of the motion of the intellect, a more profound psychology, which considers the heredity of human thought as the prime element of intelligent being, finds in it a solution to most of its problems. Thus it is that the heroism of virtue or the inspiration of genius is not the thought of an individual but rather the thought of past ages. Whether we have thought or not, someone has thought for us before we came into the world. At the bottom of every moral act, however spontaneous it may be, however isolated it may be, there thus necessarily lies a sense of duty, i.e., of submission.

What would happen if man could make himself so submissive that he wholly rid himself of freedom? Clearly, according to what we have said, this would be the highest degree of human perfection. Every movement of his soul would then be produced by the principle which produced all other movements of the world. Thus, instead of being separated from nature, as he now is, man would fuse with it. Instead of the feeling of his own will, which excepts him from the general order of things, which makes him a being apart, he would find the feeling of universal will, or, what is the same thing, the intimate feeling, the profound awareness of his real relation to the whole of creation. Thus, instead of the individual and solitary idea which fills him now, instead of this personality which isolates him from all his surroundings and places a veil over all the objects before him, and which is nothing but the necessary condition of individuation and hence the effect of his violent separation from general nature—by abdicating his fatal actual *self*, man would recover the idea, the vast personality, all the power of pure intelligence in his innate bond with the rest of things. Then he would no longer feel himself living that narrow, petty life which compels him to draw everything to himself, to see only through the prism of his artificial reason. Instead, he would feel himself living the life which God Himself made for him the day when He drew him out of Nothing. It is that primordial life which the total exercise of our faculties is destined to find once more. A great genius said long ago that man has a recollection of a better life: this great idea was not cast on the earth in vain; but what he did not say, what he should have said—and this is the conclusion which neither that great genius nor any other man of his age reached—is that it is up to us to find this lost life, this more beautiful life, and that we can do this without ever leaving this world.

Time and space—these are the limits of human life such as it is today. But what is there to keep me from escaping the stifling embrace of time? Whence comes my idea of time? From the memory of past events. But what is memory? No more than an act of will: this is proved by the fact that one never has more memories than one wants to have; otherwise the whole succession of events that followed one upon another in the course of my life would always be present in my memory, would always press in my head; on the contrary, in the very moments when I let my thoughts flow most freely I entertain only the memories which coincide with the actual state of my soul at that time, with the feelings which move me, with the ideas which are on my mind. We compose images of the past just as we do of the future. Then why could I not drive back the ghost of the past which stands motionless behind me, just as I can eradicate, if I wish, the moving vision of the future which floats before me and escape that intermediary moment which is called the present, a moment so short that at the very instant when I pronounce the word that denotes it, it is no more? We ourselves make time, that is certain: God did not make time; He allowed man to make it. But then, where would time be? That fatal thought, time, which obsesses me and oppresses me on all sides, would it not vanish completely from my mind? This imaginary reality, time, which dominates and crushes me so cruelly, would it not be wholly dispersed? Then there would no longer be a limit to my existence, no longer any obstacle to infinite life; my gaze would plunge into eternity: the terrestrial horizon would disappear, the vault of the heavens would no longer join the earth at the end of the immense plain which stretches before my eyes. I would see myself in that unlimited duration, undivided into days, hours, and fleeting instants, forever one, where there is no longer motion or change, where all individualities are lost one in another, where, finally, eternal objects endure. Every time that our mind knows how to disengage itself from the chains it has forged for itself, it conceives this kind of time just as well as that in which it lives now. Why does our mind again and again leap away from the immediate succession of things measured by the monotonous beat of the pendulum? Why does it leap again and again into that other world where the fatal voice of the clock is no longer heard? Because the infinite is the natural atmosphere of thought; because there is the only true time; because the other time is only that which we create for ourselves, I know not why.

As for space, thought does not reside in space, everyone knows that. Thought naturally accepts the conditions of the tangible world, but it does not inhabit this world. Hence, whatever reality space may be supposed to have, it is no more than a fact external to thought and has nothing to do with the being of the mind: an inevitable form if you will, but only a form, in which the external world appears to us. Thus, even less than time can space enclose the new life of which we are speaking here.

This is that higher life toward which man must strive—the life of perfection, of certainty, of clarity, of infinite knowledge, but most of all of perfect submission; a life which man possessed in the past, but which is still promised to him. And do you know what this life is? It is Heaven—there is no other heaven but this. We are allowed to enter it right now, do not doubt this. It is nothing but the complete renewal of our nature within the given order of things, the last stage of the labors of intelligent being, the final destiny of spirit in the world. I do not know whether each one of us is called to fulfill this immense career, to reach the glorious goal which is its end, but what I do know is that the final end of our progress can be none other than a complete fusion of our nature with universal nature, for only in that way can our spirit rise to the perfection of things which expresses the *very words* of the Supreme Intellect.[5]

But[6] in the meantime, while we have not reached the end of our pilgrimage, before this great fusion of our being with universal being is realized, can we not fuse at least with the intellectual world? Have we not in us the power to identify ourselves to an indefinite extent with beings similar to ourselves? Have we not the faculty of taking over their needs, their interests, of appropriating their feelings, and this to the point of living only for them, of feeling only through them? Of course we have. Sympathy, love, charity, whatever name you give to this unique capacity of ours to fuse with what is going on around us, it is certain that that capacity is inherent in our nature. We can, if we wish, so well mingle with the moral world that nothing can happen in it—so long as we know about it—such that we do not feel it as something happening to ourselves. Indeed, it is not even necessary that worldly events should particularly concern us; the general, the profound idea of the concerns of men, the intimate awareness of our real link with humanity, alone suffices to make our hearts beat with the destinies of all the human race, to make our every thought, our every action, accord with the thoughts and actions of all men in harmonious concert. By cultivating this outstanding property of our nature, by developing it more and more in our souls, we shall reach heights

---

[5] Two things must be noted here: first, that I do not intend to say that Heaven is wholly in this life, but only that it begins in this life, since, from the day when the Savior vanquished it, death has no longer existed; secondly, this is not a question of material fusion in time and space, obviously, but of fusion in idea and principle.

[6] [McNally says ("Chaadayev's Philosophical Letters," p. 61n.) that this paragraph ("But in the meantime . . . an impenetrable mystery") is crossed out in the manuscript. The Russian translation (*Literaturnoye nasledstvo*, XXII–XXIV, 35) gives no indication of this. I have found only a vertical line drawn in the margin of the manuscript. —*Trans.*]

from which the rest of the road we must cover will be wholly revealed to us. Fortunate are those mortals who, once there, can remain at that height without falling back into the low regions whence they started! Until the moment when that height was reached, our existence was but a perpetual oscillation between life and death, a prolonged agony. From that moment, true life began; from that moment it is left up to us to follow the path of the true and the good, for from that moment the law of the moral world is no longer an impenetrable mystery.

But do things happen this way in the world? Far from it. It is not a matter of imagining this law of mental nature which appears to us only so late in life and so obscurely—any more than the law of physical nature is to be imagined. All that we can do is to hold our souls open to this knowledge when it comes to offer itself to our minds. In the ordinary course of events, in the daily concerns of our minds, in the habitual sleep of our souls, the moral law is much less clearly manifested to us than the physical law. It reigns over us absolutely, that is true; it orders our every act, every movement of our reason, and, leaving with us, by a marvelous arrangement, by a perpetual miracle, the awareness of our own activity, it imposes upon us a fearful responsibility for each thing we do, for every beat of our heart, for even every one of those fugitive thoughts which no more than graze our minds in passing. But in spite of this, it escapes from our intelligence into deep shadows. And what happens? Lacking knowledge of the true principle of which he is the agent, man unwittingly makes his own law, and the law which he thus sets over himself on his own is what he calls *the moral law*, or wisdom, or sovereign good, or simply law.[7] And to this fragile work of his own hands, which he can break as soon as the fancy strikes him and which he does break at every instant of the day, in his blindness he attributes all the positivity, the absoluteness, the immovability of the true law of his being, that hidden principle of which, by his reason alone, he can evidently know nothing but its inevitable necessity, nothing more.

[7] See the Ancients.

Besides, although the moral law, like the physical law, exists outside of us independently of our knowledge, there is an essential difference between these two laws. Countless multitudes have lived and live with no idea of the material forces which move the world of nature; God willed it that human reason should discover all that for itself and little by little. But however degraded an intelligent being may be, however limited his faculties, he cannot be wholly deprived of some knowledge of the principle which makes him act. Deliberation, judgment, necessarily presuppose the notion of good and evil. If you take this notion away from man, he will not deliberate, he will not judge, he will no longer be a rational being. Thus, God could not let us live a single instant without it; He made us this way. And this imperfect idea, placed in our souls in a manner we cannot understand, makes up the whole of intellectual man. You have just seen what could be derived from this idea if it could be found in its pristine purity, as it was given to us in the beginning, but we must [now] see what we can learn by seeking the principle of all our knowledge in our own nature alone.

Sokolniki, 1 June

The will is only a certain mode of thought. . . . In whatever way
. . . the will be conceived, whether as finite or infinite, it requires
a cause by which it may be determined to . . . action, and therefore
. . . it cannot be called a free cause but only necessary or compelled.

—SPINOZA, De Anima[1]

We have seen that every natural phenomenon can be viewed as a
syllogism; but it can also be viewed as a numerical figure. Either
one lets nature work in terms of figures and watches it work—this
is observation—or one figures it in the abstract—this is computation—or, again, one takes as units the quantities found in nature
and computes them; then one applies the computation to observation and science is completed. This is the whole sphere of positive knowledge. But it must be noted that there are no quantities
as such in nature; if there were, an analytical deduction would be
equivalent to a divine *fiat*, for it would in no way fail of absolute
certainty, hence, of omnipotence.[2] Impotence is error: there is
nothing above absolute Truth. True quantitative values, that is,
absolute units, exist only in our minds; in the universe there are
only numerical appearances. It is these appearances, in terms of
which materiality presents itself to our observation, which give us
the notion of numbers. This is the basis of mathematical thought.
The numerical expression of things is but a mental construct

---

[1] [*Ethics*, I, Prop. XXXII, W. H. White translation. The ellipses are not indicated in the manuscript. —*Trans.*]

[2] In such a case it would be algebra, not faith, that moved mountains.

which we build from these data furnished by nature. We first transform the data into abstractions; we then conceive them as quantitative values; and then we make of them what we will. Mathematical certainty thus also has its limitations. Let us be sure to bear this in mind.

It is certain that in its application to phenomena of nature the science of numbers fully satisfies empirical reasoning as well as the material needs of man. But in the abstract order of things it is far from satisfying the demands of certitude required by the mind. Geometrical reason, rigid, immovable, such as most geometers conceive it, is both simpleminded and impious. If there were complete certainty in mathematics, numbers would be real things. This is how they were understood, for example, by the Pythagoreans, the Cabbalists, and others of the same sort, who attributed all kinds of powers to numbers and who found in them the principle and substance of all beings. These people were quite consistent: they conceived nature as composed of numerical values and they did not worry about anything else. But we others who see in nature more than figures, we who believe seriously in God, are being absurd when we decide to arm the hand of the Creator with a compass; we forget that measure and limit are the same thing, that infinitude is the first attribute of divinity, the attribute which constitutes, as it were, His whole divinity; that in making the Supreme Being a geometer we take His eternal nature from Him and bring Him down to our level. It is the pagan notions which still dominate us unawares that make us fall into this kind of error. It is not true that number is in the Divine Mind; creations flow from God like water from torrents, without measure and without end. Man requires, however, a point of contact between his limited intelligence and the infinite intelligence of God, separated by infinity though they be. That is why he so loves to imprison divine power within the proportions of his own nature. And this, too, is true anthropomorphism, a thousand times worse than that of those simple hearts who, in their eagerness to approach God and because they cannot imagine a moral individual in a form other than that which they know, reduce divinity to a being similar to themselves. Actually, philosophers do no better. "They attribute to God"—as a great and experienced thinker has said—"a reason similar to that which they themselves possess. Why? Because they know of nothing in their own nature more perfect than their reason. But Divine Reason is the cause of everything and human reason is but an effect: what, then, can these two reasons have in common? At best," this thinker said, "what there is in common between the constellation of the dog which shines in the sky and the dog which runs about in the street: merely the name."[3]

As you see, all the positive qualities of those sciences we call exact come from the fact that their objects are *quantities,* that is, limited things. It is only natural that the mind, since it can embrace such objects completely, reaches its greatest certitude in its knowledge of them. But you also see that in spite of our role in the production of these truths, we still do not derive them from ourselves. The first ideas which suggest them to us are thus given to us from without. Hence, the logical consequence derived from the very nature of that knowledge which, of all knowledge that we have, is the most susceptible of certainty, is that such knowledge concerns only limited things, that its source does not lie immediately in our brain, that in this order of ideas we use our faculty only on the finite, and that in this order we invent nothing. But what happens if we wish to apply the method relating to this order of ideas to our other objects of knowledge? We find that the form of the known object, whatever it may be, must necessarily be that of a finite thing; that its place in the intellectual sphere must be outside us. Such are the natural conditions of certainty. But, if this is so, then what is our position with respect to intellectual things? First, what is the limit of the data of psychology and morality? There is none. Second, where does the moral fact occur? Within us. Thus, can the method of the mind in the order of

---

[3] Spinoza. [*Ethics,* I, Prop. XVII, Scholium. Although Chaadayev put the passage in quotation marks, it is a paraphrase. —*Trans.*]

positive ideas be of use in this other order? Impossible. Well, then, how will any evidence be obtained? Personally, I do not know. What is strange is, simple as this deduction may be, philosophy has never made it. It has never been willing clearly to make this essential distinction between the two spheres of human knowledge; it has always confused the finite with the infinite, the visible with the invisible, the sensuous with what is not an object of sensation; and, if it has sometimes changed its vocabulary, nevertheless, it has never, in the recesses of its thought, doubted for an instant that the moral world, like the physical world, can be known only by studying it, ruler in hand, by calculating, measuring intellectual dimensions as one does material ones, experimenting on intelligent being as on inanimate being. Strange indolence of the human mind! In order to avoid the work required for a clear understanding of the higher world, the human mind denatures that world, denatures itself, and then goes on its way as if this did not matter. We shall see why it acts in this fashion.

You must not imagine that natural science consists only of observation and experiment. One of the secrets of its great method is that only truly observable objects are observed by it. This may be a negative principle, but it is more powerful, more fertile than the positive principle itself. It is to this principle that modern chemistry owes its progress; it is this principle which produces in general physics that horror of metaphysics which, since Newton, has become its main rule and the basis of its method. Now, what does this all mean? Nothing more than that the perfection of these sciences, all their powers, come from the fact that they know enough to circumscribe themselves perfectly within this legitimate circle. As for the procedure of observation itself, what is it? What do we do when we observe the movement of the stars along the vault of the skies or that of vital forces in an organism, when we study the powers that move bodies or those that agitate the integrating molecules of which they are composed, when we consider chemistry, astronomy, physics, physiology? We conclude from what has been to what will be; we connect events which immediately succeed one another in nature and we deduce the result which is presently to come. This is the required cycle of the experimental method. But in the moral order, do you know anything which happens by virtue of a constant, irrevocable law such that it would give us grounds to conclude similarly from one fact to another and thus to predict with certainty a posterior event by means of a prior one? By no means. On the contrary, nothing happens there but by virtue of free and divergent wills which recognize no law but their own whim; everything there is the effect of the will and freedom of man. Of what use would the experimental method be there? None whatsoever.

Such is the lesson we learn from the natural progress of the human mind in the realm of knowledge in which it is fitted to reach its highest certainty. Let us proceed to the moral which follows from this knowledge.

The positive sciences have, of course, always been studied, but as you know it is only within the last century that they have suddenly risen to the height where we see them today. Three things gave them the impetus which brought them so rapidly to this height: *analysis*[4] created by Descartes, *observation* by Bacon, celestial *geometry* by Newton. Analysis, since it is completely restricted to mathematics, does not concern us here; note, only, that it brought into the moral sciences an element of false rigor which has immensely hindered their progress. The new way of approaching the natural sciences, conceived by Bacon, is of the utmost importance for all philosophy, for it is this that has given science that empirical tendency which for so long wholly characterized modern thought. But in the study we are making it is the law in virtue of which all bodies gravitate toward a common center which especially interests us. Hence, it is this law which must now concern us.

At first sight universal gravity seems to contain all the forces of nature; but it is not the only force of nature, and that is precisely why the law it obeys, from our point of view, is so profound. At-

4 [Analytic geometry? —*Trans.*]

83

traction by itself not only does not explain the world, but explains nothing at all. By itself it would make of matter but a uniform and inert mass. All motion in nature is a product of two forces attracting all that is movable in two different directions, and it is especially in cosmic motion that this principle is most clearly seen. But once astronomers recognized that heavenly bodies were subject to the law of gravitation, and since the effects of this law could be precisely determined, the whole system of the world became a problem of geometry, and, by a kind of mathematical fiction, the most general law of nature is today conceived as Attraction or universal Gravity. That other force, without which gravity would be powerless, is *Initial Impulse* or *Projection*. Hence the two moving forces of nature are *Gravity* and *Projection*. And in the clear notion, such as science gives it to us, of the simultaneous action of these two forces is contained the whole doctrine of the *Parallelism* of the two worlds. All we need do now is assimilate it to the combination of the two forces we recognized earlier in the intellectual order and see what the results will be; of these we are conscious of the one, our *free will*, while the other, which rules us unawares, is the action on our being of an *external power*.[5]

---

[5] Without doubt, in the realm of tangible things the extent of the applications of the law discovered by Newton is enormous, and these applications will become daily still more numerous, but it should not be forgotten that the law of falling bodies was found by Galileo and that of planetary motion by Kepler. Thus, Newton merely had the fortunate inspiration of combining one of these laws with the other. But everything concerned with this famous discovery is important. A renowned geometer, for example, deplored the fact that certain formulae used by Newton in his work were unknown to us. True, no one doubts but that science would have infinitely to gain from the discovery of these talismans of genius. But can one seriously believe that all the secret of Newton's genius, all his powers, are to be found only in his mathematical proceedings? Do we not know that there was something else in this high intelligence besides talent in computation? I ask you, has ever a thought of such dimension as that involved here come to an impious mind? Has ever truth of such greatness as this been given to the world by an unbelieving mind? How can one imagine that when Newton fled the epidemic which was ravaging London and took refuge in Cambridge, and that when there, the law of materiality flashed in his mind and the veil of nature was torn asunder before him, there were only numerical figures in his pious soul? Strange. There are still people in the world who cannot refrain from smiling in pity when they think of Newton commenting on the Apocalypse. Men do not realize that it was Newton as he [really] was, with a genius as submissive as it was vast, as humble as it was

We know attraction through an infinity of its effects: it constantly happens before our eyes; we measure it; we have a perfectly certain knowledge of it. This, as you see, corresponds wonderfully to the idea we have of our own power. Of Impulsion we know nothing but its absolute necessity, just as we know nothing more of divine action upon our souls. Yet, we are just as convinced of the one of these forces as of the other. Thus, in both cases, clear and precise knowledge of one thing, vague and obscure knowledge of the other, and *absolute certainty* of both. Such is the immediate application of this manner of conceiving the material order of the world, and you see that it presents itself quite naturally to the mind. But we must also consider the fact that astronomical analysis extends the law of our solar system to all stellar systems that fill the spaces of the sky, that the molecular theory makes it the principle of the very formation of bodies, and that we are fully authorized to view the law of our system as a universal principle of all creation—or almost so. Then this point of view has immense implications.

Moreover, all the lines we draw between different beings, all the imaginary distinctions we set up among them for our convenience and according to our whim, is not all this absolutely nothing in comparison with the creative principle? Have we not, whatever we do, the intimate feeling of a reality superior to the apparent reality which surrounds us? And that other reality, is it not the only truly real *objective* reality, which comprehends being as a whole and fuses even ourselves in the general unity? There all differences, all limits imposed by the mind because of its imperfection and of the inborn limitations of its nature are engulfed, and from then on there is, in all the infinity of things, but one

---

powerful, who alone was able to make the great discoveries in which the whole human species takes pride, and by no means the presumptuous man that men want him to have been. Again [I ask], when has one seen, I do not say an atheist, but a mind merely cold to religion, push science as he did beyond the bounds which had seemed prescribed to it? [As the Russian editor observes (*Literaturnoye nasledstvo*, XXII–XXIV, 41 and 70, n. 14), Newton did not flee from London to Cambridge but from Cambridge to his native home of Woolsthorpe in Lincolnshire. —*Trans.*]

unique and universal fact. Indeed, the intimate feeling of our own nature, just as much as the sight of the universe, allows us to conceive created being in no other way than in a state of continuous motion. This is the universal fact. The idea of motion must therefore, in philosophy, naturally precede any other idea. But this idea must be sought in geometry, for it is only in geometry that one finds it divested of all arbitrary metaphysics; it is only in linear motion that we can grasp the absolute notion of any motion whatever. And then? The geometer can conceive no motion but communicated motion. He is therefore obliged to assume that the *moved* body is inert of itself and that all motion is the effect of an impulse impressed from without. In the highest abstraction, as in nature, we are thus always brought back to an external and initial action, regardless of the object under consideration. The idea of an action, taken separately from all power, from all cause to be found in the object in which the motion occurs, is thus logically inseparable from the idea of motion itself. And this is also why the human mind has such difficulty ridding itself of that old error that all its ideas come from the senses. This is quite simple: there is nothing in the world which we are more inclined to doubt than our own power; hence what is positively absurd in the system of the sensationalists is merely that it attributes to a material thing an immediate action on an immaterial thing, thus making bodies interact with minds, instead of making things of the same nature come into contact with one another, as in the physical system, namely, minds with minds. Finally, we should be clear on this: in the pure idea of motion, materiality signifies nothing at all; the whole difference between material and moral motion consists in the fact that the elements of the former are space and time whereas time alone is the element of the latter. Now, it is evident that the idea of time is sufficient by itself to give us that of motion. The law of motion is, therefore, the universal law of things, and what we have said of physical motion applies perfectly to mental or moral motion.

What must we conclude from all this? That there is no difficulty in considering the activity of man as that of an *accessory* cause, a power which acts only by virtue of its combination with another superior power, just as the force of attraction acts only in combination with the force of projection. This is what we were driving at.

It may appear that there is no place for the philosophy of the *Ego* in this system. That is a mistake. On the contrary, such a philosophy fits in quite well with this system, but it is reduced to its proper value. From what we have just said of the double action which rules the worlds, it in no way follows that our own activity is nil. Hence, it is very useful to consider the power we have and to try our best to understand it. Man is incessantly pushed by a power of which he is unaware, granted, but this external force acts on him by means of knowledge. Thus, by whatever manner an idea may come into my head, it is because I know this idea that I find it there. But to know is to act. Thus, I truly and constantly act; at the same time as I am dominated by something more powerful than myself, I *know*.[6] One fact does not destroy the other: they follow each other without denying each other. Both are equally proven to me. But if you ask me *how* that force acts on me from without, that is quite a different question, and you well know that this is not the time to discuss it; let a higher philosophy answer this. Common reason does nothing but point out the external force and posit it as one of its fundamental beliefs. The rest does not concern it. But who is not aware of alien thoughts entering his mind, of submitting to the views and opinions of others? What thinking man does not full well conceive the working of a reason subordinated to another [reason] and yet retaining its full power, its full faculties? Thus, it is certain that the great problem of free will, as abstruse as it may be, would not be difficult if only we would fully assimilate the idea that the nature of intelligent being consists only of its knowledge and that, so long as an intelligent being knows, he loses none of his nature no matter how his knowledge comes to him.

[6] [The Russian editor (*Literaturnoye nasledstvo*, XXII–XXIV, 43 and 70, n. 18) points out that this is an indirect allusion to Descartes' *Cogito.* —*Trans.*]

The fact is that the Scottish school, which has for so long lorded it over the philosophical world, has confused all questions of the nature of ideas. As you know, it claims to give the origin of every human thought, and to explain everything by indicating the thread which binds present perception to a preceding perception. Once these philosophers had arrived at the origin of a certain number of ideas by means of their Associationism, they concluded that everything that happened in our minds was produced by this principle, and from then on they would take account of nothing else. They thought that everything was reducible to the fact of consciousness and on this fact they erected empirical psychology. But, I ask you, is there anything in the world which we feel more strongly than the incessant production of ideas in our brain, a production in which we play no part? Is there anything of which we are more certain than of this continuous work of our intellect which takes place without our having any hand in it at all? Besides, the problem would be no nearer solution if we did manage to refer all our ideas to one group of ideas whose origin was completely known to us. Granted that nothing happens in our minds which is not somehow or other related to what has previously happened there, it by no means follows that every change in my thought, every turn it takes, is produced by my own power. Thus, there is room for an immense action wholly distinct from my own. The empirical theory therefore does no more than state certain phenomena of our nature; as for the total phenomenon, it gives no account of it at all.

Finally, the proper activity of man is such only when it is in conformity with law. Whenever we act contrary to law, it is no longer we who are determining ourselves, but the things around us that are determining us. When we give ourselves over to those alien influences, when we go outside the law, we annihilate ourselves. But in our submission to divine power we never have complete awareness of this power; thus, it can never encroach on our freedom. Our freedom hence consists only in that we do not feel our dependence; this is all we need in order to consider ourselves

88

perfectly free and responsible for everything we do, for every idea we think. Unfortunately, this is not how man conceives his freedom. *He believes himself free*, says Job, *like the young of the wild ass.*[7]

Yes, I am free. How could I doubt it? Do I not know, as I write these lines, that it is in my power not to write them? If some Providence has irrevocably ordered my life, what matters it, if I cannot feel its power? But another idea is associated with that of my freedom, a fearful idea, the terrible, inexorable consequence of the idea of freedom, that of the abuse of freedom and of the *evil* which follows upon its abuse. Suppose that a single molecule of matter should once have one voluntary motion; that, for instance, instead of tending toward the center of its system, it should deviate in the slightest manner from the radius on which it is situated. What would happen? The whole economy of the world would at once be upset. Every atom in infinite space would be displaced. More, all bodies would collide haphazardly and would mutually destroy one another. Well, do you realize that that is what each of us does every moment of the day? We do nothing but have voluntary motions, and each time we shake the whole universe. And it is not merely our external motions which cause this frightful destruction in the heart of creation, but every pulsation of our soul, every one of our most intimate thoughts. Such is the spectacle we offer to the Supreme Being. How can He allow it? Why does He not sweep this world of insurgent creatures out of space? Even stranger, why did He give them this mighty power? He willed it this way. *Let us*, He said, *make man to Our image and likeness.*[8] This image of God, this likeness, is our freedom. But, uniquely made creatures that we are, we are also made such that we know that we are resisting our Creator. How can we doubt, then, that if He willed to clothe us with His amazing power which seems to contradict the whole order of the world, He did not also will to regulate it and to enlighten us on its use?

[7] [See Job 11:12. —*Trans.*]
[8] [Genesis 1:26. —*Trans.*]

First, all mankind, in the person of him who contained within himself all future generations, heard the Word of God; then God deigned to enlighten some chosen men so that they might preserve Truth on earth; finally, God found one of us worthy of being invested with all His authority, of being initiated into all of His secrets, so much so that he was *one* with God, and God charged him with the task of teaching us all that we can know of the divine mystery. This is what we are taught by Scripture. But does not our reason tell us the same thing? If God did not instruct us, could the world, could we, could anything subsist a single moment? Would not everything at once fall back into chaos? Most certainly; and when our reason is not blinded by its deceptive self-confidence, when it is not wholly drowned in its pride, it tells us exactly what faith tells us, namely, that God must necessarily have taught and led man from the first day of man's creation, that God has never ceased to teach and lead him, that He will never cease doing so until the end of time.

Sokolniki, 30 June

Much of the soul they talk, but all awry. —Milton[1]

As you see, everything brings us back to this absolute principle, namely, that human reason cannot give itself a law, any more than it can give one to any created thing. Like the law of physical nature, the law of moral nature is thus given to us once and for all; there is no reason why, if we find the one ready-made, we should not find the other ready-made as well. Like the light of those suns which revolve in other skies but whose rays, although weakened, still reach us, so also does the light of the moral law shine for us from a distant and unknown region: it is ours to have our eyes open to receive it when it comes to shine before us. As you have seen, we have reached these conclusions from logical inferences which led us to discover certain elements of identity between the material order and the intellectual order. The psychology of the schools starts from approximately the same point, but it does not reach the same conclusions. It takes from natural science only [the method of] observation, that is to say, what is least suitable to the subject of its study. Thus, instead of rising to the true unity of things, it merely lumps together what ought to remain eternally separated; instead of finding the law, it finds chaos. Doubtless, there is an absolute unity in the totality of beings: this is precisely what we ourselves are seeking as best we can to demonstrate. What is more, this is the *credo* of any sane

[1] [*Paradise Regained*, IV, 313. —*Trans.*]

philosophy. But this unity is objective unity, wholly beyond sensible reality. It is an immense, undoubted fact which sheds an ineffable light on the great ALL, which gives to logic both premises and conclusions, but which has nothing in common with the kind of pantheism which is professed by the majority of contemporary philosophers—a grievous doctrine which today communicates its false light to all philosophical trends, so that in our times there is no longer any system which, in spite of its fine promises of spiritualism, does not end up treating mental fact exactly as if it were dealing with material fact.

Mind by its very nature tends to unity. But unfortunately man has not yet well understood in what the true unity of things consists. To convince yourself of this, consider how the majority of minds conceives the immortality of the soul: An eternal God and a soul eternal as He is, an absolute infinity and another absolute infinity next to it: is that possible? Is not absolute infinity absolute perfection? How then can there be two eternal beings, two perfect beings side-by-side? Yet such is the fact. Since there is no legitimate ground for admitting, in a being formed of intelligence and matter, the simultaneous annihilation of the two natures that constitute it, it was natural enough for the human mind to arrive at the idea of the survival of one of these natures over the other. But that was as far as it should have gone. Even if I were to live a hundred thousand years after the moment I call death—which is nothing but a physical phenomenon having nothing to do with my intellectual being—there would still be a long distance from there to eternity. Like all the instinctive ideas of man, the idea of immortality was at first a simple and reasonable one; but once fallen on the over-fertile soil of the Orient, it grew disproportionately and, ever growing, finally attained the status of that impious dogma that confuses creation and Creator, that breaks down the barrier which eternally separates them, burdens the spirit with the immense weight of an endless future, and mixes and scrambles everything. Then, introduced into Christianity along with many elements which Christianity inherited from the pagans, this idea appropriated all the backing of that new power, and by these means managed wholly to subjugate the human heart. Yet everyone knows that the Christian religion considers eternal life a reward for a life that was perfectly holy. Thus, since man must earn eternal life, he clearly cannot previously have possessed it; if eternal life is the future reward of a perfect life, how can it be attained at the end of an existence spent in sin? Amazingly, the human mind, enlightened by the highest of lights, nevertheless cannot grasp the whole Truth: it ever vacillates between the true and the false.

It must be admitted that every philosophy necessarily imprisons itself within a fatal circle from which it cannot escape. In morals it always first prescribes a law for itself and then sets about obeying it, no one knows how or why. In metaphysics it always first posits a principle and then derives from it a whole world of things of its own creation. Thus, there is always a *petitio principii*, but this is inevitable: else what would be reason's role in all this? Obviously, nothing at all.

For instance, the most positive, the most rigorous philosophy of our time proceeds as follows. It begins by positing that, since our reason is the given implement for knowledge, it is our reason which we must first of all learn to know; without such knowledge, it argues, it would be impossible for us to use this implement properly. Then it sets about dissecting, dismantling this reason as best it can. But by what means is this preliminary work, this indispensable work, this anatomy of intelligence performed? Is it not by means of this same reason? Thus, reduced in its very first and most important operation to using a tool which, by its own admission, it does not yet know how to use, how will it manage to reach the knowledge it seeks? There is no conceivable answer. Nor is that all. Surer of itself than were all the philosophies that preceded it, it declares that the mind must be handled exactly like external objects. Thus, the same eyes with which you see the world will enable you also to see your own being. Just as you set the world before yourself, so you can set yourself before yourself; just as you reflect on the world, just as you experiment on the world, reflect and experiment on your own being. Since the law of identity is common to nature and intellect, you may operate on either one in the same manner. Since you conclude to a general phenomenon from a series of identical phenomena in the material order of things, what is to prevent you from concluding in like manner, in the intellectual order, from a succession of similar facts to a universal fact? Just as the physical fact is [thus] known to you in advance, so, with equal certitude, can you predict the moral fact: one should act in psychology just as one acts in physics. Such is empirical philosophy.

Fortunately, this philosophy is today no more than the eccentric opinion of a few retarded minds who still obstinately persist in remaining in their ancient ruts. A new light is already dawning amidst our darkness, and all that is going on today in the area of philosophy, even that eclecticism which is so benevolent and obliging that it seems to aspire only to its own self-effacement, all concurs to bring us back into better paths. Among the intellectual currents of our times one must be particularly singled out.[2] This is a sort of subtle Platonism, a recent creation of Germany, that profound and contemplative land; it is a transcendent idealism, full of high rational poetry, which has already shaken the foundations of the ancient monument of philosophical superstitions. But as yet it lives only in the ethereal regions where breathing is difficult. It seems to soar in its diaphanous atmosphere, now lit by I know not what gentle and delicate light, now eclipsed in a dim or dark twilight, like one of those fantastic mirages which sometimes float in the southern sky only to disappear an instant later leaving no trace either in the air or in the memory. Let us hope that this beautiful and grandiose thought will soon descend into habitable regions; then we shall greet it with a most enthusiastic welcome. Meanwhile, let us leave it to pursue its vagabond course while we continue along the surer path which we have marked out for ourselves.

[2] [The philosophy of Schelling. —*Trans.*]

If we conceive the motion of the moral world as the effect of a primitive impulse, just as we conceive the motion of the physical world, then does it not follow that these two motions, as they continue, are also subject to the same laws, and that therefore all phenomena of the mind are but the result of this analogy?[3] Just as the collision of bodies carries onward in nature this first impulse communicated to matter, so the collision of minds carries onward the motions of mind. Just as everything in nature is bound to all that preceded it and to all that follows it, so every human individual and every human thought are bound to all human beings and to all human thoughts which came before them and which will come after them. Just as nature is one, so *the whole succession of men,* according to Pascal's colorful expression, *is one man who exists always,*[4] and each of us directly participates in the intellectual work which is being achieved through the ages. Finally, just as a certain plastic and constant labor of material elements or atoms, namely the generation of physical beings, makes up material nature, so a similar labor of intellectual elements or ideas, namely the generation of minds, carries onward intelligent nature; and just as I conceive all tangible matter as a single whole, so I should conceive the totality of minds as one unique mind.

The main vehicle for the procreation of mind is, naturally, speech; without it you can explain neither the origin of intelligence in individuals nor its development in mankind. But speech alone is not enough to produce the great phenomenon of universal mind. It does not alone provide all the communication there is

[3] [". . . *ne sont que le résultat de cette analogie.*" The Russian translation, however, reads: ". . . can be understood according to this analogy" (*Literaturnoye nasledstvo,* XXII–XXIV, 48). —*Trans.*]

[4] [The editor of the Russian translation notes (*ibid.,* pp. 49 and 74, n. 9) that this phrase is taken from "Fragment de Préface sur Le Traité du Vide" (*Oeuvres de Blaise Paschal,* ed. Léon Brunschvicg and Pierre Boutroux [Paris, 1908], II, 139). Chaadayev's rendering is inaccurate. Pascal's text reads: "*toute la suite des hommes . . . doit estre considérée comme un mesme homme qui subsiste toujours*" (The whole succession of men . . . must be considered as one and the same man who subsists always). Brunschvicg's edition notes (p. 139, n. 1) that this notion was common in and shortly after Pascal's day. He cites, in particular, Fontenelle. See p. 135 (*Letter VII*), below, for another paraphrase of this same text. —*Trans.*]

among men, nor, therefore, embrace all the mental activity that takes place in the world. A thousand invisible bonds unite the thoughts of a rational being to those of another. Our most intimate thoughts find all sorts of ways of reproducing themselves outside our minds; by spreading abroad, by crossing one another, they fuse, combine, pass from one mind to another, germinate, fructify, and finally engender general reason. Sometimes an idea seems, when it manifests itself, to make no impression on its surrounding objects; still the motion has been communicated, the collision has taken place; in due time it finds a congenial idea which it moves by its contact and then you see it return to the light of day and produce some unexpected effect upon the intellectual world. You are familiar with the following experiment in physics: several balls are slid on a horizontal wire; the first is then drawn aside;[5] it is the last one that moves, the intermediary ones remain at rest. That is how an idea is transmitted through the minds of men.[6] How many great and beautiful thoughts, originating who knows where, have invaded countless multitudes and generations! How many profound truths live, act, rule, or shine among us, mighty powers or brilliant lights, of which we know neither whence they came nor how they traversed time and space! "Nature," Cicero somewhere remarks, "has made the human face such that it can represent the secret feelings of our hearts: whatever affection we feel, our eyes always express it."[7] That is perfectly true; everything, in an intelligent being, translates his most intimate thought. The whole man communicates himself to his peers, and thus minds are generated. For mind is produced no more miraculously than other things—there is generation there just as everywhere else. A single law presides over all production, of what-

[5] [Chaadayev should have added: "and pushed forcefully against the next." The experiment illustrates Newton's law of conservation of momentum. —*Trans.*]

[6] As is known, the famous proof of the existence of God attributed to Descartes was invented by St. Anselm in the eleventh century. It had remained buried in a corner of the human mind for nearly five hundred years when Descartes came and delivered it over to philosophy. [Presumably, Chaadayev means six hundred years. —*Trans.*]

[7] [*De Legibus*, I, 26–27. Chaadayev's rendering is a paraphrase. —*Trans.*]

ever kind: nothing is generated but by the contact or fusion of beings; no force or power acts in isolation. It must merely be remarked that the event of generation itself occurs in a region screened from our direct perception. Thus, as, in the physical world, we see the effects of the different powers of nature such as attraction, assimilation, affinity, etc., but reach at last a fact which cannot be grasped, namely the act which confers physical life, similarly, in the mental world, we see the effects of the different human faculties, but in the end reach something which transcends the domain of immediate perception, namely the act which confers mental life.

As for this universal mind which corresponds to universal matter, in the heart of which moral phenomena take place just as physical phenomena take place in the heart of materiality, this is simply the totality of all the ideas that live in human memory. An idea must go through a certain number of generations to become the patrimony of mankind. In other words, an idea comes within the domain of general reason only in the state of a tradition. But we are not speaking here of merely those traditions which history or science brings to the human mind and which are but a part of universal memory. There are traditions which were never [truths] recited to the assembled people or sung by rhapsodes, which were never engraved on columns or on parchment, whose dates were never checked by computation and the names of stars, which criticism never weighed on its partisan scale; but which an unknown hand places within the soul, which a mother's first smile, a father's first caress bring to a newborn child. These are the powerful memories in which the experience of ages is united. Every individual gathers them up in the air he breathes. This is the *milieu* in which all the marvels of the intellect occur. Doubtless, this hidden experience of the ages does not come as a whole to every fraction of mankind, but it forms the mental substance of the universe. It runs in the blood of all human races, it mingles with their fiber; finally, it carries on those other traditions, yet more mysterious, which have no source on earth, which were the starting point for all societies. It is a fact that in the tribe most remote from the great movement of the world one always finds a certain number of ideas, more or less clear, of the Supreme Being, of good and evil, of justice and injustice. Without such notions the tribe could not have survived, any more than it could survive without the crude food it receives from the ground it treads upon and from the trees that shelter it. Whence come these ideas? No one knows: traditions, that's all. There is no way to reach their source; children have learned them from their fathers and mothers, that is their whole genealogy. Then centuries descend upon these primitive ideas, experience accumulates over them, sciences rise on them, the human mind grows on this invisible base, and that is how you get by means of facts to the same point we reached through reasoning, to that initial impulse, without which, as we have seen, nothing in nature would move, and which is as necessary here as there.

Can you conceive, I ask you, an intelligent being possessed of no idea at all? Can you conceive reason existing in man before he used it? Can you imagine something existing in a child's head prior to what has been taught him by those who attended his entry into life? There have been children who grew up among the beasts of the forest, sharing their customs, who have been known later to recover their mental faculties; but these children were not abandoned from the first days of their existence. The young of the most robust of animals would die without fail if it were forsaken by the female as soon as it was born; man, of all animals the feeblest, unable to do without suckling for the first six or seven months of his life, whose skull is still soft several days after birth, would be all the more incapable of surviving the first period of life without the arms of a mother to hold him. It follows that these children received the seed of intellectual nourishment before they were taken from their parents. If a man were, from the moment he opened his eyes to the light, separated from the authors of his days and from all human beings, if he had never once seen the countenance of one of his own kind nor heard a single sound of his voice, and if he lived thus to the age of reason, I guarantee that between that mammal and the others which the naturalist places in the same category there would be no difference at all. Is it not absurd to think of every human individual as starting his species anew, like a brute? Yet this is the hypothesis on which the whole ideological edifice is based. It is assumed that this little formless creature, whose umbilical cord still binds him to his mother's womb, is an intelligent being. But how is this known? Do you recognize, in the galvanic shuddering that agitates him, the celestial gift which has been imparted to him? Do you discover, in the stupid expression, the tears, the piercing screams, the being made in the image of God? I ask you, will such a being ever have an idea which has not come to him from the small number of notions which his mother, his nurse, or any other human creature has caused to enter into his brain during the first days of his existence? The first man was not a howling child but a man ready-made; he could therefore quite well resemble God, and in fact did so. But it is certainly not the human embryo which is made in God's image. What constitutes the true nature of man is the fact that, of all beings, he is the only one who can receive unlimited instruction: this is his greatness, this is his superiority over all created things. But to rise to the state of intelligent being a ray of the light of Supreme Reason must shine on his brow. On the day when man was created God spoke to him, and man listened to Him and understood Him: this is the true genesis of human reason; psychology will never find a more profound one. Later, man lost in part the faculty of hearing the voice of God: this was the natural result of the gift of unlimited freedom he had received. But he did not lose his memory of the first divine words that sounded in his ears. Thus, it is the same word of God, spoken to the first man, which, transmitted from generation to generation, strikes upon [the ear of] the child in his cradle, brings him into the world of minds, and makes of him a thinking being. The procedure God used to draw man from nothing is thus that which He still uses today to create every new intellect. It is always that of God speaking to man, through the medium of those made in his likeness.[8]

As you see, the notion of mankind coming into the world with a ready-made intellect thus has basis neither in experience nor in thought. The great law of the constant and direct action of a supreme principle is thus merely reproduced in the general life of man, as it is reproduced in all creation. There it is a force contained in a *quantity*, here it is a principle sustained in a *tradition*, but it is always the same fact: an external activity acting on all being of whatever kind, first instantaneously, then continuously and permanently.

Turn back upon yourself as you will, dig into the most secret recesses of your heart, you will never find anything there but the thought which we have inherited from those who came before us on earth. That understanding which man dissects and takes apart will never be but the understanding of all the generations which have succeeded one another from the first man down to our own; and when we reflect on the faculties of our mind we merely use, as best we can, that same universal reason to observe that part of it which we have assimilated in the course of our private lives. What is the faculty of the soul? It is an idea, an idea which we find ready-made in our mind, ignorant of how it came to be there, and which produces another idea. But the first idea, whence would you expect it to have come to us if not from that ocean of ideas in which we swim? If we were deprived of contact with other minds, we would be chewing grass instead of speculating on our nature. If the thought of man is not the thought of mankind, then there is no conceivable thing for it to be. As in the rest of the created world, so in the mental realm, nothing can be conceived as completely isolated, as completely self-subsistent. Finally, if it is true that in supreme or *objective* reality man's reason is but the perpetual reproduction of the thought of God, then it is also certain that his actual or *subjective* reason is but the reason he has made for himself by virtue of his free will. Of course, the schools make nothing of this: there is but one, unique reason; for them

8 ["*His likeness*"? —*Trans.*]

man as we see him is man as he came from the hands of his Creator; created free, he did not misuse his freedom; endowed with a
will, he remained unchanged, obeying an irresistible force, like an
inanimate object; the countless errors he has committed, the
crude superstitions to which he has given birth, the crimes with
which he has defiled himself, none of this has left a mark on his
spirit. He appears now just as he was the day when the breath of
God gave life to his earthly form, as pure, as chaste as in that time
when nothing had yet tarnished his young nature. For the schools,
man is always the same; he has been the same at all times and is
the same in all places; we are as we must be; and that mass of incomplete, fantastic, incoherent ideas which we call the human
mind is, according to the schools, pure intellect, a divine emana-
tion from God Himself; nothing has altered it, nothing has
touched it. Behold the wisdom of mankind!

Yet the spirit of man has always felt the need to improve itself
in terms of an ideal type. Until the appearance of Christianity
man labored at nothing but the achievement of this ideal type
which forever escaped him and for which he repeatedly began to
strive. This was the great concern of Antiquity; but in those days
man had naturally to look for this ideal within himself. What is
astonishing is that even in our day philosophers sometimes persist, in the very presence of the profound teachings offered by
Christianity, in remaining within the realm to which Antiquity
was confined, that they do not think of seeking an example of perfect intelligence anywhere but within human nature, of looking
for it, for instance, in that sublime doctrine destined to preserve
among men the most ancient traditions in the world, or in that
admirable book which bears so well the seal of absolute reason,
that is, of that very reason which they seek and cannot find. If, in
good faith, you meditate no matter how little on the revealed
system, you will be struck by the great formula of intellectual perfection which dominates its every part; you will see that all the
eminent minds you meet there are but fragments of a single vast
mind which fills and pervades that world where past, present, and

future are but a single indivisible whole; you will feel that each thing there tends to make you understand the nature of a reason which is not subject to the conditions of time and space, and which man lately possessed, which he lost, which he will some day find again, and which was shown to us in the person of Christ. Note that on this point philosophical idealism in no way differs from the system opposed to it, for whether one assumes that the human intellect is a *tabula rasa* and rests content with the old adage of the sensationalists that *there is nothing in the mind which was not first in the senses,*[9] or whether one supposes that the intellect acts of its own power and repeats with Descartes, *I shut off all my senses and I live,*[10] in either case the reason involved is the same reason we find in ourselves today and not the reason which was granted to us in the beginning; thus, what is analyzed will never be the true mental principle, but that principle as disfigured, mutilated, and corrupted by the will of man.

Nevertheless, of all known systems, that one which, in order to account for intellectual phenomena, without going back to the

---

[9] [The saying is not primarily one of the Empiricists, although similar observations can be found: e.g., Locke, *Essay Concerning Human Understanding*, Bk. II, Ch. 1: "There appear not to be any ideas in the mind before the senses have conveyed any in" (ed. Alexander Campbell Fraser [Oxford, 1894], I, 141) and "We have nothing in our minds which did not come in one of these two ways (sensation or reflection)" (*ibid.*, pp. 124–25). The obvious reference is to the Scholastic dictum: "*Nihil est in intellectu nisi prius fuerit in sensu,*" or "*Nihil est in intellectu quod prius non fuerit in sensu.*" Although the remark is frequently attributed to St. Thomas, it seems to exist in this negative form neither in St. Thomas nor in Aristotle. M. John Farrelly, O.S.B., of De Sales Hall School of Theology in Washington, D. C., observes that in its positive form it has a basis in both: *Summa Theologica*, Part I, Question 84, Art. 6, Question 85, Art. 1, and *De Veritate*, Question 10, Art. 6; *De Anima*, III, 7(432a4f.). Fr. Farrelly points out that St. Thomas is speaking only of conceptual knowledge, not of connatural knowledge. (In an article in *New Scholasticism*, 1955, pp. 173–74, Fr. Farrelly argues that there are exceptions to the adage in the latter area.) Lewis White Beck finds a later version of the saying in Nicolas of Cusa (*Idiota de Mente*, Ch. 2, Heidelberg ed., V, 53): "*Quicumque igitur putat nihil in intellectum cadere posse, quod non cadat in ratione, ille etiam putat nihil posse esse in intellectu, quod prius non fuit in sensu.*" —*Trans.*]

[10] [*Meditations*, II and III (see Descartes, *Selections*, ed. Ralph M. Eaton [New York, 1927], pp. 96–97 and 107. Chaadayev's rendering is a very loose paraphrase). —*Trans.*]

very source of mental phenomena, strives in good faith to construct an absolutely abstract intellect, a purely mental nature, is assuredly the most profound and the one most fruitful in its results.[11] But since it is still man as he is that provides the materials with which the system constructs its model, it is still artificial reason that it shows us, not primordial reason. The profound thinker who was the author of this philosophy did not see that the matter was not[12] one of conceiving a mind which had a will only to seek and call forth the Supreme Mind, but [one] which, along with all that exists, had a perfectly legitimate mode of movement, and whose power consisted only in an infinite tendency to fuse with that other Mind. Had he started from this point he would certainly have reached the notion of a truly pure reason, for it would [then] be but a reflection of Absolute Reason, and the analysis of this Reason would undoubtedly have led him to immensely far-reaching results. Moreover, he would not have fallen into the erroneous doctrine of the *autonomy* of the human mind, of I know not what imperative law lying in our very reason, which gives it the power to rise of its own momentum to all possible perfection; finally, an even more arrogant philosophy, the philosophy of the *omnipotence of the human self*,[13] would not owe its birth to him.

Nevertheless, justice must be rendered to him; his achievement, as such, deserves all our respect; it is to the direction he gave

[11] [The philosophy of Kant. —*Trans.*]

[12] [The sentence in the original is unclear. It reads ". . . *n'a point vu qu'il ne s'agissait point de se représenter une intelligence qui n'eut de volonté que pour rechercher et évoquer l'intelligence suprême; mais qui, ainsi que tout ce qui existe, eut un mode de mouvement parfaitement légitime et dont le pouvoir ne consiste qu'en une tendance infinie à se confondre avec cette autre intelligence,*" and "*mais*" after the semicolon is a correction added, apparently, in Chaadayev's handwriting. The Russian translation renders the passage as follows (*Literaturnoye nasledstvo*, XXII–XXIV, 56): ". . . *ne usmotrel, shto vse delo [zaklyuchalos] tolko v tom, shtoby predstavit sebe razum, kotory by imel odno volevoye ustremleniye: obresti i vyzvat k deystviyu razum vysshi, no takoy razum, svoystvo* (mode) *dvizheniya kotorovo zaklyuchalos by v sovershennom podchinenii zakonu, podobno bsemu sushchestvuyushchemu, a vsya yevo sila svodilas by k bezgranichnomu stremleniyu slitsya s tem drugim razumom.*" The translation depends on how the reader thinks Chaadayev is interpreting Kant at this point. —*Trans.*]

[13] [The philosophy of Fichte. —*Trans.*]

to philosophy that we owe all the sound ideas there are in the world today, and even I myself am but a logical consequence of his idea. He marked out with a sure hand the limits of human reason; he showed it that it was constrained to accept its two most profound convictions without being able to prove them to itself, namely, the existence of God and the unlimited duration of its own being; he taught us that there was a supreme logic which was not of our own making and which was imposed upon us in spite of ourselves, and that there was a world distinct from the one in which we move yet simultaneous with it, that reason must recognize this world if it is not to annihilate itself, and that it is from there that we must draw all our knowledge in order to apply it to the world of actuality. Finally, one must also agree that his only mission was to open out a new road for philosophy, and if he deserves well from the mind of man it is because he made it retrace its steps.

This, then, is the conclusion of the study we have just made. All that exists in the world of ideas comes only from a certain number of traditive notions which no more belong to any mental individual than the forces of nature belong to any physical individual. The *Archetypes* of Plato, the *innate ideas* of Descartes, the *a priori* of Kant, all these diverse elements of thought which all deep thinkers were compelled to recognize as anterior to any activity of the soul, as prior to all experience, to all proper activity of the spirit, all these pre-existent germs of the mind without which man would be but a bipedal or bimanual mammal, no more, no less, in spite of his large facial angle, in spite of the size of his encephalic organ, in spite of his vertical posture, etc.—[all these germs] are comprised in the ideas which come to us from the minds which preceded us in life, and from those which were entrusted with bringing us into our personal existence. Miraculously infused into the mind of the first human being on the day of his creation by the same hand which thrust this planet into its elliptical orbit, which impressed motion upon inert matter, which gave life to organized being, these are the ideas which communicated to mind the motion which is proper to it and which pushed man in the immense cycle which he is destined to traverse. Reproducing themselves by the mutual contact of minds and in accordance with a mysterious principle which perpetuates in the created mind the action of the Supreme Mind, these ideas make mental nature endure in the same way as a similar contact and an analogous principle make material nature endure. Thus, the initial impulse continues in all things; thus, it finally resolves itself into a constant and unmediated Providence, acting on the whole universality of beings. Once this conclusion is demonstrated the remaining study is simple. We have but to seek the progress of these traditions through the history of the human race, in order to see how and where the idea originally placed in the heart of man was preserved whole and pure.

Man can well ask himself how, in the midst of so many shocks, internal wars, conspiracies, crimes and follies, so many men could cultivate both the useful and the fine arts in Italy and later in the other Christian states; this is something one does not find under the domination of the Turks. —VOLTAIRE, *Essay on Morals*[1]

Madam:

You have seen the importance of a correct understanding of the movement of thought in the sequence of historical periods. But you must also have seen that, once imbued with the fundamental idea that there is no truth in the spirit of man other than that which God placed there with His own hand at the time when He drew man out from nothing, we can hardly consider the movement of centuries in the same manner as popular history considers it. We discover then that a Providence or an all-wise Reason not only presides over the course of events but also acts directly and steadfastly on the mind of man. Indeed, if we admit that, in order for the reason of created being to be set in motion, it had to receive an external impulse; that its first ideas, its first knowledge could only have been miraculous communications from the Supreme Reason; then it follows that the power which thus fashioned it must continue to exercise upon human reason in the course of its progress that same influence which it employed at the moment when it imparted its first movement to it.

[1] [Ch. 197. *Oeuvres complètes* (Paris: Garnier, 1878), XII, 178. —*Trans.*]

106

This manner of presenting intelligent being in time and its sequence must have become familiar to you, Madam, if you have properly understood the things we previously agreed upon. You have seen that pure metaphysical reasoning demonstrates perfectly the continuity of an external action upon the spirit of man. But recourse to metaphysics is unnecessary; the inference is formal: even without such recourse, one can deny it only by denying the premises from which it follows.

If, now, we consider the mode itself of this continuous action of Divine Reason upon the moral world, we find that, in addition to its having to be, as we have just seen, in conformity with its initial action, it had also to take place in such a manner as not to destroy the freedom of human reason or to render useless the proper activity of this reason. It is therefore not at all surprising that there should have been one people among whom the tradition of the first inspirations of God was preserved in a purer and more certain form than among all others, and that, from time to time, men appeared in whom the original event of the moral order was somehow renewed. If you take away this people, if you take away these privileged men, you will have to assume that divine thought revealed itself with equal fullness, equal vitality, among all peoples, at all times in the universal life of mankind, and in each individual. This would mean, as you see, the destruction of all personality and of all freedom in the world; it would mean contradicting the given fact. It is evident that there are only as much personality, as much freedom, as there are diversity of intelligence, diversity of moral strength, diversity of knowledge. On the other hand, in assuming that there is in one nation only, or in a few isolated souls, especially charged as it were with the safeguard of this trust, an extraordinary degree of submission to primordial traditions or a particular ability to conceive the truth originally infused into the human spirit, we do nothing but assume a moral fact perfectly analogous to that which constantly passes before our eyes, namely, the possession by nations and individuals of a certain understanding of which other nations and other individuals are deprived.

Among the rest of the human race these great traditions were also preserved, varying in purity with the different situations of nations; and man has walked in the way prescribed for him only by the light of these mighty truths which a reason other than his own engendered in his mind. But there was only a single focus of light on earth. Of course this source of light did not shine as human lights do; it did not diffuse a deceitful brilliance far and wide but concentrated on a single point; it was at once luminous and invisible, like all the great mysteries of the world; ardent but hidden, like the fire of life. Everything was illumined by this ineffable light, and everything tended toward this common center, while everything appeared to shine of its own brilliance and to direct itself to ends diametrically opposed to one another.[2] But, at the time of the great catastrophe of the intellectual world, all the vain powers which man had created vanished at once, and there remained standing, in the midst of the general conflagration, only the tabernacle of eternal truth. It is in this way that the unity of history is conceived, and it is in this way that this conception grows to be a veritable philosophy of history, a philosophy which shows us intelligent being as subject to a general and absolute law as all other created things.

I would very much like it, Madam, if you could come to this abstract and religious manner of understanding history, for nothing enlarges our thought and purifies our soul as does this view, however obscure, of a Providence dominating the centuries and leading mankind to its final destiny. But in the meantime, let us try to construct such a philosophy of history as will at least diffuse over the whole vast region of human memory a light which will be for us as the dawn of the bright light of day. We shall reap all the more benefit from this preparatory study of history insofar as it constitutes in itself a complete system with which we can, if necessary, remain satisfied should something by chance occur to

[2] It is useless to seek the precise point on earth where this source was to be found, but this much is certain, that the traditions of all the nations of the world agree that man's first knowledge came from the same regions of the globe.

108

put a stop to our further progress. Meantime, Madam, please bear in mind that I am not writing from the height of a professorial chair, and that these letters are but a continuation of our interrupted talks, talks during which I experienced so many so pleasant moments and which, I like to repeat, were for me a true consolation at a time when I was in great need of it. Do not, therefore, expect to find me this time more didactic than usual, and do you, as in the past, be ready to supply your share in this meditation.

Doubtless you have yourself already noticed that the present tendency of the human mind leads it naturally to clothe all aspects of knowledge in an historical form. If we reflect on the philosophical bases of historical thought, we cannot but admit that such thought is called upon today to rise to a height infinitely greater than that on which it has remained until now. One can say that the mind feels at ease today only in the field of history; that it does nothing but constantly double back on time past and seeks to acquire new powers only by focusing them on its memories, on the contemplation of the course it has already traversed, on the study of the forces that have ruled and determined its progress through the ages. Modern science has in this case surely taken a very fortunate direction. It is time that we realized that the power which human reason draws from the narrow present does not completely constitute that reason, and that it has another power which, by gathering into a single thought both time past and time promised, makes up its true being and places it in its true sphere of activity.

But do you not find, Madam, that in general traditional history, or history as told, is necessarily incomplete: is it not the case that such history will never contain more than remains in the memory of men? Yet not everything that happens remains there. Thus, the present historical approach can never satisfy reason. In spite of the philosophical spirit which has penetrated present-day history, in spite of the useful work of criticism, in spite of the assistance which the natural sciences have recently been pleased to lend it, astronomy, geology, and even physics proper, you can see that it has been able as yet to reach neither the *unity* nor that high morality which would devolve from a distinct view of the general law of the moral movement of the ages. In its contemplation of past centuries the human mind has ever aspired to this great result; but the facile teaching which is otherwise derived from historical studies, these lessons of trite philosophy, those examples of I know not what virtues, as if virtue lay sprawled over the great theater of the world and its essential characteristic were not to remain hidden, that trivial psychological morality of history which has never made a single honest man but rather a horde of scoundrels and madmen of all kinds and which serves only to perpetuate this world's poor comedy—all that has turned reason away from the true teaching which human traditions are intended to offer to it. So long as the Christian spirit dominated science, profound though poorly articulated thought diffused over these studies something of the holy inspiration from which it itself emanated; but at that time historical criticism was still so imperfect, so many events, especially those of primitive times, still lay preserved in human memory in so disfigured a manner, that all the enlightenment of religion was unable to dissipate the abysmal darkness, and history, though illumined by a superior light, nevertheless remained earthbound. Today a wholly rational manner of looking at history would without doubt bring a completely positive result. The reason of this age requires a wholly new philosophy of history —a philosophy as little resembling the old kind of philosophy of history as the skilled analyses of present-day astronomy resemble the series of gnomonic observations of Hipparchus and the other astronomers of Antiquity. It must be noted, however, that there will never be enough facts to demonstrate everything, and that from the time of Moses and Herodotus there were enough for much to be foreshadowed. Whatever accumulation of facts is made, they will never lead to certitude; certitude can come only from the manner in which the facts are understood. This is why the experience of centuries, which taught Kepler the laws of planetary motion, did not suffice to reveal to him the general law of nature; discovery was reserved for a kind of extraordinary revelation, for a pious meditation. This, Madam, is the history we must try to understand.

And first, what significance is there, I ask you, in the comparisons of centuries and nations accumulated by a vain erudition; what in all the genealogies of languages, nations, and ideas? Will not a blind or stubborn philosophy always be able to rid itself of them with its old argument about the general uniformity of human nature? Will it not be able to rid itself of that wonderful interweaving of epochs by its theory of the natural development of the human spirit without trace of Providence, without other cause than the mechanical force of its own nature? According to such a philosophy, the human spirit is but a snowball which grows as it rolls, no more. Besides, either it sees everywhere a natural progress and a natural improvement which are, according to its views, inherent in human nature, or it finds only a pointless and irrational motion. Depending on different temperaments, somber and despairing or full of hope and thoughts of compensation, now it can see man only fidgeting stupidly like a gnat in the sun, now it sees him raising himself and ever rising higher as a result of his sublime nature: but, for this philosophy, it is always man and no more than man. Willfully ignorant, it learns nothing from that physical world which it thinks it knows, except what that world offers to the vain curiosity of the mind and to the senses. The great illuminations which this world sheds constantly from its bosom do not reach such a philosophy. And if such a philosophy decides finally to recognize a plan, a purpose, a reason in the totality of things, to submit human intelligence to it, and to accept all the resulting consequences in their relation to the universal moral order, it cannot do it so long as it remains what it is. Thus, it is vain to link together the ages or to work endlessly on facts; what is needed is an attempt to find the fundamental character of the great periods of history, to determine strictly and with complete impartiality the features of each epoch according to the laws of a high practical reason. Indeed, a careful look will show that historical material is exhausted, that nations have recited for us almost all their tra-

111

ditions, that if ages in the distant past are yet someday to be clarified (and even then it will not be by that kind of criticism which knows only how to stir up the old dust of nations, but rather by some purely logical procedures), so far as facts as such are concerned there is almost none left to exhume. *History has thus nothing left to do today but to meditate.*

If history once realized this, it would naturally find its place in the general system of philosophy and would become an integral part of it. Many things would then, of course, detach themselves from history and be handed over to novelists and narrative poets; but there would be many more which would suddenly appear out of the nebulous atmosphere where they still lie helpless and would place themselves at the most outstanding peaks of the new system. These things would no longer receive their character of truth merely from chronicle; rather, like the axioms of natural philosophy discovered by experiment and observation but reduced to formulae and equations by geometric reasoning, it would henceforth be moral reason which would place the seal of certitude upon them. Such, for instance, would be that period which is still so little understood, not for lack of facts and documentation, but for lack of thought, to which all historical times lead, where all ends, where all begins, in which one can say without exaggeration that all the past of the human race is found fused with all its future: I mean the first moments of our era. The day will come when historical thought will be unable to tear itself away from that commanding spectacle when all the early grandeur of men crumbled into dust and all their future grandeur came to light. Such also is the long period which followed upon and continued this age of man's renewal, the period of which philosophical prejudice and fanaticism made in the past so false a picture, when such brilliant lights were hidden in the depths of the darkest of nights, when such prodigious moral forces were preserved and nourished in the midst of the apparent immobility of human minds, a period which we have begun to understand only since the human mind took on its new direction.

[If history were so conceived,] then this period would appear in all its true greatness and with all its great teachings. Then gigantic figures, now lost in the mass of historical personalities, would emerge from the shadows which surround them, while many a reputation which men have for too long guiltily or stupidly venerated would be engulfed forever by nothingness. Such would be, among others, the new lot of some persons in the Bible, unrecognized or neglected by human reason, and of some pagan wise men whom our reason has surrounded with more glory than they deserved. For instance, of Moses and Socrates, it would be known once for all that Moses gave to man the true God, whereas Socrates bequeathed to him only faint-hearted doubt; of David and Marcus Aurelius, it would be seen that David was the perfect model of the most saintly heroism, whereas Marcus Aurelius was but a quaint example of artificial grandeur and of pompous and ostentatious virtue. Cato, too, would be remembered, tearing out his entrails, but only in order that we might properly evaluate both the philosophy which inspired such frantic virtue and the paltry greatness which the man had attributed to himself. Among the glories of paganism I believe that the name of Epicurus would be found freed from the prejudice which sullied it and that he would be remembered with renewed interest. Other great reputations would similarly undergo a change of lot. The name of the Stagyrite, for instance, would no longer be spoken without a kind of horror, that of Mohammed no longer without profound respect. The former would be considered as an angel of darkness, who for numerous centuries repressed all the forces of good among men; the latter as a benevolent being, one of those who contributed most to the realization of the plan formulated by Divine Wisdom for the salvation of the human race. Finally (dare I say it?), a kind of infamy would attach itself to the great name of Homer. The judgment which Plato's religious instinct led him to pass on this corruptor of men would no longer be considered one of his famous utopian sallies, but a most admirable anticipation of the thoughts of the future. The day must come when men will learn to blush at the memory of that guilty enchanter who contributed in so frightening a way to the degradation of human nature, when men will repent for the incense which they lavished upon this flatterer of their passions, who, to please them, soiled the sacred tradition of truth and filled their hearts with filth. All these ideas, which until now have no more than lightly grazed the human spirit or which at best lie lifeless in a few independent minds, would henceforth irrevocably take their place in the moral feeling of the human race, and would become so many axioms of common sense.

One of the most important teachings of history so conceived would consist in impressing upon the memory of man the respective importance of the nations which have disappeared from the worldly scene, and in filling the awareness of existing nations with the feeling of the destinies which they are called upon to fulfill. Every nation, by clearly understanding the different periods in its past life, would understand its present existence as it is in fact and would be able to anticipate the path it was to follow in the future. Thus, among all nations a truly national consciousness would be established; this would consist of a number of positive ideas, of evident truths derived from their memories, of profound convictions which would more or less dominate all minds and lead them to a single end. Then nationalities, which have up to now done nothing but divide men, stripped of their blindness and of their passionate self-interest, would join with one another to produce a harmonious and universal result; then all nations would reach out their hands to one another and walk together toward a common goal.

I know that this fusion of intellects is promised by scholars to philosophy and to the general progress of enlightenment. But if we recognize that nations, although composite beings, are, in fact, like individuals, moral beings, and that consequently an identical law governs the mental life of each, then we shall find that the activity of the great human families depends necessarily on this personal feeling which makes each consider itself distinct from the rest of the human race, having its own existence and individual interests; that this feeling is a necessary element of universal reason and constitutes as it were the "I" of the collective human being. Then, from our hopes of future felicity and indefinite perfection, we shall find that we cannot abstract great human personalities any more than other minor ones of which they are composed, and that we must consequently accept them as given principles and means to arrive at a more perfect state.

The cosmopolitan future described by philosophy is thus no more than a chimera. A domestic morality of nations, differing from their political morality, must first be worked out. Nations must first learn to know and appraise themselves just as individuals do. They must know their vices and their virtues. They must learn to repent of the sins or crimes they have committed, to repair the harm they have done, or to persist in the good path they follow. These are the necessary conditions of true perfection for nations, just as they are for individuals: in both cases, it is by doubling back on their past lives and finding their future in their past that they will learn to fulfill their destiny.

You see that in this way historical criticism would no longer be reduced to satisfying idle curiosity but would become the most august of judiciaries. It would exercise implacable justice on the fame and grandeur of every age. It would impartially scrutinize every reputation, every boast. It would accept the challenge of every phantom, of every historical marvel. It would wholly busy itself destroying the false images with which the memory of men is cluttered, so that, once the past appeared to reason in its proper light, it could deduce from it sure conclusions with respect to the present and raise its gaze with some sort of assurance to the infinite spaces of the future.

I believe that an immense glory, the glory of Greece, would then wholly vanish; I believe that the day will come when moral thought will consider this land of deception and illusion only with a feeling of holy sadness—a land whence the spirit of imposture for so long poured seduction and deceit over the rest of the world. Then the pure soul of a Fénelon will no longer be seen indolently feeding itself on voluptuous imaginings begotten of the most frightening depravity into which the human race has ever fallen, and powerful intellects will no longer permit themselves to be invaded by the sensual inspirations of Plato.[3] On the contrary, the old almost-forgotten thoughts of religious minds, the prodigious conceptions of those wise men to whom God entrusted the preservation of the first words He spoke in the presence of a creature, will then find an application as wonderful as unexpected: I am referring to some of those powerful thinkers, true heroes of the intellect, who, at the dawn of the new era, mapped out with one hand the path it must follow, while with the other they struggled against the dying monster of polytheism. And since it is probable that, in the unique visions of the future with which some privileged intellects were favored in the past, man will see primarily the expression of an intimate knowledge of the total interconnection of the ages, it will be found that these predictions in fact refer to no determinate epoch, but that they are instructions which are relevant indifferently to all times. What is more, it will be realized that, in a way, we need only look around us to see their perpetual fulfillment in the successive phases of society, like daily and luminous manifestations of the eternal law of the moral world, so that the fact of prophecy will then be found to be as sensible as the very fact of the events which carry us along with them.[4]

Finally, here is the most important lesson which I think history so conceived would teach us, and, in our system, this lesson alone gives the answer to the human riddle and sums up all the philosophy of history by making us understand the universal life of mental being: men would cease to rest content with the senseless system of the *mechanical* perfectibility of our nature, so manifestly refuted by the experience of every era. They would recognize

[3] Schleiermacher, Schelling, Cousin, etc.
[4] Among other things, people will no longer seek, as they did in former times, the great Babylon in such or such a worldly power; they will feel themselves living in the very midst of the din of its downfall, that is, they will know that the sublime historian of the future who told us of this terrible fall was thinking of the fall of no particular empire, but of that of all material societies that are or are to be.

that, left to himself, man has, on the contrary, never followed any course but that of indefinite degradation. If, as is the case, there have been, from time to time, ages of progress among all nations and moments of great lucidity in the universal life of man, sublime leaps of his reason, prodigious efforts of his nature—and they cannot be denied—still nothing proves any permanent and continuous progress of society in general. In reality, it is only in that society of which we are members, in Christian society, a society not made by human hands, that one can find a true ascending movement, a real principle of continuous progress as well as of infinite duration. We have doubtless inherited what was thought or discovered by the minds of the Ancients, we have profited by it, and we have thus sealed the link of the chain of time; but it does not follow that nations would have arrived at the stage at which they are today without that historical event, completely spontaneous, completely isolated from all its antecedents, completely outside the normal generation of human ideas and outside all natural succession of things, which separates the ancient world from the new.

Then, Madam, when the gaze of the wise man turned back toward the past, the world as it was at the time when a supernatural power gave it a new direction would reappear in his imagination in its true color, corrupt, bloody, deceitful. He would then realize that this progress of nations and of generations which he so admired actually had led them only to a brutishness infinitely below that of those peoples we call savage; and, what shows clearly how imperfect were the civilizations of the ancient world, he would find that there was no principle of duration, of stability in them. Where, he would wonder, are the profound wisdom of Egypt, the graceful charm of Ionia, the virtues of Rome, the dazzling brightness of Alexandria? How, you brilliant civilizations, ancient as the world and nourished by all powers, associated with all glories, all grandeurs, all dominions, and, in the end, with the greatest power which ever weighed upon the earth,[5] how could you have been destroyed? To what were all this labor of centuries,

[5] Alexander, Seleucids, Marcus Aurelius, Julian, Lagidae, etc.

all these superb efforts of intelligent nature leading, if new peoples, who had in no way participated in them, were one day to wipe all this out, to tear down this magnificent edifice, and to run their plows through its ruins? Had man then built only to see all the work of his hands reduced to dust? Had he accumulated so much only to lose everything in a single day? Had he raised himself to such a height only to fall still lower?

Be not misled, Madam. It is not the barbarians who destroyed the ancient world: this world was already a decaying corpse; they did no more than scatter its dust to the wind. These same barbarians had attacked ancient societies before this, without making a breach in them: history hardly remembers their first invasions. The truth is that a vital principle which had animated human society up to that time was now exhausted; that material interest, or, if you prefer, real interest, which had up to then alone determined social activity, had as it were accomplished its task and brought to completion the preliminary instruction of the human race. The human spirit, desirous as it is of getting out of its terrestrial sphere, can rise only from phase to phase toward the regions where the true principle of all things resides and therefore cannot give society its definitive form. All the history of which I am speaking to you is contained in this truth.

Unfortunately, we have for too long been accustomed to see in Europe only separate states. This is why the permanence of the new society and its immense superiority over the old could not be understood. People did not consider that, for many centuries, this new society had formed a truly federative system or rather a single nation, and that this system was dissolved only by the Reformation. When the Reformation occurred society was already built for eternity. Before that fatal event the nations of Europe considered themselves as constituting but a single social body, geographically divided into several states but morally constituting only one. For a long time there was among them no public law aside from that of the Church. The wars which took place during that time were considered internal wars. A single and unique interest animated this whole world, a single thought inspired it. This is what makes the history of the Middle Ages so profoundly philosophical: it is, literally, the history of the spirit of man. Moral, mental activity is its whole basis; purely political events have but a secondary role. This is demonstrated precisely by those wars of conviction which the philosophy of the last century held in such great horror. Voltaire very perceptively observed that conviction has caused wars only among Christians; then he rambles on in his usual fashion. Yet when one finds in history a unique phenomenon one should, I believe, above all seek to understand what caused it and what resulted from it. I ask you, could the rule of thought be established in the world in any way but by giving to the very principle of thought all of its actuality? The appearance of things has changed, if you insist; this is the result of the schism which, in breaking up the unity of thought, also broke up the unity of society. But, without any doubt, the basis is still the same, and Europe is still Christendom, no matter what it does. Doubtless, it will never return to the state of its youth and growth, but there is no doubt that some day the boundaries which divide Christian nations will again be erased and that, in a new form, the primitive principle of modern society will appear, more powerful than ever. For the Christian, this is a matter of faith: he may no more doubt this future than the past on which his beliefs are founded; but for any earnest mind I think the matter is demonstrated. Who knows but that that day is closer than one would believe? There is certainly today a religious activity going on in the depths of souls; there are back-tracking motions in the progress of science, that supreme power of the century; there is from time to time I know not what of solemn and meditative in men's souls. Who knows but that these are the antecedent signs of great moral and social phenomena which are to bring about a general revolution in all intelligent nature such that the promised destiny of man, which is today a belief of faith, will then become a probability, a certitude of general reason?

It is in the great family of Christian nations, Madam, that the special character of the new society must be studied. It is there that the true element of stability and progress which differentiates it from any other social system on earth is to be found. It is there that all the great insights of history are hidden. Thus we see [for instance] that in spite of all the upheavals which the new society has experienced, not only has it lost none of its vitality, but rather it grows daily in strength; daily in it new powers are seen more vigorous even than those which first developed in it. Thus we see, again, that the Arabs, the Tartars, the Turks not only were unable to destroy it, but that on the contrary they did nothing but consolidate it. You know that the first two of these nations attacked it before the discovery of gunpowder: hence it is not firearms which preserved it from destruction. Yet one of these nations was simultaneously invading the two remaining societies of the ancient world, India and China. These two societies also did not perish, granted, thanks to their huge populations, masses which, although inert, were capable of reaction. But their native character was lost, their vital principle was cast away to the extreme limits of the social order, so that they were nevertheless sentenced to death.

These two countries, however, were destined to serve as a great lesson from which we are bound to profit. Looking at them today we become in a sense contemporaries of that world of which we find around us only the dust; it is, thus, there that we can learn what would have become of the human race if it had not had that new impulse given it by an all-powerful hand. And note that China seems to have been in possession from time immemorial of the three great instruments which have, it is said, most accelerated the progress of the human mind among us: the compass, the printing press, gunpowder. And of what use were they to it? Did the Chinese go around the world? Did they discover a new hemisphere? Do they possess a literature more vast than that which we possessed before the invention of the printing press? In the deadly art of war did they have Fredericks and Bonapartes as we did? As for Hindustan, does anything in the world more clearly show the powerlessness and the miserable state of any society not founded on the truth emanating directly from the Supreme Reason than that abject state to which it has been reduced by the conquests first of the Tartars and then of the English? I cannot doubt that this stupid immobility of China and this extraordinary debasement of the Indian nation, which was the repository of the earliest natural insights and of the seeds of all human knowledge, contains some profound lesson and that this is why God preserved them on earth.[6]

You have often heard the fall of the Roman Empire attributed to loss of morals and to the despotism which resulted from it. But in this universal revolution it was not just Rome that was involved; it is not Rome that perished, but an entire civilization. The Egypt of the Pharaohs, the Greece of Pericles, the second Egypt of the Lagidae, all the Greece of Alexander which reached beyond the Indus, finally Judaism itself, after its Hellenization, all this had melted into the Roman mass and formed but one unit, one single society which represented all the previous generations back to the origin of things, which contained all that there had been of moral and intellectual forces in human nature up to that time. Thus, it was not an empire, it was human society that was destroyed and reborn. Ever since Europe has, as it were, encircled the globe and rebuilt a new world born from the ocean, since all other human peoples have become so subject to it that one can say that in a way they exist only at its convenience, it has become easy to under-

---

[6] May it not be the application to the collective intelligence of nations of the law whose effects we see daily on individuals, namely, that a mind which, for whatever reason, has drawn nothing from the mass of ideas spread among all the human race, which has not thus subjected itself to the working of a general law, but rather has found itself isolated from the human family and has withdrawn wholly into itself, necessarily undergoes a degradation proportionate to the degree of the insubordination of its own act? Has any nation, indeed, ever been reduced to such an abject state as to become the prey, not of another nation, but of traffickers, subjects themselves in their own country yet absolute potentates in that nation's midst? Moreover, in addition to the unheard-of degradation of the Hindus which resulted from conquest, the deterioration of Indian society dates from much further back. Its literature, its philosophy, even the language in which all this was uttered, belong to an order of things which long ago ceased to exist.

stand what was happening on earth when the old building was falling and the new miraculously rising in its place: the moral element of the universe was getting a new law, a new constitution. The materials of the ancient world doubtless served in the construction of the new, for the material basis of the moral order necessarily had to remain the same. But other human materials, wholly new, cut from a quarry undeveloped by ancient civilization, were furnished by Providence. The vigorous and concentrated abilities of the North were combined with the expansive powers of the South and Orient; the cold and serious mentality of the severe climates fused with the warm and laughing mentality of temperate zones; it would seem as if all the intellectual forces scattered over the earth had come forward and intermingled that day in order to give birth to generations of ideas whose elements had until then remained buried in the most mysterious depths of the human heart. But neither the plan of the building nor the cement which bound the diverse materials was the work of man; it was the divine idea which made everything. This is what it behooves us to understand, and this is the immense fact which purely historical reasoning, calling to its aid all the human resources which it finds existing in that era, will never be able to explain. This is the pivot around which the entire sphere of history turns and which explains and demonstrates the phenomenon of the education of the human race. The mere grandeur of that event, its intimate, necessary, and wholly Providential connection with all that preceded and followed it, would, I believe, suffice to place it beyond the ordinary course of human events; but the decisive effect of this event on the intellect, the new powers with which it enriched the intellect, the new needs which it created for it, and, above all this, that leveling of minds which it effected, in every situation, in all concerns, and in all conditions, so that man has become desirous of truth and fitted to know it, this is what impresses upon all this era an astonishingly strong stamp of Providence and of Supreme Reason. Moreover, since then has not human reason, in spite of its frequent returns toward things which are no more, which can and must be no more, however hard it tries, always fastened itself to that moment? Does not that portion of universal intelligence which today dominates and carries with it all the rest of its mass date from the first day of our era? Is not the spirit of the world today the spirit of Christianity? I do not know; possibly the line which separates us from the ancient world is not visible to all eyes, but so far as I am concerned, all my philosophy, all my morality, all my religion is contained in this. A time will come, I hope, when all reversions to paganism, especially that effected in the fifteenth century and which, I believe, is called the Renaissance of Letters, will, with all their implications and consequences, be but like guilty intoxications whose remembrance we must try to erase from the world's memory by all possible means.

We must also note that, by some sort of optical illusion, men picture Antiquity as an endless succession of ages, whereas the modern era seems to have begun but yesterday. Yet in fact the history of the ancient world, going back, for instance, to the time when the Pelasgians settled in Greece, encompasses a space of time greater by only one century than the duration of our own era. And the extent of historical times is not even that. Yet, in that short space of time, how many societies perished in the ancient world, whereas in the history of modern nations it is only the geographical boundaries of states that shift, while the society itself and the nations remain unchanged! I need not to tell you that such events as the expulsion of the Moors from Spain, the destruction of the American [Indian] populations, the annihilation of the Tartars in Russia, serve only to reinforce our argument. Thus it is that the fall of the Ottoman Empire, which is already resounding in our ears, will yet afford the spectacle of one of those great catastrophes which Christian nations are destined never to suffer. Then will come the turn of the other non-Christian nations which lie at the more remote extremities of our system. Such is the cycle of the all-powerful activity of sacred Truth, now pushing peoples back, now encompassing them within its circumference, constantly growing and bringing us nearer to the promised time. Thus is fulfilled the destiny of the human race.

The indifference with which modern civilization has for a long time been considered is wonderful. Yet you see that, to understand it properly, to explain it perfectly, is simultaneously to solve the social problem. This is why, even in the most vast and general concerns of the philosophy of history, we must, willy-nilly, come back to this civilization. After all, does it not contain all that past ages have produced; and are the ages to come to be something else than the product of this civilization? Moral being is nothing else than being as created by the ages and which the ages must complete. In human society has the mass of ideas spread over the surface of the world ever been so concentrated as in present society? Has a single thought, at any time in the universal life of man, so well encompassed the whole activity of human nature as in our own day? We are, thus, clearly heirs of all that has ever been said or done by men, and there is no point on earth not subject to the influence of our ideas; there is, thus, in the whole universe now only one intellectual power. Thus, all fundamental concerns of the philosophy of history are necessarily comprised in the single concern of European civilization. But once the words, "human perfectibility," "progress of the human spirit," have been spoken, men believe that they have said all there is to be said, that they have explained everything. One would think that man has at all times done nothing but go forward, without ever stopping, without ever going backward; that in the movement of intelligent nature there has never been a time of conflict or of reversal, only development and progress. But why, then, have those nations of which I spoke earlier not moved so long as we have known them? People say that the nations of Asia have become stationary. But why are they stationary? To reach the state in which they now are they surely had to do as we did, seek, invent, discover. Why is it then that, having reached a certain point, they stopped short and have since been unable to imagine or create anything?[7] The answer is very simple: it is that the progress of human nature is by no means indefinite, as men usually imagine. It has limits that it can never surpass. That is why the societies of the ancient world did not keep going forever. That is why Egypt, from the time when Herodotus visited it, made no progress until the Greek conquest. That is why the Roman world, so beautiful, so brilliant, which acted as a prism for all the light shed from the Pillars of Hercules to the Ganges, had, at the time when a new idea came to enlighten the human spirit, attained that state of immobility which of necessity puts a stop to all purely human progress. If only a little thought free from the prejudices of the schools—those scourges of history—is given to this moment which was so fruitful in its consequences, it becomes clear that, in addition to the excessive depravity of morals, in addition to the loss of all feeling of virtue, of freedom, of patriotism, in addition to decadence in all branches of human knowledge, there was complete stagnation in all things, and that intellects had reached the point of being able to move only in a narrow and evil circle from which they escaped only to hurl themselves into a dissolute stupidity. Once material interests are satisfied, man ceases to go forward; he is fortunate if he does not go backward! This is the case, be not mistaken; in Greece as in Hindustan, in Rome as in Japan, in Mexico as in China, all the labor of the intellect, however remarkable it may have been or even still is, was and is aimed at but one and the same thing; the most exalted and exuberant aspects of the doctrines and customs of the Orient, far from refuting this general fact, rather affirm it: anyone can see that all these outbursts of thought are but the result of the illusions and artifices of material man. The only thing that must be made clear is that this earthly interest, the eternal motive of all human activity, is not limited to mere sensu-

[7] When one says of a civilized nation that it is stationary, one must say when it became so; otherwise, no conclusion can be drawn from this fact.

ous appetites. Rather, this interest is simply the general need for well-being which, manifested in all sorts of ways, and in the most various forms, depending on the more or less advanced state of society and on different local causes, never rises to the level of the needs of purely moral being. Christian society alone is truly directed by spiritual interest. It is this which makes for the perfectibility of modern nations and in which lies the secret of their civilization. In whatever manner that other interest should appear in it, you will find that it is always subordinated to that powerful force, which takes hold of all the faculties of man, puts to use all the abilities of reason, and leaves nothing which is not made to serve the fulfillment of its destiny. This interest, certainly, can never be satisfied; it is infinite: hence, Christian nations must always go forward. And even though the end to which they aim has nothing in common with that other well-being—the only end which non-Christian nations can set themselves—they find it on their way and benefit by it. The pleasures of life which alone other nations seek, Christian nations obtain also but by another road, in accordance with the saying of our Savior: *Seek ye the kingdom of heaven, and all these things shall be added unto you.*[8] The enormous unfolding of all intellectual powers which the spirit dominating them arouses thus showers them with abundance of all goods. But it is certain that there will never be among us either Chinese immobility or Greek decadence, still less complete annihilation of civilization. You need merely look around you to be convinced. For this to happen the whole globe would have to be convulsed from top to bottom; a second revolution, similar to that which gave it its present form, would have to occur. Without another universal cataclysm it is impossible to imagine such an event. Should, for instance, one of the two hemispheres be swallowed up, what remained of our culture in the other would suffice to revive the human spirit. Never, no, never will the spirit which is to conquer the world stop or die; for that a special decree of Him

[8] [See Matthew 6:33. —*Trans.*]

who placed it in the human soul would have to come to strike it from on high. Finally, I hope, Madam, that you will find this philosophical conclusion of meditation on history more forceful, more evident, and particularly more instructive than all those which old-fashioned history draws in its fashion from its description of the centuries by appealing to soil, climate, races of men, and the famous theory of human perfectibility.

If the influence of Christianity on society and on the development of the human spirit is not yet fully undersood or appreciated, do you know, Madam, who is to blame? The men who broke up moral unity and who date Christianity only from their own time, those who call themselves the Reformers. They are clearly not interested in following the progress of Christianity through the Middle Ages; for them this immense period is thus but a void in time. How, then, can they understand the education of modern nations? Nothing, believe me, has so assisted in disfiguring the picture of modern history as has this false point of view of the Protestants. It is Protestantism that led men so to exaggerate the importance of the Renaissance of Letters, an event which, in fact, never took place, inasmuch as literature was never wholly lost. It is Protestantism that led men to dream up a number of diverse causes of progress, causes which in fact were only secondary or which are merely derivative of the single cause of everything. It is Protestantism that led men to seek the causes of the forward progress of modern nations everywhere except where they really are so that thus Christianity was disavowed. (But since a less narrow and loftier philosophy has, by a fortunate return toward the past, turned to the study of this important period, so many things, until then unknown, have suddenly been revealed to thought that the most obstinate ill will would henceforth be unable to resist these new insights. If, therefore, it is in the plan of Providence that men should be enlightened from this direction, the time is not far removed when a great light will flash out of the darkness which still partially covers the history of modern society, and it will not be long before this new philosophy of history which I want to explain to you will be understood by men of science.)[9]

You must admit that this obstinacy of the Reformers is remarkable. According to them, after the second or third century, there remained of Christianity only just enough to keep it from being utterly destroyed. The superstition or ignorance which existed in those eleven or twelve centuries seems to them such that they can see in them only as deplorable a kind of idolatry as that of the pagans. According to them, had it not been for the Vaudois the thread of sacred tradition would have been wholly broken, and if Luther had not come on the scene it would have been but a matter of days before the religion of Christ came to an end. Now, I ask you, how can anyone find the Divine Seal in this powerless, impermanent, lifeless doctrine which they make of Christianity? How can anyone find the work of God in this deceitful religion which, instead of regenerating the human race and imbuing it with a new life as it had promised, momentarily appeared on earth only to be extinguished, was born only to die immediately or to serve as an instrument for human passions? Can it be that the fate of this religion thus depended merely on Leo X's desire to complete the basilica of Saint Peter? Can it be that, had he not had indulgences sold to Germany in order to do this, there would today be no vestige of Christianity left? I doubt that anything demonstrates more clearly the radical vice of the Reformation than this narrow and niggardly way of viewing revealed religion. Is this not to belie all the promises of Jesus Christ, is this not to deny all His teaching? If it is true that His word is to last longer than heaven and earth, and if He is himself to be always present in our midst, how then could the temple built by His hands have been on the

---

[9] (Since this letter was written M. Guizot has in great part fulfilled this hope.) [The sections in parentheses are crossed out in the manuscript. I am following McNally ("Chaadayev's Philosophical Letters," p. 90) in preserving them here. —Trans.]

verge of crumbling? How could it have remained abandoned, like a house doomed to fall into ruins?

You must agree, however, that the Protestants were consistent. If they first set all Europe on fire, if they then broke the ties which united nations and which made them a single family, if they spread so much misery and shed so much blood over the earth, it was because Christianity was about to perish. After all, must not all be sacrificed to save it? But the truth is this: nothing, on the contrary, better demonstrates the divinity of our religion than its perpetual and constant influence on the human mind, an influence which, although modified to meet the needs of different times, although combined with the varying needs of nations and centuries, has, far from totally ceasing, never weakened for a single moment. It is the sight of our religion's sovereign power, acting constantly in the midst of the countless obstacles ceaselessly caused by the vice of our nature and by the baleful heritage of paganism, which most satisfies reason with respect to it.

What is meant by the assertion that the Church had degenerated from the primitive Church? Did not the Fathers, as early as the third century, deplore the corruption of Christians? Were not these complaints always repeated, in every century, at every council? Did not true piety always raise its voice against the abuses and vices of the clergy, and, when occasion arose, against the usurpations of hierarchial power? Nothing is more wonderful than the brilliant lights which shot up from time to time from within the dark night that covered the world. Now these lights were examples of the most sublime virtue, now the marvelous effects of faith on the minds of nations and individuals. The Church collected all this and made of it its strength and its wealth. Thus was the eternal fabric woven, in the way which could best give it its necessary pattern. Naturally, the primitive purity of Christianity could not be preserved forever; Christianity had to pass through all possible phases of corruption; it had to bear every imprint which the freedom of the human intellect must impress upon it.

What is more, the perfection of the Apostolic Church was that of a small community lost in the great pagan community: it could not therefore be that of the universal society of the human race. The golden age of the Church, as is known, was that of its great suffering, that during which the labor of pain which was to found the new order was still under way, during which the blood of the Savior still gushed forth. It is absurd to dream of a return to a state of affairs which was but the consequence of the immense suffering that bore down on the first Christians.

Do you wish to know, then, what was accomplished by this Reformation which boasts of having rediscovered Christianity? And, you can easily see, this is one of the greatest questions which the science of history can ask. The Reformation placed the world back into the disunity of paganism. It established once again the great national individuals, the isolation of souls and minds; once again it cast man into the solitude of his own self; once again it attempted to take from the world all the sympathy, all the harmony which the Savior had brought to it. If it accelerated the movement of the human spirit, it also took away from the consciousness of intelligent being the fruitful and sublime idea of universality and unity, the only source of the true, that is, the infinite progress of man. The real result of every schism in the Christian world is to break up the mysterious unity in which are comprised all the divine thought of Christianity and all its power. This is why the ancient Church in which Christianity matured will never compromise with new communions. Woe to it and woe to the world if it ever recognized division as a fact. All would soon again be but chaos of human ideas, but multiplicity of lies, but ruin and dust. Only the visible, tangible, plastic steadfastness of Truth can preserve the reign of spirit on earth. Only by realizing itself in the given forms of human nature can the realm of thought find permanence and duration. And then, if there is to be no more visible union, if internal community of opinion without external reality is found sufficient, what will become of the Sacrament of Communion, that marvelous discovery of Christian reason which, as it were, materializes souls in order the better to unite them? To what end unite ourselves with the Savior if we are divided one from another? It does not surprise me that Calvin, the murderer of Servetus, that Zwingli, the bully, that Henry VIII, the tyrant, together with that hypocrite Cranmer, should have failed to recognize the powers of love and union contained in the great Sacrament; but that such profound and sincerely religious minds as the many found among the Lutherans where this spoliation of the Eucharist is not part of dogma, and where their founder fought against it with such ardor, should be so strangely mistaken about the idea of that great institution and should abandon themselves to the deplorable teaching of Calvinism—this is inconceivable. It must be admitted that there is a strange love of destruction in all Protestant churches: they seem to aspire to nothing but self-annihilation, to fear being too alive, to wish to have nothing which might make them endure. Is this, then, the doctrine of Him who came to bring us life on earth and who conquered death? Are we already in Heaven that we can with impunity reject the conditions of terrestrial economy? And this economy, is it anything other than the combination of the pure thoughts of intelligent being with the necessary conditions of his existence? But the first of these conditions is society, the contact of minds, the fusion of ideas and of feelings. It is only by satisfying this condition that Truth becomes alive; that from the region of speculation it descends into that of reality; that from thought it becomes *fact*; that, finally, it acquires the character of a natural force, and that its action becomes as certain as that of any other natural force. But how could this occur in an ideal society which existed only in wishes and in the imagination of men? This is what the Church invisible of the Protestants is: in fact invisible, like non-being.

The day when all Christian communions unite will be that when the schismatic churches decide to admit in a spirit of penitence and humility, in sackcloth and ashes, that in separating from the mother Church, they had cast far from them the effect of this sublime prayer of the Savior: *Holy Father, keep them in thy name whom thou hast given me; that they may be one, as we also are.*[10]

As for the papacy, if it is, as people would have it, a human institution—if indeed things of such proportions could be the work of human hands—of what importance is this? What is certain is that in its day it derived essentially from the true spirit of Christianity, and that today, still a visible symbol of unity, it is also a symbol of reunion. On these grounds, why not concede to it a superior rank among all Christian societies? And who will not marvel at its singular destiny? Who will not marvel to see it, in spite of all its vicissitudes and all the disasters it has suffered, in spite of its own faults and guilts, in spite of all the attacks and the unheard-of triumph of unbelief, standing more steadfast than ever! Stripped of its human brilliance, it is only the stronger, and the indifference felt toward it merely steadies it the more and the better guarantees its continuance. Formerly it subsisted through the veneration of the Christian world, through an instinct among nations, which led them to see in it the cause of their temporal as well as of their eternal salvation; now it subsists by its humble attitude in the midst of earthly powers. But at all times it perfectly fulfills its destined function, it centralizes Christian thoughts even today; even today it brings them in spite of themselves toward one another; it reminds those who denied it of the unity of the supreme principle of their faith, and always, by the nature of the heavenly vocation impressed upon it, it soars majestically above the world of terrestrial interests. Even though men seem very little concerned with it today, should it, *per impossibile*, disappear from its place upon the earth, you would see the bewilderment into which all religious communities would fall when that living monument of the history of the great community was no longer present among them. This visible unity, on which they set so little store

10 [John 17:11. See also above, *Letter I*, p. 32. —*Trans.*]

today, would then be sought everywhere but found nowhere. And it is certain that the precious awareness of its future which now occupies Christian thought, and which gives it the superior life that distinguishes it from common thought, would then necessarily be wholly dissipated, just as hopes founded on the memory of an active existence are lost when that activity is found to have no result and from then on the very memory of our past escapes us, useless.

Madam:

(The more you reflect on what I was telling you the other day, the more you will find that it has all been said a hundred times by men of all parties and of all opinions, and the only difference is that we are interested in it in a way which has not yet interested others. Yet I have no doubt that if these letters should by chance see the light of day people would cry paradox. Whenever even the most common ideas are emphasized with a certain degree of conviction they are taken as strange and novel. For my part, I think that the age of the paradox and of systems with no real foundation is so much past that it is only through stupidity that people can succumb to these old eccentricities of the human spirit. Certainly, if human reason is today less vast, less elevated, less fertile than in the great centuries of inspiration and invention, it is, on the other hand, infinitely more severe, more sober, more rigorous, more methodical, finally, more exact, than it has ever been. I would add, and this with a feeling of true happiness, that reason has been for some time more impersonal than ever before: this is the surest guarantee against the rashness of private opinions.)[1]

If we have, in meditating on the memories of man, reached some insights which are our own and which do not agree with prejudice, that is because we believe that it is time frankly to take

---

[1] [This whole paragraph is crossed out in the manuscript. I am following McNally ("Chaadayev's Philosophical Letters," pp. 93–94) in preserving it here. —*Trans.*]

sides in these matters, as was done during the last century with regard to the natural sciences. It is time to consider history in all its rational ideality, just as the latter were considered in all their empirical reality. Since the subject matter of history and the means for knowing it are always the same, it is clear that the circle of historical experience must someday be completed. Applications will never end, but the rule once found, there will be nothing to add to it. In the physical sciences every new discovery opens a new horizon to the mind and uncovers a new field for observation; we need go no further than the microscope: did it not bring to light a whole world unknown to ancient scientists? In the study of nature, progress is thus necessarily infinite. But in the study of history, it is always man that is studied and it is always one and the same instrument that is used in this study. Hence, if there is a great lesson hidden in history, we must someday reach something stable which will once for all bring the experiment to a close. That fine conception of Pascal's, which I believe I have already quoted to you, *that the whole succession of men is but one man who abides always,*² must someday no longer be the figurative expression of an abstract principle, but must become the real fact of human reason; and thenceforth human reason will as it were be compelled to act only by each time shaking the whole immense chain of human ideas which stretches across all ages.

But will man ever be able to substitute for the wholly personal and solitary consciousness which he now has, that general consciousness which would make him constantly feel that he was a part in a great spiritual whole? Yes, assuredly. Just consider: in addition to the feeling of our personal individuality we carry in our hearts the feeling of being related to our country, our family, the community of views of which we are members. This latter feeling is often even stronger than the former. The seed of a higher consciousness truly resides in us, forming the essence of our nature. Our present *I* is not inflicted upon us by any inevitable law; we have ourselves placed it in our souls. It becomes clear, then,

---

² [See above, p. 95 (*Letter V*). —*Trans.*]

that man has no other mission than the annihilation of his personal being and the substitution for it of a perfectly social or impersonal being. You have seen that this is the only basis of moral philosophy.[3] You see now that it is also the basis of historical thought. According to this view, the illusions which veil or distort the different ages of the general life of man could not be considered with the cold interest of science but must be considered with the deep feeling of moral truth. How can there be identification with something which never happened? How can one become one with non-being? It is only in truth that the forces of attraction of both this and that nature make themselves felt. We must, in the study of history, make it a practice never to compromise with the reveries of the imagination, nor with the habits of memory, but rather to be as eager to seek out what is positive and certain as man has always been to pursue what is picturesque and amusing. It is no longer a matter of filling our memory with facts; there are more than enough facts there. It is sheer error to imagine that in history the mass of facts necessarily carries certainty along with it. It is not the lack of facts which makes historical understanding conditional, nor is it ignorance of them which makes for ignorance of history, but rather lack of reflection and bad reasoning. If men wanted to reach certainty and positive knowledge in this field of science only on the strength of facts, there would never be enough of them. Often a single aspect, if well understood, clarifies and demonstrates better than a whole chronicle. Therefore, here is our rule: let us meditate on the facts we know and try to have in our minds more live pictures than dead matter. Let others tire themselves digging in the ancient dust of nations; we have other things to do. We consider the subject matter of history as quite complete; but we have little confidence in the logic of history. And if, like others, we should see in the flow of time nothing but human reason and perfectly free wills, then no matter to what extent we piled up facts in our minds and how marvelously we made them derive one from another, history would offer us nothing of what

[3] See the *Second Letter.*

136

we seek; we would never see anything in it; it would be[4] [merely] the same human interplay which men have always seen.[5] It would still be that dynamic and psychological kind of history of which I spoke to you earlier, which tries to explain everything in terms of individuals and the imaginary linkage of causes and effects, in terms of human whims and the supposedly inevitable consequences of these whims, and which thus hands human intelligence over to its own law.[6]

Behold one of the most outstanding instances of the falsity of certain conceptions of history as it is today. You know that it is the Greeks who made of art a vast idea of the human spirit. Let us see what constituted this magnificent creation of Hellenic genius. The Greeks idealized the material aspect of man, enlarged it, made it divine. The natural and legitimate order of things was

[4] [The words *"de cette manière que"* have been scratched out in the manuscript and unclear words have been inserted above them. McNally ("Chaadayev's Philosophical Letters," p. 95, ll. 18–19) reads *"C'est acquit"* (which he corrects to *"C'est acquis"*). Possibly: *"C'en serait."* —*Trans.*]

[5] (One cannot accuse Herodotus or Livy or Gregory of Tours of not making Providence intervene in human affairs, but is it necessary for me to explain that it is not to the idea of that superstitious and casual intervention of God that we would like to see the human mind return?) [The footnote is crossed out in the manuscript. I am following McNally ("Chaadayev's Philosophical Letters," p. 95) in preserving it here. —*Trans.*]

[6] (In that Rome about which people talk so much, which everyone goes to see and which is so little understood, there is a unique monument which one can call an ancient fact that still endures, a fact of another age that stopped in the midst of time: the Coliseum. In my opinion there is no fact in history which suggests such profound ideas as the sight of this ruin, no fact which better sets off the character of the two ages of man and better demonstrates that great axiom of history, namely, that there was never any true progress or any true permanence in society before the Christian era. This arena to which the Roman people came in crowds to drench themselves in blood, where the whole pagan world was so well summed up in an appalling game, where all the life of those times was displayed in all its liveliest enjoyment, in its most brilliant pomp, is it not indeed standing there before us now to tell us what state the world had reached at a time when all the forces of human nature had already been made available for the building of the social edifice, a time when the fall of this edifice was already being heralded on all sides and when a new barbarian era was about to begin? More, it is there that the blood streamed which was to water the base of the new monument. Does not that building alone deserve a volume? Strange: it never inspired a single historical thought of the great truths it contains. From among the swarms of travelers that flock to Rome, there was one [Gibbon] who, from a neighboring and famous hill from which he could contemplate it in peace

inverted. That which should have remained forever in the lower region of the intellectual world was projected to the highest realms of thought. The action of the senses on the mind was infinitely increased. The great line of demarcation which separates the divine element of feeling from the human was broken. Hence a chaotic confusion of all elements of morality. The mind threw itself passionately onto the things least worthy of its concern. An unbelievable attraction spread to all that is most depraved in human nature. In the place of the primitive poetry of truth, the poetry of deceit was introduced into the imagination, and this powerful faculty, made to enable us to comprehend the incomprehensible and to make visible the invisible, was employed henceforth but to render the sensible still more sensible, the earthly still more earthly. Thus, our physical being grew as our moral being shrank. And if wise men such as Pythagoras and Plato fought against this deadly tendency of the spirit of their times, themselves more or less infected by it, their efforts led to nothing and it is only after Christianity had renewed the human spirit that their doctrines acquired true influence. This, then, is what Greek art did. It is the apotheosis of matter, this cannot be denied. Men look at the monuments which are left to us without understanding what they mean. They delight at the sight of these admirable inspirations of a genius which fortunately is no more, without any consciousness of the impurity which is born in their hearts, the falsity which is born in their minds. This is a cult, an intoxication, a fascination by which moral feeling is wholly engulfed. Yet one need but have the courage to consider rationally the feeling with which one is

---

in its amazing setting, thought, he says, to see the centuries roll past his eyes and teach him the riddle of their movement. Yet, he saw nothing there but conquerors and friars. As if nothing had ever happened there but triumphs and processions! A narrow and shabby view to which we owe the deceitful product which all the world knows; the true prostitution of one of the greatest historical geniuses of all time!) [The footnote is crossed out in the manuscript as is the last clause of the sentence to which it refers. I am following McNally ("Chaadayev's Philosophical Letters," pp. 95–96) in preserving the footnote here, but I am not preserving the clause in question since it adds nothing new to what has already been said. —*Trans.*]

filled in the midst of this stupid admiration to realize that it is produced in us by the most vile part of our being, that it is, as it were, with our bodies that we understand these bodies of marble and bronze. And observe that all the beauty, all the perfection of these figures come but from the complete stupidity imprinted upon them: should the sign of reason dare to appear there, the ideal which charms us would disappear at once. Thus we contemplate [in them] not even the features of a rational being but those of I know not what imaginary being, a kind of monster produced by the most lawless excess of the human mind, whose picture, far from filling us with pleasure, should rather repel us. This is how the most serious things of the philosophy of history are disfigured by prejudice, by scholastic habits, by the routines of the mind, by the charm of a deceitful illusion, which together make up present-day historical understanding.

You will ask me perhaps if I have myself always been a stranger to these seductions of art. No, Madam, on the contrary: before I even became acquainted with them some unknown instinct made me feel them as sweet enchantments which were to fill my life. When one of the great events of the century led me to the capital where conquest had temporarily collected all these marvels, I did as others did. Even more devoutly than they did I lavish my incense on the altar of the idols. Then, when I saw them a second time in the light of their native sun, I still delighted in them. But I also must admit that beneath this delight something bitter, like remorse, always lay hidden. Thus, when the idea of Truth came to me, I balked at none of its consequences; I accepted them all at once, without equivocating.

Let us return now to those great figures of history which history disowned or erased from human memory, and let us begin with Moses, the most gigantic and the most imposing of all historical figures.

Thanks to God, we are no longer at a time when the great legislator of the Jews was, even for those who really care to think, but one of those beings belonging to a world of fantasy, like all those supernatural pictures of heroes, demi-gods, prophets that one finds in the first few pages of any of the histories of ancient nations. He is no longer a poetic character in whom historical thought is bound to find only the lesson he portrays as a type, a symbol, or an expression of the time in which human tradition places him. No one today, I believe, doubts the historical reality of Moses. However, it is certain that the sacred atmosphere which surrounds him does him no great favor and that he does not hold his proper rank in history. The influence which this great man had over the human race is far from being properly understood and appreciated. His image has remained veiled in a mysterious enveloping light. For lack of sufficient study, Moses does not teach the lesson which results from the sight of great men in history. Neither the public man nor the private, neither the thinker nor the man of action finds in the story of Moses' life the whole lesson that could be found there. This is the result of the habits introduced into the mind by religion: by impressing upon Biblical figures a superhuman appearance, religion makes them appear quite other than in fact they are.[7] There is in the personality of Moses a strange mixture of loftiness and simplicity, of strength and guilelessness, and of harshness and gentleness, which, I think, cannot be too much pondered. There is, I believe, no figure in history that presents such an assembly of contradictory features and faculties. And when I consider this prodigious being and the influence he has exercised on men, I do not know which I should the more admire, the historical phenomenon of which he was the cause or the moral phenomenon which I find in his person. On the one hand, the immense conception of a chosen people, that is, a people endowed with the supreme mission of preserving on earth the idea of a

[7] Observe that, in reality, Biblical figures should be the most familiar to us, for there is none whose features are more clearly drawn. That is one of the great appeals of Scripture. Since people had to identify themselves to such an extent with these men, since these figures had to act directly on our most intimate feelings in order thus to prepare souls to submit to the otherwise compelling influence of the person of Christ, Scripture found the way of drawing their features so well that their pictures have become engraved upon the mind as those of men with whom we have lived on familiar terms.

single God, and the sight of the unheard-of means he employed in order to shape this nation in a manner such that this idea should remain preserved in its midst not only intact but so that it might one day appear powerful, irresistible, like a natural force, before which all human forces would disappear, before which the whole intelligent world would someday have to bow. On the other hand, the man, unpretentious to the point of weakness, the man who could give vent to his anger only when he was powerless, who could command only by exhausting admonition, who let himself be taught by the first comer. A strange genius, simultaneously the strongest and the most docile of men! He created future ages and humbly submitted himself to everything that appeared to him under the guise of truth; he spoke to men from the midst of a cloud, his voice resounded across the centuries, he struck nations like the voice of fate, yet he gave in to the first movement of a sensitive heart, to the first right reason that he met. Is this not a figure of astonishing grandeur, a unique lesson?

People have tried to diminish this grandeur by saying that Moses originally intended merely to deliver his people from an unbearable yoke, though at the same time they honor him for the heroism he displayed in this work. They have pretended to see in him only the great legislator, and today, I think, they find a marvelous liberalism in his laws. They have also said that his God was no more than a national God and that he took all his theology from the Egyptians. Now, without doubt he was patriotic, and what great soul, whatever his mission on earth, would not be? Moreover, this is a general law: he who would have an effect on men must act in the domestic sphere in which he has been placed, on the social family in which he was born; to speak clearly to the human race he must speak to his nation, otherwise he will not be heard, he will accomplish nothing. The more the moral action of man on his fellows is direct and practical, the more it is sure and strong; the more his speech is personal, the more it is powerful. Nothing better reveals the *supreme principle* which moved this great man than the perfect efficacy and correctness of the means he employed to effect the task he had set himself. It is also possible that he found among his nation or among other peoples the idea of a national God and that he made use of this datum—as he did of so many others which he must have found among his natural antecedents—to introduce his sublime monotheism into human thought. But it does not follow that on this account Jehovah was not for him, as for Christians, the God of the whole world. The more he sought to isolate and confine this great dogma within his nation, the more he employed extraordinary means to reach this end, the more one finds throughout all this labor of a superior mind the wholly universal aim of preserving for the entire world, for all future generations, the notion of a single God. What surer means was there of building an inviolable sanctuary to the true God, in the midst of the polytheism which at this time was invading all the earth, than by inspiring his people, the guardians of the sacred monument, with a racial horror of all idolatrous nations, than by linking the whole social being of this people, all its fortunes, all its memories, all its hopes with this single principle? Read Deuteronomy with this in mind and you will be surprised at the light it will shed, not only on the Mosaic system, but on all revealed philosophy.

Every word of this remarkable book reveals the *superhuman idea* which dominated the spirit of its author. From this also stem those frightful exterminations ordered by Moses, which contrast so strangely with the gentleness of his nature and which have so repulsed a philosophy more foolish than impious. This philosophy did not understand that the man who was so prodigious an instrument in the hand of Providence, the confidant of all its secrets, could act only as it did, only as nature did. Ages and generations could have no value of any kind for him; his mission was not to offer a model of justice and moral perfection, but to plant in the mind of man an immense idea which that human mind could not produce of itself. Can people believe that when he stifled the cry of his loving heart, commanded the massacre of nations, lowered on whole populations the sword of divine justice, he was thinking of nothing but finding a homeland for the stupid and recalcitrant people whose leader he was? Truly an excellent brand of psychology! In order not to rise to the true cause of the phenomenon under observation, what does it do? It avoids the effort by combining in the same soul the most contradictory features, features which experience has never shown united in a single individual.

And what does it matter, after all, that Moses should have drawn some lesson from Egyptian learning? What does it matter that he thought at first only of rescuing his nation from the yoke of slavery? Does that make it less true that, in realizing in this nation the idea which he either gathered somewhere or drew out from the depth of his soul, and in surrounding it with all the elements of preservation and perpetuity that human nature contains, he thus gave to men the true God? And that consequently the whole intellectual development of the human race deriving from this principle is uncontestably due to him?

David is one of the historical figures whose features have best been handed down to us. Nothing is more alive, more dramatic, more true than his story, nothing is more distinct than his physiognomy. The narrative of his life, his sublime songs, where the present is so wonderfully lost in the future, depict so well the intention of his soul that absolutely nothing in his being remains hidden from us. Yet it is only on profoundly religious minds that he makes an impression similar to that of the heroes of Greece and Rome. This is, once more, because all the great men of the Bible belong to a world apart: the haloes which shine about their heads relegate them quite unfortunately to a region where the mind hardly cares to travel, the region of importunate powers which rigidly command submission, where man finds himself constantly face to face with the implacable law, where there is nothing left for man to do but to prostrate himself and adore. Yet how can we understand the movement of the ages if we do not study it where the principle which produces it is most visibly manifest?

In opposing Socrates and Marcus Aurelius to these two giants of Scripture I wanted to make you appreciate by this contrast of such different degrees of greatness the two worlds from which they are drawn. First, read, if you can without the prejudice bound to his memory, the anecdotes about Socrates in Xenophon; consider how much his death added to his reputation; think of his famous demon; think of his tolerance of vice, a tolerance which he sometimes stretched, it must be admitted, to a surprising degree;[8] think of the different accusations made against him by his contemporaries; think of the word he spoke an instant before his death and which bequeathed to posterity all the uncertainty of his thought; finally, think of all the divergent, absurd, contradictory views that came from his school. As for Marcus Aurelius, again, admit no superstition. Consider carefully his book, remember the massacre of Lyon, the appalling man to whom he handed the universe, the time when he lived, the high sphere in which he was placed, all the means of greatness which his worldly position offered him. Then compare, if you please, the result of the philosophy of Socrates with that of the religion of Moses; compare the person of the Roman emperor with that of the man who, from shepherd become king, poet, and wise man, personified the vast and mysterious conception of the prophet-legislator, who made himself the center of that world of marvels in which the destiny of the human race was to be fulfilled, who, by definitively determining in his people the particularly and profoundly religious tendency which was to engross it all its life, thus produced on earth the order of things which alone could there render possible the generation of Truth. I have no doubt that you will agree that if poetic thought presents us men such as Moses and David as superhuman beings and surrounds them with a unique brilliance, common reason, cold as it is, must also see in them something more than merely great, extraordinary men. And it will, I think, appear obvious to you that in the course of the moral world these men were certainly wholly direct manifestations of the supreme law which governs

---

[8] Had I not been writing to a woman I would especially have advised the reader, to get an idea of this, to read Plato's *Symposium*.

that world, that their appearance corresponds to those great periods in the physical order which from time to time remake or renew nature.[9]

Next comes Epicurus. You know, of course, that I attach no special importance to the reputation of this figure. But you must know, first, that, with respect to his materialism, his views were no different from those of the other ancient philosophers, except that, being more frank in his judgment, more logical than most of them, Epicurus did not get embroiled, as they did, in endless contradictions. Pagan deism appeared to him for what in fact it was, an absurdity; pagan spiritualism appeared a deception. His physics, which after all was simply that of Democritus whom Bacon calls somewhere the only reasonable physicist among the Ancients, was not inferior to that of the other natural philosophers of his time, and, as for his atoms, if you disregard their metaphysical status now that molecular philosophy has become so positive, they are far from being so ridiculous as men have found them. But, as you know, Epicurus' name is primarily bound up with his ethics, and it is his ethics which has sullied it! Yet this ethics is judged in terms of the dissoluteness of his sect and the more-or-less arbitrary interpretations made after him. As for his own writings, you know that they are lost. Let Cicero shudder at the mere name of sensuous pleasure, but do you, I beg you, understand this ethics, which has been so disparaged, as it ought to be understood, that is, primarily in accordance with what we know of the person of its author, abstracting from the effect it had in the pagan world—this effect results rather from the general attitude of the human spirit in those times than from the doctrine itself. Then compare it to the other ethical systems of the Ancients. You will find that, less arrogant, less harsh, less impractical than that of the Stoics, less vague, less nebulous, less weak than that of the Platonists, it was

---

[9] Besides, nothing is simpler to explain than the enormous glory of Socrates, the only man whom the ancient world saw die for an ideal. This unique example of the heroism of idealism must indeed have strangely dazed those people. But for us who have seen whole populations give their lives for the cause of Truth, is it not madness to be mistaken about him as they were?

affectionate, benevolent, human, in such a way that it contained something of the principles of Christian ethics. You cannot mistake the fact that there was in that philosophy an essential element which was wholly lacking in ancient practical thought, an element of union, of bond, of good will among men. And there was in it, especially, an element of common sense and a lack of pride which is found in none of the contemporary philosophical schools. Besides, it made the highest good consist of peace of soul and of a gentle joy which imitated on earth the celestial bliss of the gods. Epicurus himself set the example of this peaceful existence; he lived almost obscure in the midst of the gentlest affection and of study. If his ethics had been able to settle in the minds of the people without being perverted by the vicious principle which then dominated the world, there is no doubt but that it would have shed on hearts a gentleness and a humaneness which neither the boastful ethics of the Stoa, nor the dreamy speculation of the Academicians was capable of shedding. Note further, I beg you, that Epicurus is the only one of the wise men of Antiquity whose morals were perfectly blameless, and the only one whose memory was mingled, among his disciples, with a love, a veneration which resembled a cult.[10] You understand now why we had to seek to correct somewhat our memory of this man.

We shall not go back to discuss Aristotle. Although this is one of the most important chapters in modern history, it is too vast a subject to be treated merely incidentally. Note only, if you please, that Aristotle is in a way a creation of the new reason. It is only natural that in its youth the new reason, tormented by its enormous need for knowledge, should fasten itself with all its strength to that mechanic of the mind who, by means of his cranks, levers, and pulleys, made the understanding work with prodigious velocity. It was perfectly natural too that the Arabs, who first unearthed him, should have found him so much to their liking. That improvised people had nothing of its own to which to

---

[10] Pythagoras is not an exception; he was a legendary figure to whom men attributed whatever they wished.

146

cling; a ready-made philosophy would thus suit it. But now all that is past: Arabs, Scholastics, and their common master, they have all fulfilled their various missions. From them the mind gained more stability, more confidence, its progress became more self-assured. It acquired a bearing which facilitated its movements, which speeded up its procedures. As you see, all was for the best; thanks to the powers and insights of the new reason, evil was transformed into good. [But] today we must backtrack, we must go back to the wide roads of those times when the intellect had no machine to use except the golden and azure wings of its angelic nature.

Let us turn to Mohammed. Consider the good which resulted for humanity from his religion, first because with other, more powerful causes, it assisted in the destruction of polytheism, and then because it spread, over an immense part of the world and even into climates which seemed inaccessible to the general spiritual movement, the idea of a single God and of a universal faith, and thus prepared countless peoples for the final destiny of the human race. If you consider this, you cannot but admit that, in spite of the tribute which this great man doubtless paid to the time and place of his birth, he deserves the praises of men incomparably more than does that crowd of useless sages who never knew how to give body or life to a single one of their imaginings, nor how to fill a single heart with a strong conviction, who did nothing but divide man instead of seeking to bring together the scattered elements of his nature. Islam is one of the most remarkable manifestations of a general law; to judge it differently is to deny the universal influence of Christianity from which it is derived. The most essential capacity of our religion is its ability to clothe itself with the most diverse forms of religious reasoning, to unite, when necessary, even with error in order fully to achieve its aim. In the great historical development of revealed religion, that of Mohammad must necessarily be considered as one of its branches. Even the most exclusive dogmatism should not hedge in admitting this important fact, and it certainly would admit this fact if it once properly understood what makes us view Mohammedans as the natural enemies of our religion, for it is from this alone that the prejudice has grown.[11] Moreover, as you know, there is hardly a chapter in the Koran which does not mention Christ. We are agreed that no man has a clear idea of the great work of redemption, that he understands nothing of the mystery of the Kingdom of God, if he does not see the influence of Christianity wherever the mere name of the Savior is spoken, or if he does not think of His influence as acting on all minds which, in whatever manner, are in contact with His doctrines. Otherwise, whole multitudes who call themselves Christians would have to be excluded from the number of those who benefit from the gift of redemption. And would not this reduce the Kingdom of Christ to a very small thing and the universality of Christianity to a contemptible fiction?

A consequence of the religious ferment brought into the Orient by the appearance of the new religion, Islam holds first place among those phenomena which seem at first glance not to follow from Christianity, but which assuredly do come from it. Thus, in addition to the negative effect which this religion had upon the formation of Christian society by mingling the private interests of nations in that of general salvation; in addition to the numerous materials with which Arab civilization supplied us—things which must be considered as indirect means which Providence employed to consummate the regeneration of the human race—one must find in its own action on the spirit of the nations which it conquered a direct and positive effect of the doctrine from which it is derived. This doctrine has in this case merely adapted itself to certain local or contemporary needs in order to find a means of spreading the seeds of Truth over a vaster territory. Happy they, no doubt, who serve the Lord in knowledge and firm belief! But, let us not forget, there are in the world an infinite number of powers

11 Originally Mohammedans had no ill feeling toward Christians. It is only after the long wars which they had with Christians that hatred and scorn of Christianity were introduced among them. As for Christians, it is natural that they considered them at first as idolaters, then as enemies of their religion, which, indeed, they became.

that obey the voice of Christ yet have no notion of the supreme power which sets them in motion.

Finally, we come to Homer. The question of the influence which Homer had over the spirit of man is today wholly answered. The nature of Homeric poetry is well known today; we know how it contributed to the determination of the Greek character which, in turn, determined that of the whole ancient world. We know that this poetry replaced another poetry, more elevated, purer, of which we find only shreds. We know also that it substituted a new order of ideas for another order, which was not born in Greek soil, and that these latter primitive ideas were driven back by the new outlook and, taking refuge now in the mysteries of Samothrace, now in the shade of other sanctuaries of lost truths, thenceforth existed only for a small number of elect or initiates.[12] But what is hardly known, I find, is what Homer can have in common with the times in which we live, what is left of him in the universal mental order of things. Yet this is precisely where lies the true interest of the philosophy of history, since its principal study is, as we have seen, but to seek out the permanent consequences and eternal effects of historical phenomena.

For us, then, Homer is still nothing but the Typhon or Ahriman

[12] For an idea of Homer's moral influence on the world, merely read Plutarch's treatise and the chapter of Maximus of Tyre devoted to him; then, in Heeren's book, the chapters on Greek civilization, and, especially, all that concerns this subject in Kreutzer's excellent work on the religions of Antiquity. [Arnold Hermann Ludwig Heeren (1760–1842) was a pioneer in the economic interpretation of history. His major work, to which Chaadayev is referring here, is *Ideen über Politik, den Verkehr, und den Handel der vornehmsten Völker der alten Welt* (1793–1796), translated into English as *Historical Researches into the Politics, Intercourse and Trade of the Principal Nations of Antiquity*. Georg Friedrich Creuzer (1771–1858), to whom Chaadayev is here referring, was professor of philology and archaeology at Marburg and Heidelberg and was the leader of the romantic school which interpreted myths as religious allegories. His major work, *Symbolik und Mythologie der alten Völker besonders der Griechen* (1810–1812), has been described by Pépin (*Mythe et allégorie* [Paris, 1958]) as "monumental." Creuzer believed that the mythology of Homer and Hesiod was not native to Greece, but was of Eastern origin, imported through the Pelasgians. Creuzer's interpretation of myth was in agreement with Schelling's early views; the philosopher turned strongly against Creuzer's thesis, however, in his late writings. —*Trans.*]

of the present world, as he was of the one he created. In our view the baleful heroism of passions, the turbid ideal of beauty, the unbridled love of earth: all these come from him.[13] Note that there has never been anything similar in the other civilized societies of the world. It is only the Greeks who decided to idealize and deify vice and crime. The poetry of evil is thus found only among them and the nations who inherited their civilization. One can clearly see what direction the thought of Christian nations in the Middle Ages would have taken if it had wholly given itself over to the hand that guided it. This poetry could not have come to us from our northern ancestors; the spirit of the men of the North was wholly different and tended to anything rather than to fasten itself to earth. If, instead of what happened, it alone had been combined with Christianity, the spirit of the North would rather have lost itself in the vague mists of its dreamlike imaginings. Moreover, we have nothing left of the blood that flowed in their veins, and it is not among the nations described by Caesar and Tacitus that we seek out the lessons of life, but among those of the world of Homer. Only in the last few days has a return to our own past begun to bring us back to the bosom of the family and made us bit by bit rediscover our paternal heritage. We have inherited from the nations of the North nothing but habits, traditions; but the mind is nourished only by knowledge, and the most inveterate habits are lost, the most deeply rooted traditions are erased when they are not bound to knowledge. But all our ideas, except for our religious ideas, assuredly come to us from the Greeks and Romans. Thus, Homeric poetry, which in ancient Western thought diverted the course of ideas which linked men to the great days of creation, did the same in modern Western thought. By handing itself over to us together with the science, the philosophy, and the literature of

---

[13] The effects of the poetry of Homer are naturally confused with those of Greek art, since it is the type of the latter. That is, it made Greek art, and Greek art continued its effect. As for whether or not a man like Homer ever lived, this is irrelevant. Historical criticism will never be able to erase the memory of Homer. It is thus the idea which is linked to this memory which must concern the philosopher, not the poet himself.

the Ancients, it identified us so well with them that in our present-day state we are still suspended between the world of deceit and that of Truth. Although people have little concern for Homer to-day and although he is assuredly but rarely read, his gods and heroes nonetheless contend with Christian thought for dominion. This is because there is indeed an amazing seductiveness in that poetry, wholly earthly, wholly material, prodigiously sweet to the vices of our nature, which relaxes the fibers of reason, holding reason stupidly chained to its phantoms and marvels and rocking it to sleep with its mighty illusions. So long as a deep moral feeling derived from a clear view of all Antiquity and from a complete absorption of the mind in Christian Truth has not filled our hearts with disgust and disdain for that age of deception and madness, that true Saturnalia in the life of the human race, with which we are still so infatuated; so long as some sort of serious repentance does not make us blush at the senseless worship which for too long we lavished on those detestable grandeurs, those atrocious virtues, and that impure beauty, the old evil impressions will not cease from constituting the most vital and active element of our reason. For my part, I believe that to be wholly regenerated in accordance with revealed reason we still lack some great penitence, some all-powerful expiation perfectly felt by all Christians, endured in common, like some great physical catastrophe over the whole surface of our world. I do not see how, without this, we could rid ourselves of the mud which still sullies our memory.[14] This is how the philosophy of history must understand Homer-ism; judge, then, with what favor it must look upon the figure of Homer. See if after that it is not conscience-bound to set upon his forehead the seal of an indelible brand!

We have reached, Madam, the end of the gallery. I have not

[14] That new region which has recently opened itself to historical thought and which Homer-ism has not infected is a veritable piece of good fortune for our time. Already the influence of the ideas of India on the progress of philosophy is making itself very usefully felt. May God grant it that we should arrive as soon as possible by this indirect route to the point to which a shorter road has until now been unable to lead us!

told you all I had to tell you, but I must finish. Do you know, ultimately we Russians have nothing in common with Homer, or the Greeks, or the Romans, or the Germans [*Germains*]; all that is completely foreign to us. But what would you: one has to speak the language of Europe. Our exotic civilization has so driven us toward Europe that, even though we do not have its ideas, we have no other language; we must, therefore, speak it. If the small number of spiritual habits, of traditions, of memories which we possess, if our past links us with no nation on earth, if we belong indeed to none of the systems of the moral world, we are nevertheless, by our external social life, bound to the world of the West. This bond, weak as in truth it is, without uniting us to Europe as intimately as people imagine or allowing us to feel at every point of our being the great movement which is there taking place, nevertheless makes our future fortunes depend on those of the European community. Thus, the more we seek to identify ourselves with it the better off we shall be. Up to now we have lived alone; what we have learned from others has remained external to us, like a mere ornament, without penetrating into our souls. Today the powers of the *dominant* society have so much increased, its influence on the rest of mankind has gained so much in area, that we shall soon be carried away body and soul in the universal whirlpool. This is certain; we shall assuredly not be able much longer to remain in our desert. Let us therefore do all we can to prepare the way for our descendants. We cannot leave them what we have not had: beliefs, a reason trained by time, a strongly drawn individuality, opinions developed during the course of a life which was long, intellectual, animated, active, and fertile in results. Let us at least leave them some ideas which, although we did not find them ourselves, will, by being thus handed down from one generation to another, nonetheless have something of the traditive element, and by this very means may have a somewhat greater power, a somewhat greater fertility than our own ideas. We shall thus deserve well of posterity, we shall not have passed over the earth in vain.

Letter Seven

Good day, Madam. My taking up this matter again, whenever you wish, is entirely up to you. After all, in a friendly talk where people understand each other well, to what end should one elaborate and exhaust every idea? If what I have told you is sufficient to let you find some new lesson in the study of history, some interest deeper than that normally found in it, then that is all that is necessary.

Moscow, 1829, 16 February

Yes, Madam, the time has come simply to speak the language of reason. It is no longer a matter of blind faith, of the beliefs of the heart; we must address ourselves directly to thought. Feeling could not find its way through the mass of artificial needs, of violent interests, of anxious preoccupations which invade our lives. In France, in England, life has become too complex, too selfish, too personal; in Germany it is too abstract, too eccentric for the powers of the heart to produce their legitimate effect. The rest of the world, for the moment, does not count. One must today seek to reduce everything, if possible, to a simple problem of probability of which the solution would be at the level of all intellects, would agree with all temperaments, would offend no present interest, and would thus win over the most recalcitrant minds.

This is not to say that feelings are to be forever excluded from the intellectual world. God forbid! Their turn will come again. Then they will reappear mightier, greater, purer than ever before. I do not doubt but that this time will come soon. But today, at this time, it is not given to them to move souls, and it is very important to be aware of this. If a certain awakening of the active faculties of the youth of the human race can be seen at this time, it is but the dawn of a beautiful day, the countryside is still in shadow, in dusk, and only a few high points are beginning to be colored by the first glows of the dawning day.

The material proofs of Truth are complete for those who care about it. Do you know, Madam, what I mean by material proofs of Truth? I mean the mass of historical facts, duly analyzed. They must at this time be summarized in a systematic and popular framework, be formulated in such a way that they will impress those minds most indifferent to the good, least open to Truth, or those which are still struggling in the past, in that time which is ended for the world and which certainly will never return, but which still endures for those slothful hearts and sluggish souls who never understand the present day and remain forever in yesterday.

The final proof must be drawn from the general idea of history, and this idea must henceforth be but the idea of a high psychology, which once for all conceives of man as abstract intelligent being, and never as an individual, personal being circumscribed by the given moment, like an ephemeral insect which is born and dies on the same day and which is bound to the totality of things only by the law of generation and decay. We must therefore show what really makes mankind subsist, discover for all to see the mysterious reality hidden in the depths of mental nature and which as yet is visible only to the eye enlightened by some unique light. So long as one is neither too esoteric, nor too visionary or too pedantic, so long especially as one speaks to the age the language of the age and not the ancient language of dogma which has become unintelligible, then, without doubt, this will be achieved, now that reason, science, even art, seem to be rushing passionately, as in the great age of the Savior, before another moral cataclysm.

I have often spoken to you of the influence which Christian truth has exercised on society. I have not told you all. People would not believe it, yet it is certain, this is an entirely new matter. The moral influence of Christianity is well enough appreciated, but people are hardly even aware of its truly intellectual influence, of its logical power. Nothing has yet been said of the role it had in the development and formation of modern thought. People do not realize that all our argumentation is Christian; they believe themselves still in [the realm of] the categories and syllogism of Aristotle. This is because the philosophers' and sectarians' endless disavowals of the so-called ages of superstition, ignorance, and fanaticism have made us wholly lose sight of the salutary effects of religion.

Thus, once the fever of unbelief was passed, the most just and submissive minds lost their bearings on their own terrain and had great trouble putting things straight in their minds. Moreover, it must be admitted that the study of purely human activities does not have for these minds all the interest it should have: they neglect it too much; they are so accustomed to consider only superhuman activity that they do not see the natural forces in the world, and the material economy of mind escapes them almost completely. It is time, however, that modern reason should at last know that all its power is due to Christianity. It is time that it learn it is only by means of the extraordinary tools furnished to it by revelation, by means of the bright light which revelation has cast on all objects of human thought, that the imposing edifice of the new science has arisen. This superb science must finally itself realize that it rose to such a height only thanks to the severe discipline, to that abiding principle, and especially to that instinct, that passion for Truth, which is found in the teachings of Christ.

Fortunately, we no longer live in the days when partisan obstinacy was taken for conviction, when sectarian passion was taken for [pious] ardor. There is, therefore, hope of agreement. But you can readily see that it is not up to Truth to make concessions. Truth is not a matter of etiquette; for legitimate authority to yield is to abdicate all power, to give up all activity; it is self-annihilation. This matter is not one of prestige or of some external impression. [In this matter] all prestige is forever dissipated, every illusion is forever unsuccessful. This is a matter of something very real, more real than one can say. Past existence guarantees future existence; such is the law of life. To annihilate one's past is to rob oneself of one's future. But the three hundred years' duration of the great Christian error is not a memory which cannot be erased at will. Thus, the schismatics have but to build the future they desire. The old community has, from the beginning, lived only by hope and faith in its promised destiny, whereas the schismatics have lived to this hour with no notion of the future.

First, however, there is an essential point which must be cleared up. Among the things that contribute to the preservation of Truth on earth, one of the most effective is without doubt the sacred code of the New Testament.[1] An instinctive veneration is naturally attached to the book which contains the authentic document of the establishment of the new order. The written word is not ephemeral like the spoken word. It makes a lasting impression on the mind. It subjugates it severely by its stability and the long duration of its sanctity. But at the same time it immobilizes it by codifying it, represses it by confining it within the narrow limits of Scripture, it hobbles it in every way. Nothing arrests religious thought in its sublime flight, in its infinite progress, so much as the Book; nothing so much prevents it from establishing itself in human thought in a wholly decisive manner. Everything in religious matters is today based on the letter, while the voice of reason incarnate remains silent. The pulpits of Truth no longer resound with anything but words that have no will or authority. Preaching is no longer but an incident in the achievement of the good. Yet in the end it must be admitted that the words which have been handed on to us through the letter were addressed, quite properly, only to those present, to those who heard them. They cannot, therefore, be equally intelligible to men of all times and of all places. They must necessarily be imprinted with a certain local and contemporary color which encloses them within a realm from which they can be extracted only by means of more-or-less arbitrary and wholly human interpretation. How then can you expect that this ancient word should speak to the world with always the same power as it had in the day when it was the true language of the time, the real force of the moment? Surely the world needs a new voice, which would be in accord with the march

---

[1] ["*La raison nouvelle.*" I am following the Russian interpretative translation (*Literaturnoye nasledstvo*, XXII–XXIV, 60). —*Trans.*]

of history, whose sounds would not be strange to any ear, which would vibrate equally over all parts of the earth, which the echoes of the century would vie to carry from one end of the universe to the other.

The Logos [*verbe*], the Word [*parole*], which speaks to all ages, consists not merely in the discourse of the Savior but in His entire heavenly appearance, encircled by His halo, covered with His blood, hanging on His cross, such, finally, as God once impressed it in human memory. When the Son of God said that He would send the Spirit to men and that He Himself would be in their midst eternally, do you suppose He had in mind that book that was composed after His death, where His words and deeds are more-or-less well told and where some of the writings of His disciples have been collected? Do you suppose He believed that it was this book which would perpetuate His teaching on earth? Surely this was not His thought.He meant that after Him would come men who would so well lose themselves in contemplation of Him and in the study of His perfection, who would so fill themselves with His teaching or the lesson of His life, that they would morally be *one* with Him; that these men, following upon one another across all future ages, would hand down to one another His whole thought, His whole Being; this is what He meant and what is not understood. People think that the inheritance He left is to be found entirely in those pages which so many varying interpretations have so often disfigured, so often bent to their fancy.[2]

People think that, if this book were dispersed over the earth, that would suffice to convert all the earth. A paltry notion which [merely] feeds the passions of the recalcitrants. [We know that Christianity was set up without the assistance of any book. As early as the second century, it had conquered the world. From

---

[2] [In the manuscript, the three sentences in brackets below appear as the final paragraph of the *Letter*. The editor of the Russian translation argues (*Literaturnoye nasledstvo*, XXII–XXIV, 60 and 78) that they are out of place there, and belong rather at the start of the paragraph immediately following ". . . their fancy." I have followed his suggestion of inserting the sentences in this earlier part of the text, but prefer them where I have placed them. —*Trans.*]

then on the human spirit was irrevocably submitted to it.] His divine reason dwells in men made like us, like Him, not in the volume compiled by the Church. And that is precisely why the obstinate attachment of men of tradition to that unique dogma of the real presence of the Body in the Eucharist, to that unlimited respect which they render to the body of the Savior, is so very admirable. Nothing serves better to clarify the source of Christian Truth; nothing more clearly shows how necessary it is that we should try, by all possible means, to realize in our midst the material presence of the man-God, constantly to evoke His corporeal image, so that we will have that awesome image ever before us, the eternal type and teaching of the new man. This, I think, is well worth meditating! This strange doctrine of the Eucharist, derided and scorned, everywhere handed forcibly over to the ill will of human argumentation, this doctrine is nevertheless preserved in a few minds, inviolate and pure! Why? Is it not perhaps to serve one day as an element of union among the various Christian systems? Is it not perhaps so that some day a new light may flash over the world, a light which now remains hidden in its miraculous destiny? I have no doubt of it.

Thus, although the written imprint of human thought must be considered a necessary element of the moral world, nevertheless the true principle of the contact of minds and of the universal development of rational being is to be found elsewhere, in the living Word, in that Word which is modified according to time, to place, to persons; which is always as it ought to be; which needs neither commentary nor exegesis; whose authenticity is not to be subjected to [any] canon—[in a word] it is, finally, to be found in the natural instrument of our thinking. Hence it is, let us not say heterodox, but certainly not very philosophically sound to suppose, as the sectarians do, that all wisdom is contained in the pages of a book. And finally, it is certain that there is a profound philosophy in the firm beliefs of men of the law, beliefs which lead them to recognize another purer source of Truth, another, less earthly, authority.

We must appreciate this Christian reasoning, which in these men is so sure, so correct. It is the instinct of Truth, the effect of the moral principle transferred from the realm of action to that of the mind; it is the unconscious logic of a perfectly disciplined reasoning. An extraordinary understanding of life, brought to earth by the Author of Christianity, a spirit of sacrifice, a horror of division, a passionate love of unity: this is what guides pure Christians in all things.[3] It is in this way that the revealed Idea is preserved. In this way, by means of this Idea, is effected the great fusion of souls and of the various moral powers of the world into one single soul and one single power. This fusion is the whole mission of Christianity. Truth is one: the Kingdom of God, Heaven on earth, all the promises of the Gospels are but the pre-vision and the achievement of the union of all the thoughts of men into a single thought; and that single thought is the very thought of God, that is, the *moral law realized*. All the labor of the intellectual generations is destined to produce but this final result, the terminal point and goal of all things, the final phase of human nature, the resolution [*dénouement*] of the drama of the universe, the great apocalyptic synthesis.

[3] ["*. . . ce qui guide les chrétiens pures en toutes choses*": what guides Christians with purity in all things? —*Trans.*]

Apology of a Madman

Adveniat regnum tuum

Charity, says St. Paul, *beareth all things, believeth all things, en-dureth all things.*[1] Thus, let us bear, believe, endure all things, let us be charitable. But first [let us observe that] the catastrophe which has lately shattered our philosophical existence and cast to the winds the work of a lifetime is but the inevitable result of the outcry raised at the publication of our article, of those pages, bitter perhaps, but which certainly deserved something other than the clamor with which they were greeted. The government has, after all, merely done its duty; it can even be said that the measures it took in my case were perfectly liberal, since they did not exceed public expectation. What would one wish of the best disposed of governments but that it should be in agreement with the wish of the people? The public hue and cry, however, is quite another matter. There are various ways of loving one's country. The Samoyed,[2] for instance, who loves the native snows that have made him myopic, the smoke-filled yurt[3] where he hibernates for half his living days, the rancid fat of his reindeer which envelops him in its nauseating aroma—such a man surely does not love his country in the same manner as the Englishman who takes pride in the institutions and high civilization of his happy island, and it

[1] [I Corinthians 13:17. —*Trans.*]
[2] [A group of Mongolian race inhabiting the tundras of northeastern Europe and Siberia. —*Trans.*]
[3] [Huts used by non-nomadic Samoyeds. —*Trans.*]

would be rather unfortunate if we were to cherish our native land only in the manner of the Samoyeds.

Love of country is a very fine thing, but there is a finer one, namely, love of truth. Love of country makes heroes; love of truth makes wise men, benefactors of mankind. It is love of country that divides people, that feeds national hatred, that at times covers the earth with mourning, while it is love of truth that spreads light, that creates the pleasures of the mind, that brings men closer to God. It is not by means of patriotism but by means of truth that the ascent to Heaven is accomplished. It is true that we Russians have had among us but few lovers of truth; examples of such men are lacking to us. We must not, therefore, be too offended if a nation which has never been much concerned with what may or may not be true was so angered by a rather virulent attack on its shortcomings. Nor do I hold any grudge, I assure you, against that dear public which for so long kept its claws hidden inside velvet paws. I am trying to understand my strange situation dispassionately, with no feeling of resentment at all. Must I not try to explain to myself where the man sentenced to madness stands with respect to his fellow man, to his fellow citizens, to his God?

I have never highly valued the masses; I never had democratic tastes; I never solicited the ovations of the populace or prized the opinions of the crowd. I have always thought that the human race could go forward only by following the footsteps of chosen men, the footsteps of those whose mission it was to lead it; that common reason is not, as a great writer of our days believed, absolute reason; that the instinct of the majority is necessarily more selfish, more prejudiced, more narrow than that of isolated individuals; that what is called the good sense of the people is not good sense at all; that Truth cannot be expressed by a numerical symbol; finally, that human intelligence manifests itself in all its might only in the solitary spirit [who reigns as] center and sun of his existence. How comes it then that I found myself one day face-to-face with an angry public, a public whose approval I never solicited, whose endearments never delighted me, whose whims never moved me? How comes it that an idea which was not addressed to the world, which I said a thousand times was of no concern to my contemporaries, which I willed in profound conviction to generations still to come, generations better informed—how comes it that this idea, which had already acquired a semi-public character, one day broke its bonds, escaped from its cloister, and rushed leaping into the street amid a stupified mob? Indeed, I cannot explain it, but this much [at least] I can say with perfect assurance:

Russia has longed to fuse with the West for the past three hundred years;[4] for the past three hundred years it has admitted that it was inferior to the West, has drawn all its ideas, all its teaching, all its pleasure from the West. For the past century it has done more than that. The greatest of our kings, our glory, our demi-god, the one who began a new era for us, to whom we owe our greatness and all the goods we possess, this king, one hundred years ago, in the presence of the entire world, foreswore the old Russia. With his mighty breath he swept away all our ancient institutions; he dug an abyss between our past and our present, and into it he threw pell-mell all our traditions. He went West himself and made himself the smallest of men, and he returned the greatest among us; he prostrated himself before the West and he arose our master and our law-giver; he introduced into our idiom the idioms of the West; he modeled the characters of our writing on those of the West; he scorned the clothes of our fathers and made us wear the fashions of the West; he named his new capital with a name of the West; he rejected his hereditary title and took a title that came from the West;[5] finally, he renounced his own name and signed himself with a name of the West. Since that time our gaze has been constantly turned toward the West; we have breathed nothing but the emanations which came to us from there and we fed on them alone. Our princes, who were always ahead of the people, who always dragged us in spite of ourselves on the way toward perfection, who always took the listless nation in tow,

---

4 [Since the time of Ivan III. —*Trans.*]
5 [Peter the Great took the title of Emperor for that of Tsar. —*Trans.*]

themselves imposed the ways, the language, the splendor of the West upon us. We learned to read in Western books, we learned to speak from Western men; the West taught us our own history; we drew everything from the West, we transplanted it completely, and finally we were happy to resemble the West and we were proud when it counted us among its own.

It was glorious, you must admit it, this creation of Peter the Great's, this idea of the man of genius who dictated the path we were henceforth to follow; there was profound wisdom in those words which said to us: "See that civilization over there, the fruit of so many labors, those sciences, those arts which cost so much sweat to so many generations; all that is yours if only you will cast off your superstitions, if only you will repudiate your prejudices, if only you will not pride yourselves on your barbarous past, not boast of your centuries of ignorance, aspire only to appropriate the achievements of all peoples, the riches acquired by the human spirit in all the latitudes of the globe." Nor did this great man work for his nation alone: such men of Providence are always sent for [the benefit of] the entire world; first one nation claims them, then they are absorbed by the human race, like great rivers which first fertilize vast regions and then flow into the ocean. Was that unique spectacle which he offered the universe when he left his throne and his country to hide among the lowest ranks of civilized people anything but another effort of the man's genius to quit the narrow circle of nationality and to settle in the great realm of mankind? Such was the lesson we were to learn from this sight. And we did, in fact, profit from it; up to this day we have walked along the path which the great emperor marked out for us. Our immense development is but the fruit of his far-sighted genius. Never was a people less self-infatuated than the Russian people fashioned by Peter the Great. The high intelligence of this extraordinary man perfectly foresaw what must be our point of departure. He saw that a historical foundation was wholly lacking to us, that consequently we could not rest our future on such an empty ground; he understood that, confronted by the ancient civilization

166

of Europe, we could not afford to drown ourselves in our history, we could not afford to drag ourselves, like the people of the West, through the world of national prejudice, along the narrow paths of local ideas; that we had to seize our promised destiny by a spontaneous leap. Hence, he freed us from all those antecedents which clutter historical societies and put a stop to their progress; he opened our minds to all the great and fine ideas that exist among men; he handed us the entire West, as the ages had made it; for our history he gave us its entire history, for our future he gave us its entire future.

Do you believe that, had he found in his people a rich and fertile history, living traditions, rooted institutions, he would have cast it into a new world, despoiled it of its nationality, without hesitation? Would he not rather have sought in that very nationality the means of its regeneration? And that people, would it have allowed him to ravish its past, somehow to impose the past of Europe upon it? But this was not the situation. Peter the Great found in his country only a blank sheet of paper; on it he wrote: "Europe and the West." From that time on we were part of Europe and part of the West. Make no mistake: whatever the genius of that man, his achievement was possible only in the midst of a people whose past did not imperiously determine the road it must follow, whose traditions did not have the power to create a future for it, whose memories could be erased with impunity by an audacious law-giver. If we were obedient to the voice of the prince who led us into a new life, it is because we had nothing in our past life that could justify resistance. The most profound feature of our social life is improvisation. Every fact in our history is isolated, imposed, every new idea is detached, imported. Thus, the bond between today's event and yesterday's is naturally lacking to us. But there is nothing in this outlook at which national feeling can justifiably take offense. If it is true, it must be accepted, that is all. Human logic failed us, but the logic of Providence was watching over us and leading us to its own ends. There are great nations, just as there are great historical figures: neither can be explained by the laws of our reason, but the Supreme Reason rules mysteriously over both. Such is our situation. Once again, this in no way affects national pride.[6]

The history of a people is not merely a succession of facts following upon one another but also a sequence of connected ideas. Facts must be expressed by ideas; then you have history, then the fact is not lost; it has then left its mark on the mind and remained engraved in men's hearts. Such history is not made by historians but by the course of events. Some day the historian comes on the scene, finds it ready-made, and records it, but whether he comes or not, it exists nonetheless and everyone carries it within him in the depths of his being. This is exactly the sort of history we lack. We must learn to do without it and not to abuse those who first discovered this lack. Our fanatical Slavists may well, from their diverse excavations, now and then still exhume curios for our museums and libraries, but it is doubtful that they will ever draw from the entrails of our historic soil the wherewithal to fill up the void in our souls, to condense the fog in our minds. Look at Europe in the Middle Ages: there is no event in that period which was not in some way absolutely necessary. And how many furrows this history has dug in the minds of men, how it has plowed the earth over which the human spirit moves! I well know that not all histories have the rigorous and logical progress of this prodigious period, but it is nonetheless true that this is the real character of historical development, be it of a nation or of a group of nations, and that nations lacking a past thus fashioned must seek the bases of their future progress elsewhere than in their memories. The life of nations is like the life of individuals: all men have lived, but only the man of genius has a history. That a nation, by a coincidence of circumstances which it did not create, by the effect of a geographical situation which it did not choose, should spread over an immense expanse of land, unaware of what it is doing, and that

---

[6] [Reading "*l'honneur national*" as in F309/No. 2688, p. 4 and in Gershenzon (*Sochineniya i pisma*, II, 33) for "*l'homme national*" in F357/Op 2/No. 408, p. 4 and in McNally, "Chaadayev's Philosophical Letters," p. 112, l. 29. —*Trans.*]

one day it should see itself a powerful nation—this is surely an astonishing phenomenon and can be a source of silent wonder; but what would you wish history to say? This nation's history will begin only on the day when this nation becomes conscious of the idea which was entrusted to it, which it is called upon to realize, and when it sets about to follow it with that enduring though hidden instinct which leads nations to their destinies. This is the moment I am calling up for my country with all the power of my heart, this is the task which I want to see you undertake, you my dear friends and fellow citizens, who live in a time of high learning and who have just shown me how ardently you are fired with the holy love of your fatherland.

The world has from all time been divided into two spheres, the East and the West. This is not a geographical division; it is an order of things which develops from the very nature of intelligent being. East and West are two principles which correspond to two dynamic natural forces, two ideas which encompass the whole economy of mankind. In the East the spirit of man found its power in self-concentration, in meditation, in shutting itself up within the sphere of its own activity; in the West it developed by spreading outward, by radiating in all directions, by struggling with all obstacles. Society was naturally set up on the basis of these primitive data. In the East the intellect retired within itself, took refuge in repose, hid in the desert, and allowed the power of social position to become master of all the goods of the earth; in the West the intellect spread out in all directions, embraced all the needs of men, aspired to all goods, based power on the principle of law. Still, in both these realms life was strong and fruitful; in neither was human intelligence lacking in high inspiration, profound ideas, sublime creations. The East came first and poured over the earth a flood of light from the depths of its silent meditation. Then came [the turn of] the West with its immense activity; its eager word took hold of its labors, completed what the East had begun, and finally enveloped it in its vast embrace. But in the East, the intellect, docile, kneeling before the authority of

169

time, exhausted itself in the first years of the world by its exercise of absolute submission, and one day it stopped motionless and silent, unaware of the new destiny prepared for it; while in the West it walked proud and free, bowing only before the authority of reason or of Heaven, stopping only before the unknown, its gaze ever fixed on the boundless future. And it still walks on, as you know. And you also know that since Peter the Great we believe we have been walking along the same path.

Now, however, a new school has sprung up in our midst. People no longer wish to have anything to do with the West; they want to undo the work of Peter the Great; once again they want to follow the desert road. Forgetting what the West has done for us, people insult it; without gratitude toward the great man who brought us a new life, toward the Europe which taught us, men deny both the great man and Europe. Already, in its impatient eagerness, this newborn patriotism proclaims that we are of the East. What need had we, people are saying, to seek enlightenment from the countries of Europe? We should have let time take its course; left to ourselves we would without doubt have surpassed all those nations, abandoned as they are to error and deceit. What was there for us to envy in the West? The Wars of Religion, the Inquisition, the Pope, the Jesuits? Fine things indeed! It is not the West but the East that is the home of knowledge and of great ideas. Let us then retire into the East, which neighbors us on every side, whence we formerly drew our beliefs, our laws, our virtues, everything that made us the most powerful nation on earth. The old East is passing away; we are its natural heirs; it is among us that those great and mysterious truths will be perpetuated, those truths which the East so long preserved for the benefit of mankind.

Now you can understand the source of the storm that broke over me the other day and can see how real a reaction is taking place in our midst. But this time the impulse is not from above. On the contrary, never before was the memory of our great regenerator more revered in the uppermost regions of society than it is today.

The initiative thus comes wholly from the people. God alone knows where this first act of our nation's emancipated intellect will lead us! Meanwhile, no man who seriously loves his country can remain anything but gravely affected by this apostasy on the part of our nation's most enlightened minds toward what until now was the cause of our glory and our honor, and it is the duty of a good citizen to try his best to understand this strange phenomenon.

We are situated in the east of Europe, that is undeniable, but for all that we were never part of the East. The East, as we have just seen, possesses an idea which has been imbedded in men's minds since the first days of Creation. This is a fertile idea which with time produced an immense intellectual development. It set the spiritual principle at the highest level of society; it subjected all power to a supreme, inviolable law, the law of time; it conceived social castes. Even though it constrained life within a limited circle, it still also protected it from all external disturbance. All this was wholly foreign to us. Among us the spiritual principle was never established at the top level[7] of society; the law of time, tradition, never reigned over us; we never had social castes; finally, life among us was never uninfluenced from without. We are simply a nation of the North, and in our ideas as well as in our climate far removed from the scented Vale of Kashmir and the holy shores of the Ganges. A few of our provinces neighbor the empires of the East, granted, but our centers are not there, our life is not there, and they will never be there unless the earth's axis shifts or a new cataclysm once again hurls the nature of the South into the glaciers of the polar regions.

The fact is that we have never yet considered our history from a philosophical point of view; no great event of our past has been

---

[7] [Manuscript F357/Op 2/No. 408, p. 7 has "*chez nous assis au fait de la société*" as does F309/No. 2688, p. 7. Gershenzon (*Sochineniya i pisma*, II, 36) has "*chez nous assis au haut de la société.*" The later version of the *Apology of a Madman* (Gershenzon, *ibid.*, I, 228) has, however, "*assis au faîte de la société.*" I am following this last reading (*faîte*) as the word intended, thus reading the phrase, "*chez nous assis au faîte de la société.*" —Trans.]

clearly delineated, no great period in our history has been evaluated honestly: whence our peculiar imaginings. German scholars discovered the authors of our chronicles some fifty years ago; then Karamzin recounted in resounding phrases the acts and deeds of our princes; today second-rate writers possessing neither the scholarship of the Germans nor the style of the famous prose writer claim that they are describing times and manners of which no one has retained any remembrance or love; such is the sum of our studies of our national history. It must be granted that one can hardly draw from these few things the wherewithal to give a great nation a sense of the destiny in store for it. Yet this is precisely the concern today, those are precisely the results which in our day constitute the interest of historical study. What the serious mentality of our times requires is a strict examination, an impartial analysis of the moments in the life of a nation when it lived with some intensity, great or small: its future, the elements of its possible development lie in those moments. Even if such periods are few in your history, even if your national life was not always forceful and profound, do not deny the truth, do not feed on lies, do not imagine having lived when you have [only] dragged yourselves from one grave into the next. But if then, crossing this vacuum, you reach an instant when the nation really felt itself alive, when its heart truly began to beat rapidly, and if you hear the voice of the popular tide resound and rise up around you, then stop, think, study; your labors will not be in vain, you will learn what your country can do in its great days, what it can hope for in the future. Such was, in our country, that moment which put an end to the terrible drama of the interregnum,[8] when the nation, having by itself beaten down its enemy, placed on the throne the noble house which rules over us, a unique moment which cannot be enough admired when one considers the vacuum of the preceding centuries and the wholly particular situation of our nation. It is clear that I am far from insisting, as it has been alleged, that we should despoil all our memories; I am simply saying that it is time

[8] [The "Times of Troubles," 1605–1613. —*Trans.*]

to take a clear look at our past, not to extract from it ancient rotted relics, ancient ideas eaten up by time, ancient quarrels for which the good sense of our princes has long since given satisfaction, but to know what to believe about our past. This is what I was trying to do in a work which remained unfinished and for which the part that has just now so strangely aroused national vanity was to serve as an introduction. Doubtless, this first foray of an idea poignantly felt was too passionate, doubtless there was impatience in its expression, exaggeration in the background of the thinking, but the emotion which dominates the entire piece is by no means hostile to my country: it is one of deep sorrow strongly expressed, no more.

I love my country more than anyone does, believe me; I am eager for its glory, I can appreciate the eminent qualities of my nation; but it is true that the patriotic feeling which animates me is not exactly like that of the men whose shouts upset my obscure existence and cast back onto their sea of misery my ship, which had run aground at the foot of the Cross. It is true that I have not learned to love my country with my eyes shut, my head bowed, my mouth closed. I think that a man can be of service to his country only if he sees it clearly; I believe that the time for blind love is past, that fanaticism of any sort is out of fashion; I love my country as Peter the Great taught me to love it. Mine is not, I admit, that sanctimonious, lazy patriotism which manages to see everything in a rosy light, which falls asleep over its illusions, and with which, unfortunately, many of our well-intentioned intellects are afflicted today. I think that if we have made our way after the others, it was to do better than the others, not to fall into their superstitions, their delusions, their infatuations. In my opinion it would be strangely to misconceive the role that has been allotted to us if we were to restrict ourselves to a repetition of the long series of follies and calamities which nations less favored than ours have had to undergo. I find that our situation is fortunate, so long as we know how to appreciate it, that it is a great privilege to be able to contemplate and judge the world from a level of thought unencumbered by the unrestrained passions, the paltry prejudices which invade men's minds. More: I have a deep conviction that we are called upon to resolve the greater part of the social problems, to perfect the greater part of the ideas which have arisen in older societies, to pronounce judgment on the most serious questions which trouble the human race. I have often said and I like to repeat that we are by the very nature of things made to serve as a real jury for the many suits which are being tried before the great tribunals of the world.

Indeed, observe what is happening today in those countries which I perhaps over-praised but which are nevertheless the best examples of all kinds of civilization. Should a new idea blossom there, all the selfishness, all the vanity, all the factiousness that hovers restlessly over the surface of society, throws itself upon it, seizes it, disfigures it, makes a parody of it. A moment later, pulverized by these various forces, it is carried off into abstract regions where all the sterile dust of the human spirit finally collects. In our country there are no such passionate interests, ready-made opinions, inveterate prejudices: we face each new truth with unblemished minds. In our institutions, the spontaneous works of our princes, in our mores which have been in existence for less than a century, in our opinions which have yet to take a stand about the least of things, there is nothing to hinder the gifts which Providence intends for mankind. Let but a sovereign will express itself among us and all opinions vanish, all beliefs yield, all minds open up to the new idea offered to them. Perhaps it would have been better to go through all the trials gone through by other Christian peoples, to draw from them new powers, new sources of energy, new methods, as those peoples did, and perhaps our isolated situation would have preserved us from the calamities which accompanied the long education of those peoples, but this is no longer our concern. Our concern now is but properly to grasp the present character of our country, such as it is now given, such as it is irrevocably determined by the nature of things, and to draw from it all possible benefit. History is no longer ours, granted, but knowledge is ours; we cannot repeat all the achievements of the human spirit, but we can take part in its future achievements. The past is no longer in our power, but the future is ours.

There is no doubt about it, the world is oppressed by its traditions; let us not be envious of the narrow circle within which it is floundering. Certainly, in the heart of every nation there is a profound sense of its past life which dominates its present life, an obstinate memory of bygone days which fills the present day: let us leave the nations to battle with their inexorable past. We never lived under the dominion of historical necessity; an all-powerful law never dashed us into the abyss which time digs for [historical] nations; let us not today deliver ourselves up to a sullen inevitability which we never knew; let us enjoy the immense advantage of being able to walk ahead with awareness of the course we must traverse, of obeying only the voice of an enlightened reason, of a deliberative will. Let us be aware that there is no absolute necessity for us; that we are not, thank God, placed on the steep slope which carries other nations to their unknown destinies; that it is given to us to measure every step we take, to reason out every idea that affects our intellect, that we are permitted to aspire to a prosperity vaster than that dreamt of by the most ardent ministers of progress, and that to attain its final results we need but an authoritative will, such as that which once gave us new birth.

Well! Is this a niggardly future which I am offering my country? Is this an inglorious destiny that I am calling up for it? Yet this great future which will become actual, this bright destiny which will, I have no doubt, be fulfilled, will be but the result of that special nature, that nature of the Russian people, described in my fateful article.[9] (But what, in the end, was this article?[10] It was a

---

[9] [The following passage, here enclosed in parentheses, is crossed out in the manuscript. It is not reproduced in F309/No. 2688 or in Gershenzon. I am following McNally ("Chaadayev's Philosophical Letters," p. 117) in preserving it here. I am indebted to McNally for his reading of this almost illegible passage, although I occasionally differ from him. —*Trans.*]

[10] [McNally reads (*ibid.*, p. 117, l. 9): "*Mais si donc enfin.*" I am reading "*Mais sait-on donc enfin.*" —*Trans.*]

private letter, written to a woman who had for many years been suffering from the effect of a painful emotion, of a great disappointment; this article was, by the indiscreet vanity of a journalist, handed over to the public; read and re-read a thousand times in an original version far more blunt than the weak translation in which it appeared, this article never provoked anyone's ill humor, not even that of the most idolatrous of patriots, before it was printed. In it, finally, in the midst of a few pages of profound [11], was framed a historical study where the old thesis of the historical superiority of Western nations was repeated with some warmth, possibly exaggerated. Such was that odious piece of writing, that incendiary pamphlet, which drew upon its author public [12], the strangest of persecutions.) However, I am anxious to say it and happy that I was induced to make this confession: yes, there was some exaggeration in that quasi-indictment of a great nation whose only fault was, in the end, but to have been consigned to the extremities of the civilized world, far from the centers where all lights must naturally collect, far from the foci whence they had radiated for so many centuries; there was some exaggeraton in not recognizing that we were born on a soil where empires did not flourish, which generations did not plow, where nothing spoke to us of past ages, where there was no vestige of earlier civilizations, no memory, no monument of a world that had passed away; there was exaggeration in not giving its due to that church, so humble, at times so heroic, which alone attenuates the emptiness of our chronicles, on which devolves the honor of our ancestors' every act of courage, every great sacrifice; finally, there was exaggeration, no doubt, in despairing for a moment of a nation which carried within its womb the great soul of Peter the Great. But after that it must be admitted that the whims and fantasies of our public are inconceivable.

11 [Illegible word: McNally suggests "*dévotion*" (*ibid.*, p. 117, l. 15 and p. 117n). —*Trans.*]

12 [Illegible word or phrase: McNally suggests "*l'ire*" (*ibid.*, p. 117, l. 18 and p. 117n). The space, however, suggests a longer word or two words: "*l'animosité*"? —*Trans.*]

176

As people will remember, several days before the publication in question a play was produced in our theater.[13] Well, never was a nation so flogged, never was a country so dragged in the mud, never was so much of its filth thrown [back] into the face of the public,[14] and yet never was success more complete.[15] [Can it be that a serious mind which has meditated so profoundly on his country, on its history, on the character of his nation, is to be condemned to silence because he cannot express through the mouth of some theatrical performer the patriotic feeling with which he is burdened! What is it that makes us so tolerant of the cynical lesson of the comedy and so suspicious of that austere expression and its incisive analysis? You must admit it is because we have as yet little more than an instinctive patriotism, because we are still far from the deliberate patriotism of older nations which have been fashioned by the work of the mind, enlightened by the light and the study of learning. We are still at the stage of loving our country in the fashion of those adolescent nations which thought has not yet troubled, which are still seeking their idea, the role which they are called upon to play on the worldly scene. Our intellectual powers are as yet hardly accustomed to serious things. In short, the work of the mind has as yet hardly existed among us. We have reached with amazing speed a certain degree of civilization which justly deserves the admiration of Europe. Our might terrifies the world, our empire stretches over one-fifth of the globe; but all that, we must confess, we owe only to the authoritative will of our princes and the assistance of the physical conditions of the country we inhabit.

Fashioned, molded, created by our rulers and our climate, we

---

13 [Gogol's *Inspector General*. —*Trans.*]

14 [The French is ambiguous: *"jamais on ne jeta tant de son ordure au visage du public."* Never did an author hurl so much of his filth onto the face of the public? —*Trans.*]

15 [The rest of the essay here enclosed in brackets is not in the manuscripts; it exists only in the later version of *Apology of a Madman* printed by Gagarin and reproduced by Gershenzon in the first volume of his edition of Chaadayev's writings (*Sochineniya i pisma*, I, 219–34). It is translated here because of its possible interest to the reader. —*Trans.*]

have become a great nation only by dint of submission. Scan our chronicles from beginning to end: on each page you will find the profound effect of authority, the ceaseless action of the soil, and hardly ever that of the public will. However, it is also true that, in abdicating its power in favor of its masters, in yielding to its native physical climate, the Russian nation gave evidence of profound wisdom. It thus recognized the supreme law of its destiny: a strange resultant of two elements belonging to disparate realms which it can misunderstand only at the expense of falsifying its own nature, of repressing the very principle of its possible progress. A rapid glance cast over our history from the point of view we have taken will, I hope, show us this law in all its clarity.

II

There is one fact which absolutely dominates our progress through the ages, which runs through our whole history, which encompasses in a way all its philosophy, which occurs at all periods of our social life and determines their character, which is both the one essential element of our political greatness and the true cause of our intellectual weakness: this fact is the fact of geography.[16]]

---

[16] [As Gagarin notes (Gershenzon, *Sochineniya i pisma*, I, 234, n.) this latest manuscript ends here and there is no indication that it was ever continued. —*Trans.*]

Bibliography

THE BIBLIOGRAPHY appended to Charles Quénet's book, *Tchaa-daev et les Lettres philosophiques: contribution à l'étude du mouvement des idées en Russie* (Paris, 1931), pp. i-lv, is definitive up to the date of its publication. It is sufficiently comprehensive to satisfy the most demanding scholar. The present bibliography will therefore list only major texts of Chaadayev's and major works on Chaadayev written prior to 1931 and will concentrate on important material published since.[1]

Manuscripts:

Sobraniye Dashkova (Dashkov Collection), F93/Op 3/Nos. 1350–1356: Chaadayeva, P. Ya., "Filosoficheskiye pisma," Institut Russkoy Literatury, Akademiya Nauk (Institute of Russian Literature, Academy of Sciences), Leningrad.

This collection includes complete texts of all eight *Letters*, with the exception of the first three manuscript pages of *Letter II* (pp. 52–57 in the present volume). *Letters III, IV, V,* and *VIII* are in Chaadayev's own hand; *Letters I, II, VI,* and *VII* are in that of a copyist. *Letters VI, VII,* and *VIII* have corrections in Chaadayev's handwriting.

[1] In addition to Quénet's bibliography, the Chaadayev bibliography by Robin Kemball in *Studies in Soviet Thought* (V, 3 [Sept., 1965], 243–45) should also be noted. This is an excellent selective bibliography listing primarily works published (or republished or published in translation) in Russian or English between 1945 and 1964.

Arkhiv Pypina (Pypin Archives), 250/542: "Pismo Chaadayeva, ne voshedsheye v 'Oeuvres choisies,' Kopiya Zh." Institut Russkoy Literatury, Akademiya Nauk, Leningrad.

This is a copy by Mikhail Zhikharev of the first three manuscript pages of *Letter II*.

F357/Op 2/No. 408: "Apologie d'un fou." Institut Russkoy Literatury, Akademiya Nauk, Leningrad.

A manuscript copy with corrections in Chaadayev's handwriting.

F309/No. 2688: "Apologie d'un fou." Institut Russkoy Literatury, Akademiya Nauk, Leningrad.

A manuscript copy incorporating most of the corrections made by Chaadayev in F357/Op 2/No. 408, above.

Published texts:

Gagarin, I. S. [ed.]. *Oeuvres choisies de Pierre Tchadäief, publiées pour la première fois par le P. Gagarin de la compagnie de Jésus*. Paris-Leipzig, 1862.

This work contains *Letters I, VI,* and *VII* and a late version of the *Apology of a Madman*.

Gershenzon, M. O., ed. *Sochineniya i pisma P. Ya. Chaadayeva*. 2 vols. Moscow, 1913–1914.

This work contains *Letters I, VI,* and *VII* and a late version of the *Apology of a Madman* in Vol. I. An early version of the *Apology of a Madman* is printed in Vol. II.

McNally, Raymond T., ed. "Chaadayev's Philosophical Letters Written to a Lady and His Apologia of a Madman," *Forschungen zur osteuropäischen Geschichte* (Osteuropa-Institut an der Freien Universität Berlin, Historische Veröffentlichungen). Berlin, 1966. Vol. XI, 34–117.

This edition includes all eight *Letters* and an early version of the *Apology of a Madman*. Three other manuscript texts of *Letter I* and one of *Letter III*, in addition to those listed above, are mentioned on pp. 118 and 123.

Bibliography

"Lettres philosophiques," "Apologie d'un fou," *De Pouchkine à Gorki en douze volumes.* Editions Rencontre, Lausanne, 1966. Vol. II, 23–105 and 107–127.

This is a reprinting of the Gagarin version and thus contains only *Letters I, VI,* and *VII* and the *Apology of a Madman.*

TRANSLATIONS

Into English:

Blinoff, Marthe. *Life and Thought in Old Russia.* Pennsylvania State University, 1961.

Short extracts.

Edie, James M., James P. Scanlan, and Mary-Barbara Zeldin, eds., with the collaboration of George L. Kline. *Russian Philosophy.* Chicago, 1965; London, 1967; revised, Chicago, 1969. Vol. I.

Complete translation of *Letter I* and selections from *Letters III, V, VI,* and *VIII,* by Mary-Barbara Zeldin.

Kohn, Hans. *The Mind of Modern Russia.* New Brunswick, N. J., 1955.

Short extracts.

Moskoff, Eugene A. *The Russian Philosopher Chaadayev: His Ideas and His Epoch.* New York, 1937.

Long extracts from *Letters I, VI,* and *VII* and from the *Apology of a Madman* included in a critical study.

Raeff, Marc. *Russian Intellectual History.* New York and Chicago, 1966.

Complete translation of *Letter I* by Valentine Snow.

Riha, Thomas. *Readings in Russian Civilization.* Chicago and London, 1964. Vol. II: *Imperial Russia.*

Extracts from *Letter I* and the *Apology of a Madman* as well as from letters to A. I. Turgenev.

Into German:

Falk, Heinrich, S. J. *Das Weltbild Peter J. Tschaadajews nach seinen acht "Philosophischen Briefen."* Munich, 1954.

Complete texts of *Letters II, III, IV, V,* and *VIII* translated into German from the Russian translation of the French originals published in *Literaturnoye nasledstvo,* XXII–XXIV (see below).

Into Russian:

Gershenzon, M. O., ed. *Sochineniya i pisma P. Ya. Chaadayeva.* Moscow, 1913–1914. Vol. II.
Translations of *Letters I, VI,* and *VII,* and the *Apology of a Madman.*

Shakhovskoy, D. I., ed. "Neizdannyye 'Filosoficheskiye pisma' P. Ya. Chaadayeva," *Literaturnoye nasledstvo.* Moscow, 1935. Vols. XXII–XXIV, 18–62.
Translations of *Letters II, III, IV, V,* and *VIII.*

There are also a number of printings of *Letters I, VI,* and *VII* and the *Apology of a Madman* in Russian translation, starting with Herzen's reproduction of *Letter I* in *Polyarnaya zvezda,* Book VI (1861), as well as two other German translations. For these the reader is referred to Quénet, *Tchaadaev et les Lettres philosophiques,* pp. xi-xiv.

MAJOR CRITICAL WORKS AND BIOGRAPHICAL MATERIAL
PRIOR TO 1931

By contemporaries of Chaadayev:

Herzen, A. I. *Byloye i dumy.*[1] Part IV, Chs. xxix and xxx.

Longinov, M. N. "Vospominaniye o P. Ya. Chaadayeve," *Russki vestnik,* XLII (1862), 119–60.

———. "Epizod iz zhizni P. Ya Chaadayeva (1820 goda)," *Russki arkhiv,* VI, No. 7 (1868), 1317–28.

Nadezhdin, N. I. "Dve stati yevo, napisannyya po povodu 'Filo-

---

[1] *My Past and Thoughts: The Memoirs of Alexander Herzen,* trans. by Constance Garnett; 2nd ed., revised by Humphrey Higgens, with an Introduction by Isaiah Berlin (4 vols.; New York and London, 1968).

soficheskavo pisma' P. Ya. Chaadayeva," *Russkaya starina*, XXXVIII, No. 8 (1907), 237–58.

Sverbeyev, D. N. "Vospominaniya o Pyotre Yakovleviche Chaadayeve," *Russki arkhiv*, VI, No. 6 (1868), 976–1001.
Reprinted in *Zapiski Dmitriya Nikolayevicha Sverbeyeva*, Vol. II, Moscow, 1899.

Tyutchev, F. I. "Pisma F. I. Tyutcheva k P. Ya. Chaadayevu," *Russki arkhiv*, III, No. 11 (1900), 410–21.

Zhikharev, M. I. "Pyotr Yakovlevich Chaadayev," *Vestnik yevropy*, VI, Nos. 7 and 9 (1871), 172–208 and 9–54.
Selections from this article were reprinted by Ch. Vetrinski in "Melochi o P. Ya. Chaadayeve: iz rukopisi S. P. [*sic*] Zhikhareva," *Vestnik yevropy*, LI, No. 2 (1916), 396–401.
There are also a number of poems and letters by Pushkin addressed to Chaadayev. The reader is referred to Quénet's bibliography, pp. xxxvi-xxxix, and to Quénet's discussion of the relations of Pushkin and Chaadayev (*Tchaadaev et les Lettres philosophiques*, Ch. i, secs. 9–10, pp. 31–51).

By later authors:

Gershenzon, M. O. "Pyotr Yakovlevich Chaadayev tridtsatykh i sorokovykh godov," *Vestnik yevropy*, XLI, No. 4 (1906), 528–78.
———. *P. Ya. Chaadayev: Zhizn i myshleniye*. St. Petersburg, 1908; reprinted, The Hague, 1968.

Kovalevski, M. "Ranniye revniteli filosofii Shellinga v Rossii. Chaadayev i Ivan Kireyevski," *Russkaya mysl*, XXXVII, No. 12 (1916), 115–35.

Koyré, Alexander. *La philosophie et le problème national en Russie au début du XIXᵉ siècle*. Paris, 1929.
———. "Russia's Place in the World: Peter Chaadayev and the Slavophils," *The Slavonic Review*, V (March 15, 1927), 594–608.

Lemke, M. K. "Chaadayev i Nadezhdin (po neizdannym materialam)," *Mir Bozhi*, XIV, Nos. 9–12 (1905), 1–33, 122–56, 137–62, 91–108.

Reprinted with variants in Lemke, *Nikolayevskiye zhandarmy i literatura 1826–1855 gg.* (St. Petersburg, 1908; 2nd ed., 1909).

Milyukov, P. N. *Glavnyya techeniya russkoy istoricheskoy mysli XVIII i XIX stoleti.* Moscow, 1897; 2nd ed., St. Petersburg, 1898; 3rd ed., St. Petersburg, 1913.

Plekhanov, G. V. "P. Ya. Chaadayev," *Sovremenny mir*, I (Jan., 1908), 176–96.

A review of Gershenzon's *P. Ya. Chaadayev: Zhizn i myshleniye* (see above).

Quénet, Charles. "Tchaadaev dans la Russie intellectuelle de la première moitié du XIXe siècle," in *Mélanges publiés en honneur de M. Paul Boyer.* Paris, 1925.

Winkler, M. *Peter Jakovlevič Čaadaev: ein Beitrag zur russischen Geistesgeschichte des XIX Jahrhunderts.* Berlin, 1927.

MAJOR CRITICAL WORKS SINCE 1931

Falk, Heinrich, S. J. *Das Weltbild Peter J. Tschaadajews nach seinen acht "Philosophischen Briefen."* Munich, 1954.

Grigoryan, M. M. "Chaadayev i yevo filosofskaya sistema," in *Iz istorii filosofii.* Moscow, 1958. Vol. II.

———. *Glavnye techeniya idealizma v Rossii sorokovykh godov XIX veka.* Moscow, 1956.

Hare, Richard. *Pioneers of Russian Social Thought.* 2nd ed., New York, 1964.

Kemball, R. J. "Čaadaev's 'Lettres philosophiques' and 'Apologie d'un fou': More Recent Source Material," *Studies in Soviet Thought*, VIII (June–Sept., 1968), 173–80.

———. "Russian 19th-Century Thought—Recent Source Material," *Studies in Soviet Thought*, VII (Sept., 1967), 227–33.

Koyré, Alexander. *Etudes sur l'histoire de la pensée philosophique en Russie*. Paris, 1950.

The section on Chaadayev (pp. 19–102) reprints the article published in *Le Monde slave* (X, Nos. 1 and 2 [1933], 52–76, 161–85; see below) on pp. 19–52 and 97–102. The article has, however, been considerably revised to take into account work done on Chaadayev's manuscripts since its original publication. A number of passages from the article have been omitted and lengthy footnotes added.

———. "Petr Čaadaev," *Le Monde slave*, X, Nos. 1 and 2 (1933), 52–76, 161–85.

Reprints short passages from "Russia's Place in the World: Peter Chaadayev and the Slavophils," published in English translation in *The Slavonic Review* (V, March 15, 1927; see above).

Krestova, L. "P. Ya. Chaadayev," *Molodoy bolshevik*, III, No. 1 (1941), 39–48.

Lavrin, Janko. "Chaadayev and The West," *The Russian Review*, XXII (July, 1963), 274–88.

McNally, Raymond T. "Chaadaev's Evaluation of Peter the Great," *Slavic Review*, XXIII (March, 1964), 31–44.

———. "Chaadayev's Evaluation of Western Christian Churches," *The Slavonic and East European Review*, XLII (June, 1964), 370–87.

———. "The Significance of Chaadayev's *Weltanschauung*," *The Russian Review*, XXIII (Oct., 1964), 352–61.

Moskoff, Eugene A. *The Russian Philosopher Chaadayev, His Ideas and His Epoch*. New York, 1937.

Scheibert, Peter. *Von Bakunin zu Lenin: Geschichte der russischen revolutionären Ideologien, 1840–1895*, I: *Die Formung des radikalen Denkens in der Auseinandersetzung mit deutschem Idealismus und französischem Bürgertum*. Leyden, 1956.

Schelting, Alexander von. *Russland und Europa im russischen Geschichtsdenken*. Bern, 1948.

Schultze, B. "Die Sozialprinzipien in der russischen Religionsphilosophie," *Zeitschrift für katholische Theologie*, LXXIII (1951), 385–423.

———. "Ein beachtlicher Text Čaadaevs über Leibeigenschaft in Russland," *Ostkirchliche Studien*, III (1954), 193–204.

———. "P. J. Čaadaev (circa 1794–1856), erster russischer Geschichtsphilosoph, über die Eucharistie," *XXXV Congreso Eucaristico Internacional* (Barcelona, 1952), II (1952), 692–96.

———. *Russische Denker: ihre Stellung zu Christus, Kirche, Papsttum*. Vienna, 1950.

Shkurinov, P. S. "Genrikh Falk v roli istorika russkoy filosofii," *Voprosy filosofii*, No. 6 (1954), 146–50.

A review of Falk's monograph (see above).

———. *Mirovozzreniye P. Ya. Chaadayeva*. Moscow, 1958.

———. *P. Ya. Chaadayev: Zhizn, deyaltelnost, mirovozzreniye*. Moscow, 1960.

Solovyova, V. "Chaadayev i yevo 'Filosoficheskiye pisma,'" *Pod znamenem marksizma*, XVII, No. 1 (1938), 63–83.

Valuable discussions of Chaadayev can also be found in George Florovsky's *Puti russkavo bogosloviya* (Paris, 1937), N. O. Lossky's *History of Russian Philosophy* (New York, 1951), T. G. Masaryk's *The Spirit of Russia*, Vol. I, trans. Eden and Cedar Paul (2nd. ed., London, 1955), and V. V. Zenkovsky's *A History of Russian Philosophy*, Vol. I, trans. George L. Kline (New York and London, 1953).

Index

A priori ideas. *See* Ideas, primordial
Absolute Reason. *See* Supreme Reason
Abyssinians, 44
Academy. *See* Platonism
Accessory cause, 23, 87
Ahriman, 149–50
Alexander I (Tsar 1801–1825), 5, 7, 18–19, 42, 42 n. 4
   capitulation to Napoleon at Tilsit, 4
   Congress of Troppau, 7
Alexander the Great, 117 n. 5, 121
Alexandria, 117
ALL. *See* Unity, of reality
Analysis, 27, 70–71, 83, 169–71
   astronomical. *See* Geometry, celestial
Ancient philosophy, 57–58
Ancient world, 43, 53, 101, 110, 118, 123, 125, 149, 152
   and Christian world. *See* Christian society, contrasted with non-Christian
   fall of, 121
   influence of, 150–52
Ancients, the, 70 n. 3, 71–72, 77 n. 7, 117, 145
Anselm, Saint, 96 n. 6
Anthony, Saint, 59
Anthropomorphism, 80–81
Apocalypse, 80 n. 5
Apocalyptic synthesis, 25, 160
Apology of a Madman
   description of the *Philosophical Letters* as incomplete, 20 n. 58, 173
   modification of views of the *First Philosophical Letter*, 4, 10 n. 20,

Apology of a Madman (cont.)
   11 n. 22, 15–16, 26–28
   writing of, 14–15
Aquinas, Saint Thomas, 102 n. 9
Arab civilization, 148
Arabs, 146–47
Archetypes. *See* Ideas, primordial
Aristotle, 58, 102 n. 9, 113, 146–47, 155
Asia, nations of, 124
Associationism, 88
Athens, 3, 6
Atoms, 145
Attraction. *See* Gravitation
Autonomy, 103. *See also* Freedom; Law, moral

Babylon, 116 n. 4
Bacon, Sir Francis, 71, 71 n. 4, 145
Barbarian invasions, 41, 46, 118, 137 n. 6
Barbarism, 35, 42
Bards, 41
Basil, Saint, 54
Beck, Lewis White, 102 n. 9
Belinsky, Vissarion Grigoryevich (1811–1848: major literary and social critic of the 1830's and 1840's), 9
Benkendorf, Count Alexander Christophorovich (1783–1844: Head of the "Third Section"), 12–13
"Benkendorf, Memorandum to." *See* Chaadayev, P. Ya., "Memorandum to Benkendorf"
Bering Straits, 42

Bible, 101, 113, 157. *See also* New Testament; Old Testament; Scripture
Biblical figures, 140, 140 n. 7, 143. *See also* individual names
Boldyrev, A. V. (1780–1842: Rector of Moscow University), 12
Bonaparte. *See* Napoleon Bonaparte
Borodino, battle of, 5, 19
Bosphorus, 58
Brutus, 6
Byloye i dumy. See Herzen, A. I., *My Past and Thoughts*
Byzantium, 21, 42

Cabbala, 80
Calvin, John, 131
Calvinism, 131
Cambridge (England), 84 n. 5
Catastrophe, moral, 89, 119, 144–45, 151, 155. *See also* Revolution, moral
Categorical imperative, 103
Catherine II (the Great, Empress 1762–1796), 18
Cato, 113
Causality. *See also* Determinism; Law; Mechanism
    principle of, 22
Cause, accessory. *See* Accessory cause
Celts, 41
Censorship, 13
Chaadayev, Michael Yakovlevich (brother of P. Ya. Chaadayev), 5, 7, 7 n. 12, 8–9, 15, 15 n. 35
Chaadayev, Peter Yakovlevich:
    Alexander I, product of his reign, 19
    ancestry, 4, 5, 5 n. 8
    arrest: 1826, 8–9; 1836, 13
    attempt to clear himself, 12–13, 20 n. 59
    author of a chapter in P. Y. Yastrebtsov's *On the System of the Sciences which must be Known by those Children of Today who are to Constitute the Most Cultured Class of our Society*, 10, 15
    Borodino, present at, 5, 19
    and his brother:
        correspondence with, 7, 15
        relations with, 7, 8, 9, 15
    Circourt, A. de, letter of 1846 to, 17, 17 n. 46

Chaadayev, Peter Yakovlevich (*cont.*)
    contemporaries' opinions of, 3, 4, 9–10
    Crimean War, on, 18
    death of, 19
    Decembrist connections, 5, 8–9
    declared insane, 12
    education of, 5, 19
    Eugene Onegin, model for, 6 n. 9
    European travel, 5, 8
    financial difficulties, 8–9, 19
    and Gogol, N. V., defense of *Selected Passages from Correspondence with Friends*, 17
    health, 8–9, 12–13, 19
    and Herzen, A. I., letter of 1851 to, 18, 18 n. 51
    influence of:
        French Revolution of 1830 on, 10
        Kant, I., on, 104
        Karamzin, N. M., on, 11, 11 n. 22, 15–16
        Kireyevsky, I. V., on, 16
        Pushkin, A. S., on, 6, 16
        Schelling, F. W. J. von, on, 8
    influence on:
        Kireyevsky, I. V., 10 n. 20
        Pushkin, A. S., 6
        Slavophiles, 16
        Westernizers, 16
        Yastrebtsov, P. Y., 10
    intellectual solitude, 19
    Karamzin, N. M., acquaintance with, 6
    and Khomyakov, A. S., 3, 3 n. 1, 3 n. 4, 4 n. 5, 14, 14 n. 33, 17–18, 18 n. 49
        letter of September 26, 1849, to, 17–18, 18 n. 48
    last public statement, 18, 18 n. 50
    "Letter to an Undetermined Correspondent," 18, 18 n. 50
    liberal sympathies, 5
    "Memorandum to Benkendorf," 10, 10 n. 20, 11 n. 22, 15–16
    military career, 5–8
    moderator, 16–17
    modification of views, 4, 9 n. 16, 10 n. 20, 15–17, 26–28
    and Nicholas I:
        letter of July 15, 1833, to, 11 n. 22, 15

Index

Chaadayev, Peter Yakovlevich (*cont.*)
"Observations on Two Passages from A. S. Khomyakov's Pamphlet in reply to Laurentie," 18, 18 n. 49
open letters, 4, 10, 14–15, 17, 17 n. 46, 17 n. 47, 18, 18 n. 48, 18 n. 49, 18 n. 50
and Orlov, A. F., letter (undated) to, 18, 18 n. 51
Paris, enters with Alexander I, 5
on patriotism. *See* Patriotism; Chauvinism
Philosophical Letters. See also First Philosophical Letter; Philosophical Letters
attempts at publication, 11
complete nature of the series, 20, 20 n. 58
described as incomplete in the *Apology of a Madman*, 20, 20 n. 58, 173
estimate of the *First Philosophical Letter*, 175–77
philosophy of history. *See* Philosophy of history
and Pushkin, A. S., 6, 10
letter of June 17, 1831, to, 20 n. 58
letter of July 6, 1831, from, 10 n. 59, 11 n. 24
letter of September 18, 1831, to, 10, 10 n. 18, 16, 16 n. 41
subject for his poems, 6 n. 9
reading, 10–11
religious concern. *See* Religion
return to society, 1831, 9
Roman Catholicism. *See* Roman Catholicism
Russian civilization. *See also* Russia, specific headings; Russian society; Russian Orthodox Christianity critique of, 8–9, 11, 20–21, 25–28
Russian Orthodox Church, critique of. *See* Russian Orthodox Christianity
Schelling, F. W. J. von, acquaintance with, 8, 10
search of house, 12, 13
Semenovsky Regiment:
joined, 5
mutiny of, 7

Chaadayev, Peter Yakovlevich (*cont.*)
and Slavophiles. *See also* Chaadayev, P. Ya., influence on Slavophiles; Slavophiles
influence on government in Crimean War, 18, 18 n. 50
social connections, 5
and Stroganov, Count S. G., letter of November 8, 1836, to, 14, 15 n. 34
study of:
French philosophers, 10
Karamzin's *History of the Russian State*, 11, 11 n. 22, 15–16
Peter the Great, 6, 16, 18
science, 10–11
on sudden death, 19
suicide:
thoughts of 9, 19. *See also* Chaadayev, P. Ya., health
symbol of protest, 4, 19
testament, 19
and Turgenev, A. I.:
letters of 1835 to, 10 n. 20, 11 n. 22, 15, 15 n. 38, 19, 19 n. 57
letters of 1836 to, 15 n. 36, 16, 16 n. 42
letter of 1837 to, 15, 15 n. 39
and Turgenev, N. I., acquaintance with, 5, 9
violence, opposition to, 17
and Vyazemsky, Prince P. A., letter of April 29, 1847, to, 17, 17 n. 47
Westernism, 5, 10, 16–19, 26–28. *See also* Chaadayev, P. Ya., influence on Westernizers; Western civilization; Westernizers
Westernizers. *See* Chaadayev, P. Ya., Westernism; Chaadayev, P. Ya., influence on Westernizers; Westernizers
world view. *See Philosophical Letters*, a world view
"Chaadayev's Philosophical Letters Written to a Lady." *See* McNally, Raymond T.; Titles of *Philosophical Letters*, variants
Chauvinism, 17–18, 26–27, 50, 130, 163–64, 167, 173–74, 176
China, 41, 120, 125–26
Chingis-Khan, 5 n. 8
Chosen people, 140. *See also* Jews; Ju-

Chosen people (*cont.*)
daism; Nations, providential role of
Christ, 90, 101–102
effect of name of, 48
empire of, 48
in Koran, 148
source of unity, 25
teachings, 156
Christendom. *See* Unity, Christian
Christian era:
beginning. *See* Church, early Christian
ethics. *See* Ethics, Christian
ritual, 33
society:
contrasted with non-Christian, 70
n. 3, 123–27
progress of, 25, 46–50, 57–58,
124–27
unity. *See* Unity, Christian
world. *See* Christian, society; Unity Christian; Unity, of nations
Christianity. *See also* Protestantism;
Reformation, the; Roman Catholicism; Russian Orthodox Christianity
influence of, 22, 45–46, 48–50, 127,
147–48, 155–56, 160
mission, 160. *See also* Providence
moral system, 44–46, 155
progress. *See* Christian society, progress; Progress
prophecies, 49, 65–66
revelation and history:
roles of, 44, 158. *See also* Revelation
and Scripture, pre-dates, 158
and slavery, 57–58
universality of, 148
Church, 44
ancient. *See* Church, early Christian
Apostolic. *See* Church, early Christian
early Christian, 24, 46, 112, 129–30
golden age of. *See* Church, early Christian
institutional expression of unity, 25
and public law, 118
Scripture, compiled by, 159
social system, 21, 32, 118
total historical system, 21
universal, 44, 160
Church Fathers, 54, 116, 129

Cicero, 37, 37 n. 2, 96, 96 n. 7, 145
Circourt, Anne Marie Joseph Albert,
Comte de, 17, 17 n. 46
Civilization, 21–22, 34, 44. *See also*
Ancient world; Chaadayev, P. Ya.,
Russian civilization; Critique of Russian society; Eastern civilization;
Western civilization
Coliseum, 137 n. 6
Commission of inquiry. *See First Philosophical Letter*, commission of inquiry into the publication
Communication. *See* Ideas, transmission of; Motion, transmission of
Compass, invention of, 120
Computation. *See* Mathematics
Congress of Troppau, 7, 8
Consciousness, 88
Conservation of momentum, law of.
See Momentum, law of conservation of
Contemporary reality, emptiness of, 21,
34–35, 56–57
Councils, Church, 46
Cousin, Victor, 116 n. 3
Cranmer, Thomas, 131
Creuzer, Georg Friedrich, 149 n. 12
Creative principle, 85. *See also* Ideas,
origin; Ideas, primordial; Motion,
source of
Crimean War, 18
Critique of Russian society, 13–14. *See
also* Chaadayev, P. Ya., Russian civilization; Russia, specific headings;
Russian society; Russian Orthodox
Christianity
Custine, Astolphe, Marquis de:
Journey for Our Time, 13, 13 n. 29,
17, 19, 19 n. 53
Khomyakov, A. S., reply to. *See*
Khomyakov, A. S., "The Opinions
of Foreigners on Russia"
supporter of *First Philosophical Letter*, 13, 13 n. 29

David, 113, 143–45
Decembrist Revolt, 4, 8–9, 14
Decembrists, 5, 8–9, 14
Degradation, 117
Democritus, 145
Descartes, René, 83, 87 n. 6, 96 n. 6,
102, 102 n. 10, 104

Destiny of man. *See* Plan of Creation; Providence

Destiny of nations. *See* Nations, providential role of; Plan of Creation; Providence

Destiny of universe. *See* Plan of Creation; Providence

Determinism, 23, 87. *See also* Law; Mechanism
and free will, 61–62, 83, 137

Deuteronomy, 142

Deutsch, Babette, 6 n. 9

Disunity:
caused by chauvinism, 50, 130, 164
caused by Reformation, 24, 118, 130
pagan, 24, 130

Divine Mind. *See* Supreme Reason

Divine Reason. *See* Supreme Reason

Divine Will. *See* Providence

Divine Wisdom. *See* Providence; Supreme Reason

Dogma, 44, 131, 155. *See also* Eucharist; Revelation; Scripture

Druids, 41

Eastern civilization, 41, 92, 125, 148, 169–71. *See also* Byzantium; Russia and Eastern civilization
contrasted with Western civilization, 27, 41, 169–71

Ecclesiastical hierarchy:
reaction to *First Philosophical Letter*. *See First Philosophical Letter*, reaction of ecclesiastical hierarchy

Education, 21, 33–37, 42, 46, 167–68, 174, 177

Ego. *See* Self

Egoism, 25, 73, 154–55. *See also* Self-interest

Egypt, 117, 121, 125

Egyptian learning, 143

Egyptians, 141

Eighth Philosophical Letter. See Letter VIII

Empiricism, 22, 80, 86, 88, 102, 102 n. 9

Empiricists, 102 n. 9

Epicurus, 113, 145–46

Ethics:
Christian, 43–45, 63–66, 93
Epicurus', 145–46
philosophical. *See* Moral philosophy

Ethics (*cont.*)
Platonist, 145–46
Socrates', 144
Stoic, 145–46

Eucharist, 25, 130–31, 159

Eugene Onegin, 6 n. 9

Euphrates, 58

Europe. *See* Western civilization

European civilization. *See* Western civilization

Experimentation, 82–83, 112

External action, 22, 84, 91, 95–100, 106–109. *See also* Determinism; Initial impulse

Faith:
and reason, 22, 64–65, 67, 90, 154
unity of. *See* Unity, of faith
and works, 21, 68, 74

Falk, Heinrich, S. J., 20 n. 58

Families of mankind, 34, 121 n. 6. *See also* Unity, Christian

Family of nations, 21. *See also* Unity, of nations

Farelly, M. John, O. S. B., 102 n. 9

Feeling, 67–68, 154. *See also* Religious feeling

Fénelon, François de Salignac de la Mothe-, 115–16

Feral children, 98–99

Fichte, Johann Gottlieb, 103, 103 n. 13

Fifth Philosophical Letter. See Letter V

Figures:
Biblical. *See* Biblical figures; individual names
historical. *See* Historical figures; individual names

Finite, and infinite, 82

First Philosophical Letter, 4, 20–22, 26, 128 n. 10, 163–65, 173–77
Chaadayev's estimate of, 175–77
circulation in manuscript copies, 10, 165
commission of inquiry into the publication, 12
exaggerated criticism of Russia, 27, 176
and Gogol's *Inspector General*, 11, 27, 177, 177 n. 13
modification of views. *See Apology of a Madman*, modification of views of the *First Philosophical*

First Philosophical Letter (cont.)
Letter; Chaadayev, P. Ya., modification of views
publication, vii, 7, 10–16, 20 n. 58,
20 n. 59, 163–65, 176–77
reaction of:
ecclesiastical hierarchy, 12
government, 12–13, 26–27, 163
public, 11–12, 21, 26–27, 163–
65, 170–71, 176
supporters, 13–14
First man, 20, 23, 64, 74, 90, 99, 104,
106
Fontenelle, Bernard Le Bovier de, 95 n.
4
Fourteenth of December. *See* Decembrist Revolt
*Fourth Philosophical Letter. See Letter
IV*
France, 154
Frederick the Great, 120
Free will, 22–23, 62, 83–84, 137
in history, 25, 100
Freedom, 23, 62, 73, 88–90, 99, 101,
107, 129
and law. *See* Law, moral
and passivity, 70, 73
French civilization, 39
French philosophers. *See* Chaadayev,
P. Ya., study of French philosophers
French Revolution, 1830, 10
Fusion, 45, 73, 76, 76 n. 5, 85, 112,
114, 160, 165. *See also* Synthesis;
Unity
of moral forces, 21, 22, 160

Gagarin, Prince Ivan Sergeyevich, S. J.
(1814–1882), vii, vii n. 2, viii, x,
10 n. 20, 177 n. 15, 178 n. 16
Gagarin-Gershenzon. *See* Gershenzon,
M. O.
Galileo, 3, 84 n. 5
Ganges, 125, 171
Geometry, 84, 86
celestial, 83, 85
Germains. See Germans
German philosophy, 94, 154
German scholars, 172
German universities, 19
Germans, 41, 152. *See also* Northern
nations
Germany, 41, 94, 128, 154

Gershenzon, M. O. viii, x, 27 n. 68,
168 n. 6, 171 n. 7, 175 n. 9, 177 n.
15
Gibbon, Edward, 137 n. 6
Gnossos, 53
God. *See also* Ideas, primordial; Initial
impulse; Providence; Supreme Reason
existence, 96 n. 6
man in the likeness, 89, 99–100
nature of, 74, 80–81
thought of, 100, 104
Godunov, Boris (Tsar 1598–1605), 58
Gogol, Nicholas Vasilyevich (1809–
1852)
Inspector General, 11, 27, 177, 177
n. 13
*Selected Passages from Correspon-
dence with Friends*
Chaadayev's defense of. *See* Chaadayev, P. Ya., and Gogol, N. V.:
defense of *Selected Passages
from Correspondence with
Friends*
Good:
absolute, 60
general, 60
ideas of, 69
sovereign. *See* Law, moral
Gratieux, A., 3 n. 1, 3 n. 4, 4 n. 5, 14
n. 33
Gravitation, 22–23, 83–90, 110. *See
also* Motion
Greece, 115, 121, 123, 125–26, 143,
152
critique of, 137–39, 150, 150 n. 13
influence of, 150, 152
Greek character, 149
Gregory Nazianzen, 54
Gregory of Tours, 137 n. 5
Griboyedov, Alexander Sergeyevich
(1795–1829), 5, 14
Guizot, François, 128 n. 9
Gunpowder:
invention of, 120

Habit, 36–37. *See also* Order in life
Heaven, 75–76, 76 n. 5
Heeren, Arnold Hermann Ludwig, 149
n. 12
Hegel, Georg Wilhelm Friedrich, 9
Henry VIII, 47, 131

Index

Herodotus, 110, 125, 137 n. 5

Herzen, Alexander Ivanovich (1812–1870: leader of the Westernizers), 9, 17

Byloye i dumy. See Herzen, A. I., *My Past and Thoughts*

Chaadayev's disavowal of his characterization, 18, 18 n. 51

Chaadayev's letter of 1851 to. *See* Chaadayev, P. Ya., Herzen, A. I.

friendship with Chaadayev, 17

liberalism, 17

My Past and Thoughts, 4 n. 5, 4 n. 6, 14, 14 n. 32, 19, 19 n. 54

opinion of Chaadayev, 3–4, 4 n. 5, 4 n. 6, 13–14, 14 n. 32, 17

supports *First Philosophical Letter,* 13–14, 14 n. 32

Hindus, 121 n. 6

Hindustan. *See* India

Hipparchus, 110

Historical figures, 113. *See also* Russia, leaders; individual names

providential role of, 24–25, 28, 40–41, 139–49, 164–68, 176, 178

Historical mission. *See* Historical figures, providential role of; Nations, providential role of; Providence

History:

Ancient contrasted with Christian, 43, 113, 116–18, 123–24, 137 n. 6

Christian, 43, 45, 116–119, 150. *See also* Church, early Christian; History, Ancient contrasted with Christian; History, mediaeval; Religion, historical development

Christian interpretation of. *See* Philosophy of history

central fact of. *See* Church, early Christian

critical role of, 115, 137–51

fundamental rule of explanation, 24

goal of. *See* Plan of Creation; Providence

as history of ideas. *See* Ideas, and history; Philosophy of history

interest in, 109

lessons of, 21, 38, 42, 73, 114, 116–18, 120–21, 135, 166

Mediaevel, 112, 119, 127, 168. *See also* Church, early Christian; His-

History (*cont.*)

tory, Christian; Religion, historical development

and moral philosophy, 23, 115–16

philosophy of. *See* Philosophy, of history

philosophical presentation of, 109–12, 127, 136

popular, 106. *See also* History, traditional presentation

of religion. *See* Church, early Christian; History, Ancient contrasted with Christian, History, mediaeval; Religion, historical development

religious presentation of, 109–12, 127, 136

science of, 135

traditional presentation of, 109–12, 127, 136

unity of. *See* Unity, of history

History of the Russian State. See Karamzin, N. M.

Homer, 113–14, 149–52

Hottentots, 43

Humility. *See* Submissiveness

Hussars, 3, 6–7, 12

Idea:

divine, 25. *See also* Plan of Creation; Providence

revealed, 49

superhuman, 142

universal, 43. *See also* Plan of Creation; Providence

Ideal type, 101. *See also* Christ

Ideas:

and history, 22, 26–28, 35, 43, 46, 140–42, 166, 168–71, 178. *See also* Philosophy of history

impressed by God. *See* Ideas, origin of; Ideas, primordial

interconnection. *See* Ideas, transmission of

origin of, 23, 25, 64, 71–73, 86, 99–100, 106. *See also* Ideas, primordial

patrimony of. *See* Ideas, primordial; Tradition

primordial, 20, 25, 38, 63–65, 72–73, 78, 90, 95–105, 106–107

transmission of, 20, 23, 25–26, 32,

193

Ideas (cont.)
  34–38, 64, 72–73, 78, 86, 89–90,
  95–105, 106–109
Identity, law of, 94
Idolatry, 128
Ilissus, 53
Imagination, 41
Immortality, 92–93, 104
Impulse, divine. See Initial impulse
India, 120–21, 121 n. 6, 125, 151 n.
  14
Indian (American), 41, 123
Individuals and nations. See Parallel-
  ism, individuals and nations
Indulgences, 128
Indus, 121
Infinite, and finite, 82
Infinity, 80
Initial impulse, 21–23, 25, 84–86, 90,
  95–100, 105, 106
Innate ideas. See Ideas, primordial
Inquisition, 47, 170
Inspector General. See Gogol, N. V.,
  Inspector General
Interaction, of mind and body, 86
Intuition, 71
Ionia, 117
Islam, 147–49
Isolation, 15, 22, 25, 73, 121 n. 6, 130,
  135–36, 155, 174–75. See also Rus-
  sia, isolation
Ivan III (Grand Duke of Moscow
  1462–1505), 26, 165 n. 4

Jagatay, 5 n. 8
Japan, 125
Japanese, 44
Jerusalem, 45
Jesuits, 17, 170
Jews, 24. See also Chosen people; Ju-
  daism; Moses; Nations, providential
  role of
John Chrysostom, Saint, 54
Journey for Our Time. See Custine, A.,
  Journey for Our Time
Justice, 38
Judaism, 121. See also Chosen people;
  Jews; Moses; Nations, providential
  role of
Julian the Apostate, 117 n. 5

Julius Caesar, 150

Kant, Immanuel, 102–104
Karamzin, Nicholas Mikhailovich
  (1766–1826: historian and poet),
  6, 15–16, 172
  History of the Russian State, 11, 11
  n. 22, 15–16
Karlsbad, 8
Kashmir, Vale of, 171
Kepler, Johannes, 84 n. 5, 110
Khomyakov, Alexis Stepanovich (1804–
  1860: leader of the Slavophiles), 3,
  3 n. 1, 3 n. 4, 4 n. 5, 9, 14, 14 n. 33,
  17–18, 18 n. 48, 18 n. 49. See also
  Chaadayev, P. Ya., and Khomyakov,
  A. S.
  "Opinions of Foreigners on Russia,
  The," 17
  Reply to Laurentie. See Khomyakov,
  A. S., Western Communions, On;
  Chaadayev, P. Ya., "Observations
  on Two Passages from A. S. Khom-
  yakov's Pamphlet in reply to Lau-
  rentie"
  on Russian Orthodox Church. See
  Russian Orthodox Christianity
  Western Communions, On, 18, 18
  n. 49
Kingdom of Christ. See Kingdom of
  God
Kingdom of God, on earth, 22, 25, 32,
  44, 48, 130, 148, 160
Kingdom of Heaven, 71
Kireyevsky, Ivan Vasilyevich (1806–
  1856: major Slavophile figure), 9.
  See also Chaadayev, P. Ya., influence
  of Kireyevsky, I. V.
  on mission of Russia. See Russia,
  mission
  "Nineteenth Century, The," 10
Koran, 148
Koyré, Alexander, 10 n. 20
Kreutzer. See Creuzer, Georg Friedrich
Kulm, battle of, 5

Lagidae, 117 n. 5, 121
Lapps, 43
Latin peoples, 38. See also Southern
  nations

Law, 22–23, 70, 72–73. *See also* Parallelism, moral and physical worlds and freedom. *See* Freedom; Law, moral

moral, 22, 62, 70, 77–78, 88–90, 91, 116, 160

physical, 22, 77–78, 83–89, 91, 95, 111

Laws of motion. *See* Law, physical; Motion

Leaders. *See* Historical figures; Russia, leaders; individual names

Learning, capacity for, 99

Leo X, Pope, 128

Letter I. See First Philosophical Letter

Letter II. See Second *Philosophical Letter*

Letter III, 22

Letter IV, 22–23, 61 n. 5

Letter V, 23, 61 n. 5, 132 n. 2

Letter VI, 20 n. 59, 23–24

Letter VII, 20 n. 59, 23–24, 95 n. 4

Letter VIII, 24–25

Letters on Philosophy to Countess N. N., vii n. 1

Liberals, 5

Limitations:
recognition of, 35
spatial 22, 74–75
temporal, 22, 74

Lincolnshire, 84 n. 5

Lithuania. *See* Chaadayev, P. Ya., ancestry

Livy, 137 n. 5

Locke, John, 102 n. 9

Logic, 39, 71, 155. *See also* Analysis; Order in life; Syllogism; Synthesis

Logos. *See* Word

London, 84 n. 5

Love, 76

Luther, Martin, 128, 131

Lutherans, 131

Lyon, massacre of, 144

McNally, Raymond T., viii, viii n. 5, ix, ix n. 13, x n. 15, 56 n. 2, 62 n. 7, 65 n. 9, 76 n. 6, 128 n. 9, 134 n. 1, 137 n. 4, 137 n. 5, 137 n. 6, 168 n. 6, 175 n. 9, 175 n. 10, 176 n. 11, 176 n. 12

Major Works of Peter Chaadayev. See Philosophical Letters, translations

Man, 89, 99–100. *See also* Plan of Creation; Providence; Self

Man-God. *See* Christ

Mankind:
development of. *See* Education
unity of. *See* Unity, of human beings

Marcus Aurelius, 113, 117 n. 5, 143–45

Masses, 40–41, 163–64. *See also First Philosophical Letter*, reaction of public; Historical figures; Public, critique of; Russia, leaders

Materialism, 44, 125–26, 138. *See also* Greece, critique of

Mathematics, 61, 70, 79–80

Maximus of Tyre, 149 n. 12

Mechanism, 83, 111, 137. *See also* Law; Progress

"Memorandum to Benkendorf." *See* Chaadayev, P. Ya., "Memorandum to Benkendorf"

Memory, 74

Mental world. *See* Parallelism, moral and physical worlds; Worlds, moral and physical

Metaphysics, 23, 82, 93, 107

Metternich, Prince Clemens Wenceslas, 7

Mexico, 125

Milton, John, 91, 91 n. 1

Mind:
and body, 86
cosmic. *See* Unity, of moral world; Unity, of reality; Universal mind; Worlds, moral and physical
tendency to unity. *See* Unity, tendency of mind

Minds, contact of, 76, 76 n. 5, 86, 95–102, 135–36, 138

Mission. *See* Historical figures, providential role of; Man; Nations, providential role of; Philosophy, mission of; Providence
of Christianity. *See* Christianity, mission

Mohammed, 113, 147–49

Modern society. *See* Christian society; Contemporary reality

Molecular theory, 85, 89

Momentum, law of conservation of, 96, 96 n. 5
Mongol rule, 35–36, 43
Mongols, 121, 123
Monotheism, 24, 142, 147
Montaigne, Michel de, 68
Moors, 123
Moral knowledge, essential to man, 78
Moral law. See Law, moral
Moral nature, contrasted with physical nature, 62, 79–90, 91. See also Parallelism, moral and physical worlds; Worlds, moral and physical
Moral philosophy, 22, 60, 93. See also Ethics
and history, 23
and science, 22, 60–66, 79–90, 91
Moral revolution. See Catastrophe, moral; Regeneration; Revolution, moral
Moral world. See Moral nature; Parallelism, moral and physical worlds; Worlds, moral and physical principle of. See Motion
Morality:
of nations. See Nations, morality of
source of, 72–73
Mosaic system, 142
Moscow, 8–9, 11, 153
intellectual life of, 3, 4, 9–10, 19
Moscow University, 5, 12
Moses, 24, 110, 113, 139–45
Motion, 85–86. See also Law, physical
principle of physical and moral worlds, 23, 25, 69, 83–89, 95
source of, 25, 71, 86, 95, 105–106
transmission of, 23, 86, 95–105, 106–109
voluntary, 89
Mysteries of Samothrace, 149

Nadezhdin, Nicholas Ivanovich (1804–1854: poet, editor of Telescope), 12–13, 20 n. 59
Napoleon Bonaparte, 4, 120
National consciousness, 114
National prejudice. See Chauvinism
Nations:
growth of, 35–37, 40–41, 46–47, 130, 167–68, 172, 174, 177
and individuals. See Parallelism, in-

Nations (cont.)
dividuals and nations
morality of, 37, 115
providential role of, 24–26, 41, 107–108, 114–15, 121, 140–41, 148, 167–68
Natural development, theory of. See Mechanism; Progress
Natural philosophy. See Science
Nature. See Parallelism, moral and physical worlds; Worlds, moral and physical
Nazianzen, Gregory, 54
Necropolis, 51
New order, 44, 49, 112, 121, 138
New Testament, 62–64, 157–59. See also Bible; Scripture
Newton, Sir Isaac, 82–83, 84 n. 5, 96 n. 5
Nicholas I (Tsar, 1825–1855), 3, 9, 11–14
Chaadayev's letter of July 15, 1833, to. See Chaadayev, P. Ya., and Nicholas I, letter of July 15, 1833, to
Nicolas of Cusa, 102 n. 9
"Nineteenth Century, The," 10
Nizhni-Novgorod, 4
Nomads, 35
North America, 41
Northern nations, 38, 42, 171. See also Germans
Numerology, 80

Observation, 70, 82–83, 91, 112. See also Scientific method
"Observations on Two Passages from A. S. Khomyakov's Pamphlet in reply to Laurentie." See Chaadayev, P. Ya., "Observations on Two Passages from A. S. Khomyakov's Pamphlet in reply to Laurentie"
Oder, 42
Old Testament, 62–63. See also Bible; Scripture
On the System of the Sciences which must be Known by those Children of Today who are to Constitute the Most Cultured Class of our Society. See Yastrebtsov, P. Y.
Ontological Argument, 96 n. 6

Open letters. *See* Chaadayev, P. Ya., open letters

"Opinions of Foreigners on Russia, The," 17

Order in life, 33, 35–37, 39, 43, 54. *See also* Tradition

Orient. *See* Eastern civilization

Orlov, Prince Alexis Fyodorovich (1788–1861: successor of A. S. Benkendorf as Head of the "Third Section"), 18, 18 n. 51

Orthodoxy. *See* Russian Orthodox Christianity

Ottoman Empire, 123

Paganism, 24, 43, 92, 113, 123, 130, 145

Pantheism, 23, 92

Papacy, 24–25, 132–33, 170

Parallelism:
individuals and nations, 35–39, 114–15, 167–68, 177
logic and morality, 71
moral and physical worlds, 22–24, 36, 69–72, 77–78, 83–90, 91, 95–97, 100–102, 104–105, 144–45, 151

Paris, 5

Pascal, Blaise, 95, 95 n. 4, 135, 135 n. 2

Passivity. *See* Freedom, and passivity; Reason, obedient; Submissiveness

Past, influence of, 156. *See also* Ideas, transmission of; Tradition

Patriotism, 16, 19, 141, 177. *See also* Chauvinism
blind. *See* Chauvinism; Slavists, official
England, 163
enlightened, 26–27, 163–64, 171, 173–74, 177
mature. *See* Patriotism, enlightened

Pavlov, Nicholas Philipovich (1805–1864: poet and critic), 17

Pelasgians, 123, 149 n. 12

Perception, 86, 88, 102. *See also* Ideas, origin; Ideas, primordial

Perfectability. *See* Progress

Perfection. *See* Progress

Pericles, 6, 121

Personality, 21, 107. *See also* Self

Peter the Great (Tsar, 1682–1725), 6, 16, 18, 26–28, 42, 42 n. 3, 165, 165 n. 5, 166–68, 170, 173, 176

Petitio principii, 93

Petrine period, 14

Phaedrus. *See* Plato, *Phaedrus*

Pharoahs, 121

Philosophical Letters. *See also* under individual *Letters*
analysis of, 20–28
Chaadayev's attempts at publication, 11
circulation in manuscript copies, 10, 165
complete nature of the series, 20, 20 n. 58
completed, 9
modification of views. *See Apology of a Madman*, modification of views of *First Philosophical Letter*; Chaadayev, P. Ya., modification of views
objections to *First Philosophical Letter*. *See First Philosophical Letter*, reaction
revisions. *See Apology of a Madman*, modification of views of *First Philosophical Letter*; Chaadayev, P. Ya., modification of views
titles. *See* Titles of *Philosophical Letters*, variants
translations, vii, viii, viii n. 3, viii n. 6, viii n. 7, viii n. 8
a world view, 4, 20–28

Philosophical Letters addressed to a Lady. *See* Titles of *Philosophical Letters*, variants

Philosophical Letters to Madame ***. *See* Titles of *Philosophical Letters*, variants

"Philosophical Letters written to a Lady." *See* Titles of *Philosophical Letters*, variants

Philosophical morality. *See* Ethics; Moral philosophy

Philosophy:
circular, 93
of history, 16, 23–28, 35–50, 106–153, 155, 165–78
mission of, 70

Photius (Patriarch of Constantinople 858–891), 41–42, 42 n. 5
Physical world, principle of. *See* Motion, principle of physical and moral worlds; Worlds, moral and physical
Physics, 70, 145. *See also* Law, physical; Motion; Science; Worlds, moral and physical
Pillars of Hercules, 125
Plan of Creation, 22–23, 43, 46, 111, 113–15, 122, 127, 136, 147, 157, 175. *See also* Providence
Plato, 3, 65, 74, 104, 113, 116, 138
  dialogues, 53
  Phaedrus, 53–54
  Republic, 3
  Symposium, 53–54, 144 n. 8
Platonism, 94, 145–46
Platonist ethics. *See* Ethics, Platonist
Plutarch, 149 n. 12
Polytheism, 116, 142, 147
Post-Napoleonic generation, 9
Pre-Petrine Russia, 18. *See also* Slavophiles
Primitive peoples, 41
Primordial ideas. *See* Ideas, primordial
Prince. *See* Historical figures; Masses; Russia, leaders; individual names
Principle, of the created world. *See* Motion, principle of physical and moral worlds
Printing press, invention of, 120
Progress, 21–22, 25, 44, 73, 111, 114–21, 124–27, 137 n. 6
Projection, *See* Initial impulse
Propulsion. *See* Initial impulse
Protestantism, 18, 127–31, 156–57, 159. *See also* Reformation, the
Providence, 20, 22–26, 41, 43, 45, 60–61, 64, 69, 76, 88–90, 100, 105, 106–109, 111, 113–22, 132, 140–42, 147–48, 157, 165–68, 174–75
  and mechanism, 111, 124–27
  and revelation. *See* Revelation, and Providence
Public. *See also First Philosophical Letter*, reaction of public; Historical figures; Masses; Russia, leaders
  critique of, 163–65, 176
Public Welfare, Union of, 8
Pushkin, Alexander Sergeyevich (1799–1837), 6, 6 n. 9

Pushkin, Alexander Sergeyevich (*cont.*)
  correspondence with Chaadayev. *See* Chaadayev, P. Ya., and Pushkin
  critique of Chaadayev's manuscript, 11 n. 24, 20 n. 59
  death of, 13
  Eugene Onegin, 6 n. 9
  Peter the Great, commission to write a history of, 16
  influence on Chaadayev. *See* Chaadayev, P. Ya., influence of Pushkin, A. S., on
  letter of October 19, 1836 (drafts), 11 n. 25
  letter to P. A. Vyazemsky of August 3, 1831, 11 n. 24
  poems on Chaadayev, 6 n. 9
  and publication of *First Philosophical Letter*, 11, 11 n. 25
Pythagoras, 65, 138, 146 n. 10
Pythagoreans, 80

Quantity, 23, 79, 81, 100
Quénet, Charles, vii n. 1, 3 n. 2, 4 n. 7, 5 n. 8, 6, 6 n. 10, 6 n. 11, 7 n. 13, 7 n. 14, 8 n. 15, 10 n. 17, 10 n. 21, 11 n. 22, 11 n. 23, 12 n. 26, 12 n. 27, 13 n. 29, 15, 15 n. 37, 15 n. 40, 16 n. 43, 17 n. 44, 19, 19 n. 52, 19 n. 55, 20 n. 59

Real Presence. *See* Eucharist
Reality, 85
  unity of. *See* Unity, of reality
Reason, 67
  absolute. *See* Supreme Reason
  all-wise. *See* Supreme Reason
  artificial, 70, 74
  cognitive activity of, 22
  and divine thought, 100
  and faith. *See* Faith, and reason
  and feeling, 154
  human, 100
  logical activity, 22
  moral activity, 22
  natural, and revealed. *See* Reason, and revelation
  obedient, 22, 69, 71–72. *See also* Analysis; Submissiveness
  objective, 100
  origin, 99–100

Reason (*cont.*)
principle of Western civilization, 41
pure, 67, 103
reproduces the thought of God, 100
and revelation, 24, 63–64, 156. *See also* Faith, and reason
spontaneity of, 61, 107
subjective, 100
Supreme. *See* Supreme Reason
universal, 70, 73–74
Reasoning:
geometrical. *See* Reasoning, mathematical
mathematical, 70, 80
Redemption, 45
Reformation, the, 24, 118, 127–31. *See also* Protestantism; Religion, historical development
Regeneration, 68, 73–75, 121, 138, 144–45, 151. *See also* Revolution, moral
Religion, 20, 32, 42. *See also* Protestantism; Reformation, the; Roman Catholicism; Russian Orthodox Christianity
effect on society. *See* Christianity, influence of
historical development, 42–43, 45–47, 112, 118–20, 123–24, 127–32, 140–42, 147–49, 160
Homeric, 149
primitive Greek, 149
and science, 79–90. *See also* Faith, and reason
wars of, 47, 119, 170
Religious:
faith. *See* Faith
feeling, 21, 32–33, 67–68
life, 21–22, 32–35, 52–57, 59–60, 68
persecutions, 46–47. *See also* Islam; Inquisition; Religion, wars of
practice, 21, 33
thought, 33
wars. *See* Religion, wars of
Renaissance, 123, 127
Republic (Plato), 3
Revelation, 24, 59, 156
accessibility of, 59
New Testament, 63–64
Old Testament, 63–64

Revelation (*cont.*)
partiality of, 107
personal, 33
primordial, 64
and Providence, 22, 44
and reason. *See* Reason, and revelation; Faith, and reason
Revizor. See Gogol, N. V., *Inspector General*
Revolution:
French, 1830, 10
moral, 36, 46–47, 89, 119, 155. *See also* Regeneration
of 1848, 17–18
physical, 36, 89
political, 46–47
Roman Catholicism, 12, 17–18, 25
Roman civilization, influence of, 150, 152
Roman Empire, fall, 121–23, 125
Rome, 3, 6, 117, 125, 137 n. 6, 143, 152
Russia:
and Antiquity, 152
and Byzantium. *See* Russian Orthodox Christianity
Destiny. *See* Russia, mission
and Eastern civilization, 34, 41, 170–71
education of. *See* Russia, intellectual development
future. *See* Russia, mission
geographical situation, 27, 41–42, 171, 178
history. *See* Russia, intellectual development
humility, 28, 176
immaturity, 21, 37–40. *See also* Chaadayev, P. Ya., critique of Russian civilization; Russia, intellectual development; Russian, and Western civilization
intellectual development, 3–4, 9–10, 16, 21, 34–37, 40, 42, 164, 167–68, 177
isolation, 15–17, 21, 25, 34–38, 41–43, 152, 173–74
leaders, 21, 26–28, 41–42, 165–68, 176–78. *See also* Historical figures; Peter the Great
a lesson for others, 21, 38, 42

Russia (cont.)
mission, 16, 26–28, 38, 41–42, 174–75, 178
and Western civilization, 21, 26–28, 34, 39–43, 152, 165–68, 170, 176
Russian Christianity. See Russian Orthodox Christianity
Russian Church. See Russian Orthodox Christianity
Russian national self-consciousness, 21
Russian Orthodox Christianity, 13, 13 n. 29, 15, 17–18, 21, 25, 27–28, 42–44, 58, 119, 176. See also Russia, intellectual development
Russian society. See also Chaadayev, P. Ya., critique of Russian civilization; Critique of Russian society; Russia, specific headings
emptiness, 34–37, 52
instability, 34–36

Sacrament of Communion. See Eucharist
Saint Peter's Cathedral, 128
Saint-Simon, Claude-Henri, Comte de, 9
Samoyed, 163, 163 n. 2, 163 n. 3, 164
Scalds, 41
Scandinavians, 41
Schelling, Friedrich Wilhelm Joseph von, 8–10, 94, 94 n. 2, 116 n. 3, 149 n. 12
Schism. See Disunity; Russian Orthodox Christianity
Schismatics. See Protestantism; Reformation, the
Schleiermacher, Friedrich Daniel Ernst, 116 n. 3
Scholastics, 102 n. 9, 147
Schools, philosophy of the, 91, 100–101, 125
Science, 70, 71, 135, 145
axioms of, 112
Chaadayev's study of. See Chaadayev, P. Ya., study of science
divine, 64
fundamental principles of, 22. See also Motion
and moral philosophy. See Moral philosophy, and science
physical, contrasted with historical. See History, and moral philoso-

Science (cont.)
phy; History, science of
and religion. See Religion, and science; Faith, and reason
Scientific method, 22, 79–90, 91
and mental reality, 92
and moral philosophy, 22, 60–65, 79–90, 91
Scottish philosophy, 88
Scripture, 140 n. 7, 144, 157
intelligibility of, 24, 90, 155, 157
and revelation, 24
and Spirit of God, 158
Second Philosophical Letter, 22, 136 n. 3
Secret societies, 5, 8
Sectarians. See Protestantism; Reformation, the
Selected Passages from Correspondence with Friends. See Chaadayev, P. Ya., Gogol, N. V., defense of Selected Passages from Correspondence with Friends
Seleucids, 117 n. 5
Self, 22, 87, 104, 135–36
existence of, 23
Self-interest, 60, 72, 136. See also Egoism
Semenovsky Regiment, 5, 7, 8
Sensationalists. See Empiricism
Serfs, 35–36, 57–58
Servetus, Michael, 131
Seventh Letter. See Letter VII
Shcherbatova, Princess Anna Mikhailovna (aunt of P. Ya. Chaadayev), 5, 9, 19
Shcherbatova, Princess Natalia Mikhailovna (mother of P. Ya. Chaadayev), 5
Shakhovskoy, D. I., vii n. 1, viii, ix, ix n. 14, 56 n. 2, 61 n. 5, 62 n. 17, 65 n. 9, 76 n. 6, 84 n. 5, 87 n. 6, 95 n. 3, 95 n. 4, 103 n. 12, 157 n. 1, 158 n. 2
Shuisky, Prince Dmitry Ivanovich (d. 1613), 58
Sixth Philosophical Letter. See Letter VI
Slavery, 57–58
Slavists:
fanatical. See Slavists, official
official, 16–17, 26–27, 168

Index

Slavophiles, 3, 10, 16, 18, 28
 attack of Gogol, 17
 influence on government in Crimean
  War, 18
 patriotism, 19
Slavophilism, 17
Snow, Valentine, viii
Social feeling, 135–36
Socrates, 3, 65, 113, 143–45, 145 n.9
Sokolniki, 78, 90
Southern nations, 40. See also Latin
 peoples
Space, 22, 74–75
Spain, 123
Speech, 95–96, 99, 155. See also Ideas,
 transmission of; Motion, transmis-
 sion of; Word
Spinoza, Benedict de, 79, 79 n. 1, 81,
 81 n. 3
Spirit, reign of. See Kingdom of God
Stability. See Order in life; Russian so-
 ciety, instability
Stagnation, of nations, 124–27
Stagyrite. See Aristotle
Stankevich, Nicholas Vladimirovich
 (1813–1840: intellectual critic), 9
Stoics, 72. See also Ethics, Stoic
Stroganov, Count Sergey Grigoryevich
 (1794–1882: professor, President of
 Moscow University, 1837–1874).
 See Chaadayev, P. Ya., and Stro-
 ganov, Count S. G., letter of No-
 vember 8, 1836, to
Submissiveness, 22, 33, 60, 69–75, 84
 n. 5, 107, 156. See also Analysis;
 Reason, obedient
 and freedom, 73, 88–90
Superhuman beings, 144
Superstition, 35, 47, 128, 155
Supreme Being. See God; Supreme
 Reason
Supreme Intellect. See Supreme Rea-
 son
Supreme Mind. See Supreme Reason
Supreme Reason, 33, 44, 60, 76, 80–
 81, 99, 103–104, 106, 113, 121–22,
 159. See also God
Syktyvkar. See Ust-Sysolkst
Syllogism, 39, 72, 79, 155
Sympathy, 76
Symposium. See Plato, Symposium

Synthesis, 27, 71, 169–71. See also
 Apocalyptic synthesis; Fusion; Submissiveness; Unity

Tabula rasa, 102
Tacitus, 150
Tartars. See Mongols
Tasso, Torquato, 45
Telescope, vii, vii n. 1, 10–11, 11 n. 25,
 14, 14 n. 30, 15
Texts:
 history of, vii–x
 used, viii–x
Third Philosophical Letter. See Letter
 III
Thomas Aquinas, Saint, 102 n. 9
Tilsit, battle of, 4
Time, 74–75, 86
 limitation by, 22, 74
 man-made 74
"Times of Troubles," 172, 172 n. 8
Titles of Philosophical Letters, variants,
 vii n. 1, viii n. 5
Tradition, 23, 25–26, 34–38, 52, 64,
 97–105, 106–109. See also Ideas,
 transmission of; Motion, transmission of; Order in life
Transliteration, xi
Transmission. See Ideas, transmission
 of; Motion, transmission of; Tradition
Troppau. See Congress of Troppau
Truth:
 historical grounding of, 24, 164
 nature of, 72, 156–60
 and patriotism. See Patriotism, enlightened
 proofs of, 154–55
 social realization of, 21, 32
 source of, 159
 transmission of. See Ideas, transmission of; Motion, transmission of
Truths. See Ideas
Turgenev, Alexander Ivanovich (1785–
 1846: social and literary critic), 19
 acquaintance with Chaadayev, 10 n.
  20, 11
 Chaadayev's letters to. See Chaadayev, P. Ya., and Turgenev, A. I.,
  specific letters to
Turgenev, Nicholas Ivanovich (1789–
 1871: Decembrist), 5, 9

"Two Letters on History addressed to a Lady." *See* Titles of *Philosophical Letters*, variants
Typhon, 149–50

Unbelief, 156
Union of mankind. *See* Unity, of human beings
source for, 135–36
Union of Public Welfare, 8
United States of America, materialistic civilization of, 41
Unity, 21–22, 85–86, 160. *See also* Apocalyptic synthesis; Fusion; Synthesis
common goal of, 24, 45, 119
Christian, 24–25, 42–43, 45, 119, 123–24, 130–33
of Creation, 23, 91, 95, 135
Eucharist as expression of. *See* Eucharist
of faith, 45
of families, 24
first concrete expression of, 24
historical focus of, 25
of history, 23, 25, 95, 108–109, 116, 123–24, 135
of human beings, 23–25, 42, 73, 95, 112, 115, 135
of human faculties, 25
institutional expression of, 25
of language, 45
love of, 160
of matter and spirit. *See* Eucharist; Unity, of reality
of moral authority, 45, 118
of moral world, 21, 95, 97, 101, 135
of nations, 24, 38–39, 42–50, 114–15, 118–19
objective, 92
of physical nature, 23, 95
principle of, 20, 32, 85
of reality, 23, 25, 73, 85, 91–92, 95, 135
of Roman Empire, 121
tendency of mind toward, 160
of thought, 21, 23, 32, 43, 45, 95, 114, 119, 135, 135 n. 2
of time. *See* Eucharist; Unity, of history
of wills, 73
Universal mind, 95, 101

Universal social system. *See* Church; Kingdom of God; Unity
Universal will, 73
Ust-Sysolsk, 13
Utility, 60
Uvarov, Count Sergey Semyonovich (1786–1855: Minister of Education), 13

Vaudois, 128
Venevitinov, Dmitry Vladimirovich (1805–1827: poet, critic), vii n. 1
Vernadsky, George, 5 n. 8
Voltaire, François Marie Arouet de, 106, 106 n. 1, 119
Vyatka, 14
Vyazemsky, Prince Peter Andreyevich (1792–1878: poet, literary critic), vii n. 1, 11 n. 24
Chaadayev's letter of April 29, 1847, to. *See* Chaadayev, P. Ya., and Vyazemsky, Prince P. A., letter of April 29, 1847, to

Wars of religion. *See* Religion, wars of
Western civilization, 21, 26, 28, 38–39, 41, 44, 48, 52, 56, 121, 124, 152, 165–71. *See also* Russia, and Western civilization
Eastern, contrasted with. *See* Eastern civilization, contrasted with Western
materialism of, 174–75
Western Communions, On. See Khomyakov, A. S., *Western Communions, On*
Westernism. *See* Chaadayev, P. Ya., Westernism
Westernizers, 3, 10, 16–18, 28
attack of Gogol, 17
Wisdom, Divine. *See* Providence; Supreme Reason
Woe from Wit. See Griboyedov, A. S.
Woolsthorpe, 84 n. 5
Word (Logos), 44, 90, 99–100, 158–59
Word:
living and written, 158–59
written, 157
Worlds:
moral and physical, 22–24, 63, 69, 82–83. *See also* Parallelism, moral and physical worlds

Index

Worship, 33, 45

Xenophon, 144

Yakushkin, Ivan Dmitriyevich (1793–1857: Decembrist), 5

Yastrebtsov, P. Y. *See also* Chaadayev, P. Ya., influence on Yastrebtsov, P. Y.
On the System of the Sciences which

Yastrebtsov, P. Y. (*cont.*)
must be Known by those Children of Today who are to Constitute the Most Cultured Class of our Society, 10, 15

Zoroaster, 65, 149–50

Zhikharev, M. I. ("nephew" and biographer of Chaadayev), ix, 4, 11, 19

Zwingli, Ulric, 131

has been set on the Linotype in eleven point Electra with two-point spacing between the lines. Weiss Series I and II were selected for display. The book was designed by Jim Billingsley, composed and printed by Heritage Printers, Inc., Charlotte, North Carolina, and bound by the Becktold Company, St. Louis, Missouri. The paper on which the book is printed is designed for an effective life of at least three hundred years.

THE UNIVERSITY OF TENNESSEE PRESS

KNOXVILLE

DATE DUE